Spinning the Threads of Uneven Development

Spinning the Threads of Uneven Development

Gender and Industrialization in Ireland during the Long Eighteenth Century

Jane Gray

LEXINGTON BOOKS
Lanham • Boulder • New York • Toronto • Oxford

LEXINGTON BOOKS

A division of Rowman & Littlefield Publishers, Inc.
A wholly owned subsidiary of The Rowman & Littlefield Publishing Group, Inc.
4501 Forbes Boulevard, Suite 200
Lanham, MD 20706

PO Box 317
Oxford
OX2 9RU, UK

British Library Cataloguing in Publication Information Available

Library of Congress Cataloging-in-Publication Data

Gray, Jane, 1963–
Spinning the threads of uneven development : gender and industrialization in Ireland during the long eighteenth century / Jane Gray.
p. cm.
Includes bibliographical references and index
ISBN: 978-0-7391-0947-2
1. Linen industry—Ireland—History—18th century. 2. Sexual division of labor—Ireland—History—18th century. 3. Rural industries—Ireland—History—18th century. 4. Industrialization—Ireland—History—18th century. 5. Ireland—Economic conditions—18th century. I. Title.
HD9930.I732 G73 2005
338.4'76771164'0941509033—dc22 2004029941

Printed in the United States of America

♾™ The paper used in this publication meets the minimum requirements of American National Standard for Information Sciences—Permanence of Paper for Printed Library Materials, ANSI/NISO Z39.48-1992.

Contents

Illustrations

FIGURES

MAPS

Tables

Chapter One

Introduction

The story of recent social and economic change in Ireland has often taken the form of a myth. According to the myth, Ireland was a stagnant agrarian society until the 1960s, when enlightened government policies, together with changing social attitudes, finally set in motion the processes of industrialization and modernization. Thus Ireland is seen as a latecomer (O'Malley 1989) to the industrial transformation that had already occurred in Britain and other West European countries by the nineteenth century.[1]

Yet throughout the eighteenth-century Ireland's single largest export was an industrial commodity, namely, linen cloth destined almost exclusively for British markets. The cloth was woven in rural households throughout much of the province of Ulster and parts of Connaught, and to a lesser extent, in parts of Leinster and Munster as well (map 1.1). Before the establishment of mechanized spinning in the 1830s, even greater numbers of widely dispersed households produced linen yarn that supplied Irish and British looms. Thus, from the middle of the eighteenth to the middle of the nineteenth centuries, almost all households in the northern half of Ireland, and many households in the southwest, had at least some connection to the commercial linen industry. Women and children comprised the industrial labor force in the majority of these households. Rural industrialization had profound effects on the social and economic structure of both spinning and weaving districts. With the mechanization of spinning and its spatial concentration around Belfast, large areas of the Irish countryside experienced deindustrialization and impoverishment.

The story of the linen industry thus belies the modernization myth of agrarian timelessness. This book explores the part played by rural industrialization in the incorporation and subsequent peripheralization of Ireland in

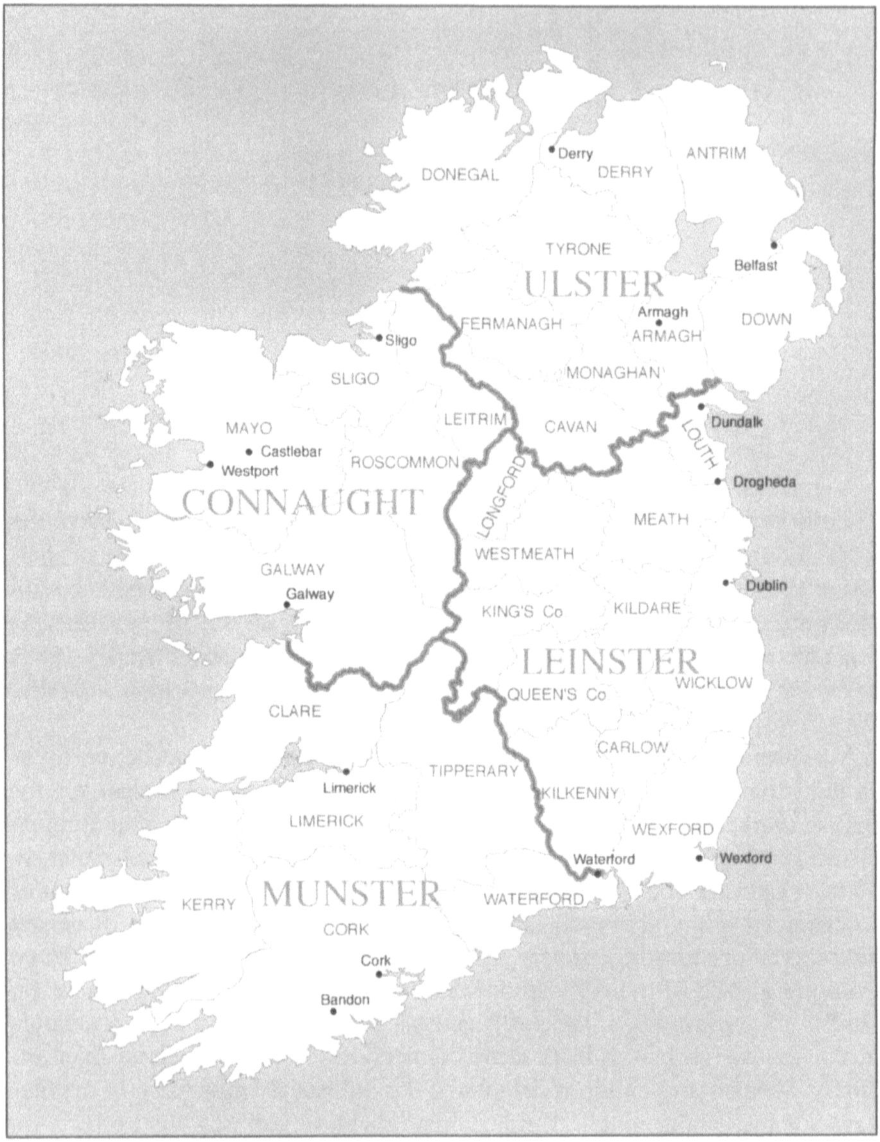

Map 1.1. Ireland: Counties and Provinces

the eighteenth and early nineteenth century world economy, and in the development of regional disparities within Ireland. Its central argument is that gender relations were at the heart of these uneven patterns of development during the transition to industrial capitalism, conceived as a *world-historical* process, rather than as a separate occurrence in individual countries.

Scholars have begun to explore the salience of gender in the political economy of Ireland in relatively recent times.[2] This book seeks to expand on that literature by demonstrating the multilayered significance of gender in the Irish linen industry: as an axis of social organization with independent causal effects on the trajectory of rural industrialization and the transition to the factory; as a negotiated set of customs, ideas, and values governing the division of labor; and as an identity structuring the differential experience of capitalist transformation. Each of these layers was dynamically related to the other two in the changing relations between women and men during the period under consideration.

In developing the argument in this book I engage with four broad areas of scholarship that have influenced research and writing on historical capitalism over the past twenty-five years. These fall under the headings of protoindustrialization, the evolution of the modern world system, working-class formation, and the family strategies approach to household production and consumption. In the following paragraphs I give a brief account of each of these perspectives, highlighting their strengths and weaknesses and showing the points of intersection between them. I argue that in order to make sense of the great transformation that ushered in the modern capitalist era, scholars must make a renewed effort to open the "black box" of the family-based household production unit (De Vries 1993, 117), and I propose a theoretical strategy for doing so.

CAPITALISM BEFORE THE FACTORY: PROTONDUSTRIALIZATION IN THE MODERN WORLD SYSTEM

A number of scholars have applied the concept of "protoindustrialization" to the Irish linen industry.[3] Franklin Mendels introduced the term in 1972. He argued that this first phase of industrialization was characterized by the rapid growth of traditionally organized, market-oriented rural industries, and by the emergence of a dynamic interaction between industrial regions that were no longer self-sufficient in food, and the commercial agricultural regions that emerged to supply them. Based on his research on Flanders, Mendels argued that population growth sustained protoindustrial expansion by ensuring a permanent oversupply of labor. He hypothesized that this occurred because protoindustrial producers remained subsistence oriented, with a high preference for leisure. Thus instead of investing additional income from rural industry, they used it "to enter into a marriage which they would otherwise have postponed, or to have a child which they would otherwise have avoided" (1981, 248).

Almost from the beginning, the literature on protoindustrialization encompassed a "family" of diverse and sometimes contradictory theories of the transition to industrial capitalism (Ogilvie and Cerman 1996a, 3). Moreover, two decades of scholarship revealed enormous variation in the trajectories of rural industrial regions, such that none of the original protoindustrialization hypotheses has emerged unscathed (Kriedte, Medick, and Schlumbohm 1993; Ogilvie and Cerman 1996b; Lehners 2003). As we will see, research on the Irish case neither fully supports nor rejects the theories of protoindustrialization. Ogilvie (1996) and Pfister (1996) have argued for new theoretical and methodological approaches oriented toward explaining divergences among protoindustrial regions. This book makes a contribution toward that agenda.

Some of the original protoindustrialization hypotheses dovetailed with emerging directions in comparative historical sociology, and in the sociology of development, during the 1970s and 1980s. Kriedte, Medick, and Schlumbohm's work (1981) formed part of a renewal of the debate on the transition from feudalism to capitalism, which in sociology was occasioned by the dependency critique of modernization theory, and by the publication of the first volume of Immanuel Wallerstein's (1974) "Modern World System" (Brenner 1977; Medick 1981c).[4] The dependency theorists pointed out that the models of socioeconomic change prevailing in sociology were ahistorical, and that they ignored the significance of relationships *between* different world areas in the process of development (Frank 1996). Wallerstein (1974, chapter 1) took the dependency argument a step further, arguing that the solution to the problems associated with modernization theory lay in conceptualizing capitalism as a single world system dating from the sixteenth century. The system was composed of unevenly developing core, semiperipheral, and peripheral zones, linked by surplus commodity flows toward the core. In order to make the claim that production by Caribbean slaves, East European serfs, and West European tenant farmers, could all be described as capitalist, Wallerstein modified the orthodox Marxist association between "free" labor and the capitalist mode of production.

> Free labor is indeed a defining feature of capitalism, but not free labor throughout the productive enterprises. Free labor is the form of labor control used for skilled work in core countries whereas coerced labor is used for less skilled work in peripheral areas. The combination thereof is the essence of capitalism. (Wallerstein 1974, 127)

Thus for Wallerstein a combination of waged and unwaged labor was not evidence of the incomplete development of capitalism, but was rather at the heart of how capitalism works as a system. The centrality of this insight to Wallerstein's theory is often overlooked. As I will show, it has important implications for understanding how gender and household relations function under capitalism.

The authors of *Industrialization before Industrialization* (Kriedte, Medick, and Schlumbohm 1981) did not wholeheartedly embrace the world-systems perspective on capitalism—indeed one of them explicitly rejected it (Schlumbohm 1981, 94).[5] Nonetheless, their model of protoindustrialization was congruent with world-systems theory in several ways. First (like Mendels), they highlighted the importance of interregional and overseas trade in increasing the demand for industrial products (Kriedte 1981a, 33–37). Second, they drew attention to similarities between the spatial organization of production under protoindustrialization and the "new international division of labour" of the late twentieth century (Kriedte, Medick, and Schlumbohm 1993; Schlumbohm 1996b, 22). Thus they raised the possibility of structural continuities (or cycles) in the process of uneven development over time. Finally, the demoeconomic processes posited by the authors (especially Medick 1981a) dovetailed with Wallerstein's (1974, chapter 2) insistence that European proletarianization began long before the industrial revolution. This point was highlighted by Charles Tilly (1983), who argued that protoindustrialization led to major changes in the relations of production long before the factory, and that these changes "produced a scattered but fast-growing population of families that were essentially dependent on the sale of their labor power for survival—a proletariat, in the classical sense of the word."

Despite these affinities, world-systems scholars have, with few exceptions (see Perlin 1983; Sanderson 1995), paid little attention to the scholarship on protoindustrialization. Some have explicitly rejected the concept (Frank 1998; Wallerstein 1997). Moreover, despite its theoretical affinities with critical development theory, the scholarship on protoindustrialization has paradoxically suffered from the ahistorical formalism typical of stage models of socioeconomic development (Pfister 1996).

In this book I argue that the theories of protoindustrialization, with their emphasis on the dynamic interrelationship between the microlevel strategies of individual households, communities, and regions, and macrolevel processes of socioeconomic change (Schlumbohm 1996a), have the potential to address two of the major theoretical problems that have been identified within the world-systems paradigm: (1) the tendency toward functionalism (McMichael 1990; Tomich 1994) and reductionism (O'Hearn 2001) and (2) the neglect of gender as an explanatory condition (Ward 1993; Misra 2000; Dunaway 2001). In turn, the emphasis of world-systems theory on the significance of the *timing* of incorporation to the capitalist world economy, together with its insistence on the explanatory importance of relations of production and exchange across space, can help to address the problem of regional "exceptionalism" in the literature on protoindustrialization theory. Thus, in this book, protoindustrialization is understood as part of an intrinsically uneven process of capitalist development, rather than as a stage of development occurring separately in different regions and countries.[6] The uneven ways in which rural industrialization affected local economies led to different patterns of class formation in different regions.

THE UNEVEN FORMATION OF WORKING CLASSES

Over the past two decades the concept of social class has been thoroughly problematized in the field of historical sociology. In an overview, Hall (1997, 7) concluded that "[The] future of class analysis has slipped off the charts of radical social theory, along with any self-assurance about how to use class analysis to understand the past." Two related theoretical critiques contributed to this loss of confidence. First, it was argued, especially by feminist scholars, that traditional class analysis fails to capture the complexity and diversity of relationships of power and social inequality (Frader and Rose 1996; Scott 1988a). Secondly, scholars influenced by postmodernism have eschewed the idea of class as an "objective" structure—indeed some argued that this eschewal is the only way to incorporate diversity in class analysis (see, e.g., Scott 1992).

The critique of structuralist understandings of class can be traced to the enormously influential contributions of British social historian E. P. Thompson. In contrast to the orthodox Marxist assumption that the subjective dimension of class was ultimately a reflection of objective circumstances, Thompson (1966, 10) argued that class consciousness must be understood as the way that the experience of class was "handled in cultural terms"—terms that were created by past experience and by the particular cultural heritage of local groups. According to Trimberger (1982, 212), Thompson's approach represented "[A] theoretical method intended to capture historical process and to integrate an analysis of culture and human agency into a macrostructural analysis of social change." His work had a profound effect on the practice of social history for more than two decades (Koditschek 1997).

However, in a trenchant critique of Thompson's (1966) classic study of *The Making of the English Working Class*, Scott (1988a) argued that his analysis was both teleological, in that it depicted rational, secular politics as the natural culmination of working class "making," and falsely universalizing, in that it conceived of this collectivity in unified terms that preclude the incorporation of diversity. "The Making" was fundamentally a story about generic male subjects, in which particular women could only be incorporated as exceptional practitioners of the rational politics associated with men, or as examples of "the crazy strain in working class discourse." For Scott, Thompson's vision of politics included previously excluded elements—such as morality and artistic expression—by refining, rather than challenging the existing, gendered representation of class: that is, by redefining culture as "masculine." If scholars were to transcend the limitations of Thompson's analysis, they must reject the notion that consciousness is immanent in social experience (Scott 1992), and instead analyze the construction of meaning (and of political identity) as a "set of events in itself" (Scott 1988a, 89). That is, they must pay attention to discourse. According to Frader and Rose (1996, 22):

> Discourses constitute ideologies as well as cultural meanings that are articulated in material practices. These ideologies and cultural meanings are crucial in the formation of political identities, and they are the means by which some subjects are included and others are excluded from sites of power, influence and political consequence.

Scott's critique inspired a new generation of feminist scholarship that has been of crucial importance in drawing attention to the fact that social processes like class formation are not "gender neutral," and to the ways in which sexual difference has often been used to "naturalize" social inequality.[7] However, in line with other dissenting voices (Kalb 1997; Steinberg 1991), I am not convinced that materialist analysis necessarily excludes diversity, as Scott's (1988b, 1992) argument suggested. First, as Koditschek (1997, 349) pointed out, in practice the empirical scholarship on gendered class formation falls "squarely within the classical Thompsonian mold" (see also Avdela 1999).[8] Secondly, if structural change is conceived of as inherently differentiated and uneven—as in world-systems theory—then diversity can be explained without resorting to post-structuralism (Kalb 1997). However, as I argue below, to fully achieve this goal, world-systems theory must be modified to incorporate gender as an independent axis of social organization, crosscutting households and regions.

Wallerstein's argument that capitalism functioned by combining different methods of labor control created the possibility of new ways of thinking about working-class formation. In his now classic study of *Europe and the People without History*, Eric Wolf (1982, 358) rehabilitated the nineteenth-century expression "working classes" in order to convey the plurality of ways that the same relation of labor to capital was produced at different times and places. William Roseberry (1989) took the argument a step further when he challenged the orthodox Marxist notion of working-class formation as a unilinear movement from free peasant to proletarian and argued that instead we must look at how different kinds of working populations were produced by the same historical process. "Uneven development," he wrote, "has one of its most important effects within the capitalist mode of production in a process that can be called uneven proletarianization" (Roseberry 1989, 215). This argument suggested that very different kinds of workers from the traditional factory operative—such as peasants and slaves—might be included under the rubric "working class." The idea was first mooted by Sidney Mintz in 1979, when he answered a qualified "yes" to the question, "Was the Plantation Slave a Proletarian" (Chase-Dunn 1989, 40). Mintz (1985) pursued the theme in his analysis of the transatlantic sugar trade, where he demonstrated a structural continuity between the processes of proletarianization in Britain and enslavement in the Caribbean: "Slave and proletarian together powered the imperial economic system that kept the one supplied with manacles and the other with sugar and rum" (Mintz 1985, 184). More recently, Don Kalb (1997) employed insights from the world-systems perspective to analyze regionally differentiated processes of class formation in the Netherlands.

According to Tomich (1997), materialist class analysis has foundered either on the reification of theoretical categories (relations of production versus relations of exchange), or on the reification of units of analysis (the totality of the world economy versus regional specificity). He argued eloquently for a "more historically and sociologically adequate understanding of processes of world economy and world class formation," in which "the *object* of analysis is particular class relations, [but] the appropriate *unit* of analysis is the totality of relations forming the historical world economy" (Tomich 1997, 308, emphasis in original). It is my contention that attention to gender relations is crucial to understanding the interdependence between class formation in protoindustrial Ireland, and the developing world economy centered on British-dominated world trade (Tomich 1997, 304–305). The division of labor *within* linen manufacturing households—specifically, the allocation of the most labor-intensive phases of the production process to women and children—affected the overall development of the industry. An understanding of gender relations requires some theoretical attention to the family-based household that lay at the heart of production, consumption, and exchange in the linen-manufacturing districts.

GENDER, DEVELOPMENT, AND CLASS FORMATION: OPENING THE BLACK BOX

While the world-systems perspective provides us with powerful tools for analyzing local and regional diversity in development and class formation, it is relatively silent on *intrahousehold* forms of inequality (Dunaway 2001;

D. Wolf 1992). This is true despite the centrality of the household to Wallerstein's understanding of unequal exchange—that is, to the process of surplus transfer from periphery to core.[9] According to Smith and Wallerstein (1991), households survive by pooling incomes from multiple sources, including wages, profits, rents, transfers, and subsistence production. In the modern world economy, no household is either fully proletarianized—in the sense of being entirely wage dependent—or completely outside the market—in the sense of being entirely self-sufficient—although there is an overall trend within capitalism for the extent of proletarianization to increase. Nonetheless, households at the core have historically been more proletarianized than households at the periphery, which have depended on subsistence production to a greater extent.[10] All other things being equal, capitalist employers prefer to draw on labor from semiproletarian households, because their members can get by with lower wages than their proletarian counterparts (Wallerstein 1983). Thus in Wallerstein's model, semiproletarian households at the periphery, through their subsistence activities, "subsidize" both capital accumulation and the relatively high wages garnered by workers at the core.

Smith and Wallerstein's (1991) argument clearly drew inspiration from the literature on the "domestic mode of production" that flourished in the 1970s and early 1980s, partly in response to the publication of the first English translation of the work of Russian economist, A. V. Chayanov (Thorner, Kerblay, and Smith 1966). According to Chayanov, the economic activities of peasant households were determined less by market forces than by the requirements of the "family economy." Peasant households sought to balance their labor output against their subsistence needs and, other things being equal, to minimize the drudgery of their work. Thus, when market conditions were favorable, peasants might withdraw labor from production. On the other hand, under unfavorable market conditions, peasants sometimes continuously increased the allocation of labor to production, to the point of "self-exploitation."

Both kinds of behavior were irrational from the perspective of a capitalist firm, but they made sense from the perspective of a production unit oriented primarily toward the daily survival and long-term reproduction of a family. However, scholars of developing societies observed that, under certain circumstances, capital might advantageously tap into the domestic mode of production without destroying it (Wolpe 1980). Medick (1976) drew on this model of the "articulation of modes of production" in developing his account of protoindustrialization as a "transitional mode," predicated on the "peculiarly stable but at the same time flexible" relationship between merchant capital and the family economy of rural industrial producers (Medick 1976).[11]

All of these authors recognized—but most failed to problematize—the fact that the allocation of labor within household production units was *gendered.*

Smith and Wallerstein (1991) observed that there was a general tendency for men to be responsible for waged income, and women for subsistence production, without venturing an explanation of why this should be so. As Dunaway (2001, 8) observed, the world-systems perspective "admits that resource allocation is inequitable . . . but we have not prioritized that household reality in our theory or our research." Similarly, Medick (1981a, 51) recognized that in protoindustrial households, women and children "contributed a necessary share to the family wage without which the subsistence gap could never have been closed, but their labor did not result in a proportional increase in income." However, this recognition did not lead scholars to include gender inequality as an endogenous factor in their models of protoindustrial development.[12]

The idea that women's activities are determined by their biology often lies behind the failure to examine gender difference as a social construct. Deere (1979, 144) suggested that Third World rural women took responsibility for subsistence production because it was more compatible with the requirements of biological reproduction—especially given that having a large family represented a rational response to poverty. While this is clearly an important factor, by itself it fails to explain *variations* in the allocation of men's and women's labor across time and space.

In their now classic study of *Women, Work, and Family* in England and France, Louise Tilly and Joan Scott (1978) used the idea of family economy to explore how *family strategies*, including the gender division of labor, changed alongside the process of industrialization, but also varied according to the timing and nature of local patterns of industrial development, and according to the family life cycle. As Moen and Wethington (1992, 234) observed, the construct of "family strategy" has "a certain intuitive appeal, bringing the family back in as an active participant in the larger society, an actor responding to, reworking, or reframing external constraints and opportunities." However, the family strategies model has also been criticized on several fronts. First, the model assumes decisions about labor allocation are made in the interests of the household as a unit, without any explicit recognition of the possibility of coercion and exploitation (Moch 1987).[13] A related critique points to the historical evidence that preindustrial households often did not function as undifferentiated units of production (Knotter 1994). Second, it might be argued that the model underestimates the significance of cultural constructions of gender in determining both family strategies and the changing economic circumstances to which they adapted (Moen and Wethington 1992, 237; Hareven 1991).

Amartya Sen's (1990) model of the household as a site of "cooperative conflict" provides an alternative approach to family strategies that has not received the attention it deserves in sociology. Briefly, according to Sen, the gender division of labor emerges as a "bargaining" solution to two different kinds of problems faced simultaneously by household members: on the one hand they must pool their resources, a shared interest that necessitates *cooperation*; on the other hand they must divide them up, which inevitably entails *conflict* among individuals with divergent interests. Moreover, the "solution" can and usually does reinforce inequalities both within the household, and in the wider socioeconomic milieu. This is because the relative bargaining strength of different household members is affected by three factors: (1) their perceived loss of well-being should the household unit break down; (2) the extent to which they perceive their self-interest in terms of individual well-being;[14] and (3) the perceived size of their contribution to the overall well-being of the group. Crucially, Sen emphasizes that these factors take the form of *perceptions* that may not be accurate reflections of the real state of affairs. For example, because women's labor is often unremunerated, its importance to household survival is often underestimated.

The focus of Sen's argument is on how gender inequality is maintained—that is, on how "the relative weakness of women in cooperative conflict in one period tends to sustain relative weakness in the next" (Sen 1990, 138). However, in my view the strength of the model lies in its capacity to incorporate *change*. While perceptions about men and women may contribute to stabilizing the household "bargaining solution" over extended periods of time, they are subject to revision if they deviate too far from objective circumstances. For example, an increase in women's ability to earn money income may increase their bargaining power by simultaneously improving both their "breakdown position" and their perceived contribution to the family economy (Sen 1990, 148).

Sen's model is powerful because it emphasizes the contingent nature of household divisions of labor, and the agency of men and women in reproducing or changing those relationships. However, in order to connect microlevel household bargaining to larger spatial and temporal continuities, it is necessary to include a macrolevel conceptualization of bargaining outcomes and the perceptions that inform them. I argue that household strategies were stabilized in different times and places by *gender contracts*: coherent sets of cultural prescriptions governing the rights, expectations, and behavior of different family members.[15] A whole range of factors, including perceived contribution to the family economy, agricultural and landholding practices, customary and legal relationships between landlords and tenants, state policies, and of course ideological beliefs about the "natures" of men and women, affected the form taken by gender contracts. Changes in any of these factors might destabilize the existing contract, leading to the renegotiation of family strategies. Thus by combining the concepts of "cooperative conflict" and "gender contract" I aim to develop a dynamic model of the intersections between structure, culture, and agency in Irish rural industrial households.

IRISH LINEN IN THE WORLD ECONOMY

Individual households lay at the heart of the Irish linen industry during the long eighteenth century. Men, women, and children reached bargains about how to allocate their labor time—amongst work and leisure, profit and subsistence-oriented activities, agricultural and industrial tasks—and how to dispose of their income. All of these cooperative conflicts occurred in the context of the family life cycle, which was itself the subject of negotiation at critical junctures—marriage, taking in servants or sending children into service, the marriages of children, the death of a spouse, the transmission of property to heirs.

Household bargains were made in the context of world-economic processes over which rural industrial producers had no direct control. In this sense their households represented nodes on long commodity chains, linking local fairs and markets to faraway sites in Britain and the Americas. Nonetheless, their decisions were also constrained by local socioeconomic circumstances, many of which can be traced to the *timing* of incorporation to the world economy through colonization, the commercialization of agriculture, and protoindustrialization. Some local circumstances affecting household bargains—such as the quality of land—remained partly independent of world-historical change.[16] Finally, household bargains were framed by gender contracts that stabilized cooperative conflicts across time and space, but which were themselves subject to alteration in light of changing world-economic and local circumstances.

My central thesis is that the allocation of labor by gender was key to the overall development of the Irish linen industry, and to regional patterns of industrialization, deindustrialization, and class formation. The story I tell in this book uses a dynamic model of household bargaining to draw together theoretical threads from the literature on world systems and protoindustrialization, in order to link an explanation of locally divergent paths of development to an understanding of the evolving capitalist system.

Two recent studies by Denis O'Hearn (2001) and Marilyn Cohen (2003) have, in different ways, placed the Irish linen industry in the context of a critical analysis of uneven capitalist development. In his comprehensive account of Ireland's changing position in the Atlantic economy O'Hearn (2001) showed how, at different historical periods, peripheral elites were constrained in their attempts to redirect Ireland's development toward industrialization, both by the actions of powerful core elites in Britain, and by path-dependent mechanisms that tended to lock Ireland into particular economic trajectories. The linen industry developed through two cycles of industrial transformation, both of which entailed the initial subjugation of potentially core industries—wool in the first cycle, at the end of the seventeenth century, and cotton in the second cycle at the end of the eighteenth century. Their replacement, linen, did not have the same potential for market expansion and linkages to other innovative activities, according to O'Hearn. It was therefore a semiperipheral industry, characterized by slow technical change with low profit rates and wages.

Cohen's (2003, 432) article provided an account of the "historically specific space-time structuration of the Irish linen industry" across three centuries. Following the model of capitalist development associated with the "regulation school," she traced the evolution of the linen industry across three "long cycles" distinguished according to the organization of the labor process—proletarianization (1725–1825), homogenization (1880–1950), and segmentation (1951 to the present). Building on Roseberry's notion of an "historical ethnographic sensibility," she explained the temporal and spatial patterns of growth and decline in the linen industry by linking the "specificities of commodity and place . . . to wider world historical processes of capital accumulation" (Cohen 2003, 454). She identified Ireland's position as an "internal periphery" in the Atlantic economy and the gender division of labor as key historically specific factors determining the distinct development of the Irish linen industry.

O'Hearn's and Cohen's studies of the Irish linen industry are sophisticated examples of how critical scholars have begun to construct explanations of regional patterns of development that link locally specific and contingent processes to the evolving regularities of the encompassing world capitalist system. My study complements theirs by elaborating a theoretical account of the household as an arena within which *nonelite* actors affected the course of Irish economic development during the long eighteenth century. Misra (2000, 119) has pointed out that the "schism" between world-systems analysis and the feminist scholarship on development has its origins in the different units of analysis each chooses to focus on. Whereas world-systems scholars examine macroprocesses at the level of the whole system, feminist scholars explore the microdynamics of the everyday lived experience of individual women. In this book I argue that a theoretically adequate understanding of the household is necessary to bridge the macro/micro divide in the explanation of particular trajectories of development, and I treat the scholarship on protoindustrialization as a springboard toward this goal.

In chapter 2 I give an overview of the expansion of the Irish linen industry, placing it in the context of the growing Atlantic trades that were increasingly dominated by Britain. In chapter 3 I explore how the linen industry was implicated in regional patterns of development in Ireland through a comprehensive examination of the scholarship on protoindustrialization and its application to the Irish case. In chapter 4 I shift the focus to local paths of rural industrialization with an in-depth empirical examination of the historical evolution of the linen industry in County Cavan. Cavan was not a "typical" Irish linen county—it was neither at the core nor the periphery of the industry, and my choice was in part driven by the availability of data. Nonetheless, I show how a careful mesoanalysis of processes of differentiation at the local level sheds light on divergences at wider regional levels. In chapter 5 I employ the concepts of "cooperative conflicts" and "gender contracts" to make sense of these divergent developments at the level of individual household strategies. I draw on a range of evidence, including folk poetry, to demonstrate how gender functioned as a key axis of processes of uneven regional development and working-class formation in the linen districts. Finally, in chapter 6, I move to a macrocomparative analysis of the Irish, Scottish, and Flemish linen industries. I argue that the divergent development of these regions during the 'long' eighteenth century can be explained partly in terms of differences in the nature and timing of their incorporation to the evolving world economy, and partly in terms of differences in how men's and women's labor was mobilized in the articulation of household and market.

COMPETING VOICES: SOURCES AND METHODOLOGY

The problem of structure and agency is one which, as Abrams (1980) noted, every generation of social scientists rediscovers for itself. How do we conceptualize the social patterns that constrain peoples' actions with the force of external "structures," without losing sight of the fact that those very structures are produced and changed by peoples' actions? The trend Abrams observed toward fruitful interaction between history and sociology contributed two main strategies toward the structure-agency problem in the 1970s and 1980s. First, on the part of many sociologists, there was a renewed determination to "take history seriously" (Tilly 1984). This involved both an understanding that "when things happen within a sequence affects how they happen," and a recognition that "things might have been different" (Wolf 1982, 6). Second, especially on the part of historians writing in the tradition of E. P. Thompson, there was a new emphasis on subjectivity—on reconstructing the interpretations and motives that *mediated* actors' experience of, and response to historical processes. These strategies seemed to go some way toward meeting the challenge of revealing historical change as "both a chain of events and a relationship of abstract conceptions" (Abrams 1980, 14).

For some scholars, as we have seen, the analytical separation between culture and structure reified the hierarchical distinction between "real" material conditions and "ephemeral" ideologies, thus inevitably reproducing the crude economism that Thompson had rejected. By the end of the 1980s, the "solution" of treating culture as a discursive framework constitutive of, and thus logically prior to social experience, had been widely adopted (Berlanstein 1993). More recently, however, a number of critics pointed out that economism simply sneaks in at the back door—often unrecognized and unexamined—in such radical culturalist accounts (Biernacki 1997).[17]

In this book I take the view that a self-conscious analytical distinction between the abstract interpretations of sociological explanation, and the experiential interpretations that constructed historical events, is both necessary and legitimate, provided the sociologist's categories are "held tightly in check by the voices of the past" (Davis 1983, 5). The methodological strategy of this book is one of "incorporating comparison" (McMichael 1990). This approach addresses the structure/agency problem by treating units of comparison as "provisionally isolated instances" of a larger world-historical process. The goal of comparison is to differentiate "particular historical sequences and spatial configurations by locating them within the evolving ensemble of relations forming the world economy" (Tomich 1994, 355). This makes it possible to explain different paths of social change in terms of variation in the nature and timing of incorporation, specific social and environmental contexts, and gendered household strategies.

Any analysis of the strategies of historical actors requires careful attention to the question of whose voices are heard in the historical record, and whose are silent. I draw on three kinds of sources in this study: contemporary "statistical" reports, census and land valuation data, and popular poetry. Both narrative and statistical accounts from the eighteenth and early nineteenth centuries must be treated with caution, because they are usually incomplete and may often have been inaccurate. The greatest shortcoming of upper-class commentaries is the probability that the observers were biased in their judgments. Reports by contemporary British and Anglo-Irish observers naturally contain elements of ethnocentrism, and were often written from a colonial perspective (Ó'Cadhla 1999). At a deeper level, both quantitative and narrative surveys are problematic in the sense that they are implicated in a growing effort on the part of the state and ruling classes to "write the nation" (Patriarca 1994), and to regulate the lives of their citizens (Shaw and Miles

1979). The obsession of upper-class observers in the early nineteenth century with the industriousness or lack thereof of the Irish rural poor anticipated the later need of capitalist industry for an expanding labor force, and in their concern with "regularity" in everything from dress to the layout of fields these reports must be seen as part of an attempt to impose discipline from above. However, this obsession also resulted in the comprehensiveness and systematic attention to detail that make the reports valuable to the sociologist. By the middle of the nineteenth century the quality of official data collection and analysis had reached an exceptionally high standard (Mokyr 1985).

Donnelly (1997) observed that the collection of official statistics required the "invention" of categories that in turn became constitutive of social change. The problem posed by reliance on government documents and upper-class observers is closely linked to the methodological and theoretical problem of trying to apprehend simultaneously how people "make their own history" and how history happens "behind men's backs." Statistical information channels our vision away from human agency toward a deterministic understanding of social change, and just as importantly cannot provide us with a view of social change from the perspective of those whose lives were most profoundly affected. In response to this problem social scientists have turned to oral history as part of an attempt to rewrite history from below (see Cohen 1997b). Of course this is not possible for the period covered by this book. I have relied instead on published poems and songs as a unique alternative source in which the voices of some ordinary people may be heard.

A number of little books of poetry by weavers and one spinner were published by subscription in the first half of the nineteenth century. According to Hewitt (1974, 7), friends, acquaintances, and prestigious persons were "solicited to take one or more copies of the book when printed, at a stated figure, usually half a crown." Many of the poems are written in the Scots vernacular which was spoken in east Ulster. While some of the little books were published at the instigation of upper-class patrons, most of the poems and songs were originally written for a local audience. As Akenson and Crawford point out (1977, 4), community support for the rhyming weavers is evidenced by the titles by which many of them were known: Hugh Porter, for instance, was called "The Bard of Moneyslan." Furthermore, the poems are directly linked to a longer, oral tradition: Hewitt (1974, 4) argues that the rhymes are characteristically "approximate, vowel rhymes or assonances," more pleasing to the ear than to the eye.

Akenson and Crawford (1977) made a strong case that the weaver poets were representative of their particular communities in the conventional sociological sense, and they must be considered immensely valuable in "giving voice" (Ragin 1994) to those who are not often heard in upper-class narratives and official reports. Nonetheless, the poems also suppress voices. First, the weaver poets are drawn almost exclusively from the Presbyterian Scots and English-speaking communities of east Ulster where the linen industry originated at the end of the seventeenth century. Their poems tell us nothing about the lives of those Catholic and Irish-speaking people who were incorporated into the industry in growing numbers from the middle of the eighteenth century. Second, with one possible exception, there were no "rhyming spinners" (Hewitt 1974, 40–41), although late nineteenth-century folklorists collected a number of spinning songs. In their original form, these consisted of partly improvised, bantering exchanges among young women gathered together to spin (Schneider 1989). While the rhyming weavers began their versifying careers in similar settings, their female counterparts never bridged the gap between oral and written composition. This is partly because women were much less likely than men to be literate.[18]

The third way that the poems "suppress voices" is through self-censorship. The rhyming weavers were very conscious that, in publishing their work, they were exposing themselves to a "respectable" middle- and upper-class readership. To what extent did their ambition to be recognized by this new audience affect the material included in their collections? James Orr, the "Bard of Ballycarry" wrote that:

> My rude Scotch rhymes the tasteful justly slight,
> The Scotch-tongued rustics scorn each nobler flight.

To the sociologist it is tempting to treat as "authentic" only those Scots-language poems on everyday life and explicitly political subjects, and to ignore the substantial number of English language items on conventional poetic themes, such as unrequited love. But might not those quaint songs about tea, whisky, and fairs equally be written to appeal to upper-class prejudices? As Hewitt (1974, 62) observed of Orr's lines, "we can only guess what veins of irony inform that couplet."

Hugh Porter (1813), the "Bard of Moneyslan," tells us in "The Author's Preface" that:

> I made my sangs to please my sel',
> My dearest worthy frien's and ithers
> No 'just sae dear, but rhymin' brithers
> To whom, just as they are, I sent them,
> But never for the public meant them.

Of course it is only because he submitted his songs to the public that we can now read them, and so we must, to the best of our ability, take them "just as they are." The poetry's value lies less in the "representativeness" or otherwise of individual weaver poets, but in the extent to which, as popular literature, it reflected the cultural values and ideals of ordinary people of its time. My interpretations of the poems and songs inevitably depend on the sociological categories and models that I think explain what was happening in rural industrial Ireland. At the same time, the voices of the rhyming weavers act as a check on my explanations, constantly challenging me to evaluate and revise them in terms of their meaningfulness to those whose lives are being described.

NOTES

1. For an analysis of the use of this myth in state development strategies, see Gibbons (1996).

2. For useful overviews, see Daly (1997) and the introduction to Cohen and Curtin (1999).

3. This literature will be discussed in detail in chapter 2. For a summary, see the introduction to Cohen 1997b.

4. For useful summaries of these debates, see So (1990) and Peet (1991).

5. In general, they were more sympathetic to the structuralist Marxist idea of "articulation of modes of production," which some development scholars adopted as an alternative to world-systems theory. See Peet (1991) and the discussion in Chase-Dunn (1989, 20–47).

6. The potential contribution of world-systems theory to an understanding of regional industrialization in Europe was earlier identified by Pat Hudson (1989, 35).

7. For overviews, see Koditschek (1997) and Frader and Rose (1996).

8. In a review of articles on gender and work, published in the journal *Gender and History* between 1989 and 1999, Avdela (1999, 534) found that authors "insist on the importance of material circumstances and social relations, even when they take language and meaning into consideration" and that "no examples of clear-cut postmodernist approaches are to be found in the journal."

9. Indeed Wallerstein's household-based explanation is probably the least influential model of unequal exchange within the world-systems literature. For an overview, see Chase-Dunn (1989, 228–55).

10. Contemporary households in the periphery may be more likely to rely on a combination of wages and informal sector activities, such as petty trading (see Wallerstein et al. 1992).

11. Mendels (1981) also drew on Chayanov's account of the peasant family economy in his model of protoindustrialization, but unlike Medick he did not develop this into a fully elaborated theory of protoindustrialization as a socioeconomic *system*.

12. Maynes (2004) has recently highlighted the extent to which women's labor fuelled growth in European regions that relied on protoindustrial textile industries.

13. Harrison (1982) has applied this criticism to the original model of the family economy developed by Chayanov. Similar criticisms have been made of Becker's no-

tion of the "altruistic head" in his rational choice model of the family, which Moen and Wethington (1992) rightly identify as a variant of the family strategies approach.

14. Here Sen (1990, 125–26) is thinking of empirical research showing that people in traditional societies—especially women—find the idea of *personal* welfare unintelligible, and understand their interests only in terms of the well-being of the family unit.

15. The idea comes from Scandinavian theories of the twentieth century "gender system," although my usage of the term is somewhat different. It was developed "in ironical analogy with the idea of the social democratic contract." See Duncan (1996, 95–96.)

16. It must be emphasized, however, that the ecological context is not independent of human activity. For example, poor quality land may be "improved" by reclamation and drainage oriented toward commercial agricultural activity. Similarly, repeated flax cropping may diminish the fertility of the richest soil. Whether either activity occurred depended partly on the processes described in this book. Here, the concept of "ecotype" proves useful. See the discussion in Knotter (1994).

17. It is sobering to remember that the structuralist Marxist theorist Richard Johnson made precisely this point about Thompson's work in 1979. Thus the structure and agency debate appears to travel in endless circles.

18. In Ulster in 1841, 41 percent of all males above the age of five could read and write, compared to 19 percent of all females.

Chapter Two

Trade, Markets, Production

In a song first published in 1804, the weaver poet James Orr (1935) described the ruination of a weaver and his family through indulgence in drink and other vices, and their salvation through conversion to Methodism. At the beginning of Orr's tale, Christy Blair is portrayed as a prosperous weaver, employing two journeymen, and relying on the labor of his wife and children to supply and prepare yarn for the loom:

> He weav'd himsel,' an keepet thwathree gaun,
> Wha prais'd him ay for hale weel-handled yarn;
> His thrifty wife an' wise wee lasses span,
> While warps and queels employ'd anither bairn.

The household seems fairly self-sufficient, though as we will see, it is unlikely that the women and children in a single family could have spun enough yarn to keep three weavers at the loom full time. In a later stanza we learn that the family also owned two milk cows that "gaed baith for debt," the first real casualties of Christy's drinking. When finally "a was gaen he had to sell or pledge," Christy wandered into a barn where a Methodist preacher was holding forth, and decided to "join the flock." As a result of his conversion, the household's prosperity recovers and multiplies:

> They min't baith warls. In warps boil'd by their han'
> Did thrice ten shuttles lose their entrails sma';
> An' on a scoup o' cheap, but mountain lan,'
> They graz'd yell kye, an' drain'd, an lim'd the shaw.

Thus Christy's household has been transformed from what might be described as a "traditional" artisanal economy, to a "modern" capitalist one.

Now the family puts out yarn to thirty weavers in contrast to the two or three journeymen they had earlier employed, and raises beef cattle for sale in contrast to the two cows they once kept to provide milk for their own consumption. It is clear that most of the yarn put out by the family is purchased in the marketplace—"Beasts, yarn, an 'claith, aft call'd the sons awa'";—although they continue to prepare yarn for the loom at home.

Other aspects of this complex song will be explored in chapter 5. The present chapter examines the different relations of production described by Orr, placing their evolution in the context of changes in the structure of trade and marketing. I argue that, while Conrad Gill's (1925) classic account of the Irish linen industry relied too much on a linear model of capitalist development, more recent accounts have underestimated the significance of changing relations of production before the factory.

TRADE: IRISH LINEN IN THE WORLD ECONOMY, 1700 TO 1850

Rural domestic production of linen cloth and yarn expanded rapidly in Ireland from the end of the seventeenth century in response to new trade regulations and growing demand from Great Britain and the American colonies. Linen was Ireland's single largest export to Britain during the eighteenth century—a time when Irish exports in general became increasingly dependent on the British market (figure 2.1). Politically, Ireland remained an independent kingdom with its own parliament under British sovereignty until 1801, when the two kingdoms were unified under a single parliament at Westminster. After 1780 linen cloth exports increased dramatically, so that the period from 1780 to around 1825 may be considered the peak years of Irish linen production under the household system.

Like cotton and the lighter woolens, linen was "decent cloth," an inexpensive lightweight material that "enhanced the living standards of the urban middle and lower classes, and soon displaced coarse homespuns in peasant households as well" (Schneider 1989, 6). Whereas wool and, after 1790, cotton, were the leading commodities exported from Britain, linen was the most significant manufactured *import* (Davis 1969; O'Hearn 2001, chapter 3). Trade regulations favoring the Irish linen industry were thus intended to diminish Britain's dependence on imports from mainland Europe, and to offset potential competition with the British woolen industry (Harte 1973). In 1699 an Act of Parliament prohibited the export of woolen goods from Ireland. Irish linen, by contrast, had been allowed to enter Britain duty free since 1696, and in 1705 its direct shipment to British colonies was authorized (Cullen 1972, 34, 37, 59).

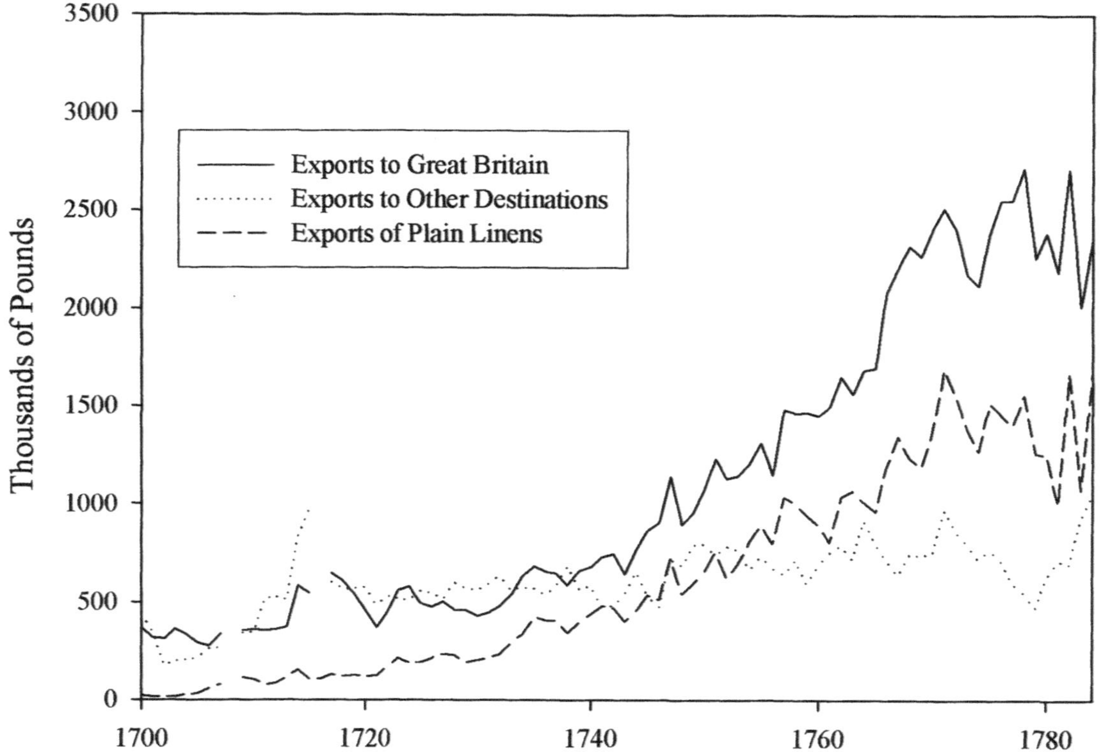

Figure 2.1. Value of Irish Exports to Great Britain and Other Destinations, 1700 to 1784
Source: Truxes 1988, Tables IIA, IIA.8, pp. 260–261, 276–277

Most Irish linens—on average more than 90 percent—continued to be shipped to Britain, where a further 20 percent were reexported, mainly to the Americas. Table 2.1 shows the main destinations of linens shipped *directly* from Irish ports. Unfortunately, this underestimates the proportions of linens that ultimately made their way to markets outside Britain. Nash (1985, 349) estimated that "from the mid-1760s to the mid 1790s, when Irish linen exports were growing at their fastest rate, the colonial market's share of total exports increased from 13 to 27 percent." According to his calculations, about 80 percent of Irish linen exports to the Americas went to the northern mainland, especially to Philadelphia and New York. Irish linens were shipped through English ports primarily because English merchant houses had greater capital and better access to shipping than their Irish counterparts (Truxes 1988, 180). The value of linens shipped *directly* from Irish ports to America represented less than 2 percent of the total export trade throughout most of the eighteenth century, although this proportion increased to an average of almost 10 percent in the 1780s and 1790s. The direct trade served mainly to reduce the cost of flaxseed from North America, by exchanging it for linens in a quasibarter arrangement (Truxes 1988, 182).

The growth of indirect exports to the Americas was at least partly stimulated by a system of bounties introduced at mid-century. The purpose of the scheme was to help British and Irish linens compete more effectively with foreign linens, which benefited from a drawback of British import duties when reexported to British colonies. There was a substantial demand from the plantation colonies for the coarse German linens known as Osnaburghs, which were used for clothing slaves. In 1743, a bounty of 1d (1 penny) a yard was allowed on exports valued at between 6d and 12d per yard. In 1745, an additional 1/2d per yard was allowed, and the scheme was extended to linen valued as low as 5d per yard, and up to 1s 6d (18d) per yard. The scheme thus favored the production and export of plain and coarse linens. In the second half of the eighteenth century, the official valuation of Irish linens ranged from 15d to 18d per yard.

There has been some disagreement on the extent of the bounty system's influence on the Irish linen industry. Gill (1925, 71) believed that it had little influence on the course of Irish trade. Following Murray (1903, 127), he pointed out that because, up to 1780, the bounties were allowed only on linens exported from British ports, the cost of carriage to England absorbed at least half the benefit to Irish exporters. More recently, however, Truxes (1988, 177) stated that "the bounty was the single most important encouragement to Ireland's transatlantic linen trade."

Throughout most of the eighteenth century, Irish linens were sent first to the Linen Hall in Dublin, where they were purchased by factors on behalf of

Table 2.1. Destinations of Linens Shipped from Irish Ports, 1710 to 1800

	Great Britain		*Americas*		*Spain*		*Baltic*		*Total*
Year	*Yards (000s)*	*%*	*Yards (000s)*	*%*	*Yards (000s)*	*%*	*Yards (000s)*	*%*	*Yards (000s)*
1710	1,528	90.5	137	8.1	24	1.4	—	—	1,689
1720	2,560	97.0	70	2.6	6	0.2	—	—	2,638
1730	3,821	92.4	218	5.3	86	2.1	9	0.2	4,136
1740	6,404	96.6	183	2.8	37	0.6	3	0.1	6,628
1750	10,857	96.9	283	2.5	43	0.4	8	0.0	11,200
1760	13,094	97.9	213	1.6	56	0.4	10	0.1	13,375
1770	19,671	95.7	827	4.0	37	0.2	21	0.1	20,561
1780	18,299	97.6	235	1.3	157	0.8	48	0.3	18,747
1790	33,361	89.4	2,821	7.6	10,380	2.7	21	0.1	37,322
1800	32,912	92.3	2,635	7.4	196	0.6	5	0.0	35,677

Sources: Truxes 1988, pp. 276–77; NLI Mss. 353–76.

English merchant houses. By the 1780s, however, there were significant changes in the system of trade. First, Belfast overtook Dublin as the most important port in the linen trade. Second, the merchants who exported the cloth from Belfast were increasingly able to do so on their own account, thus bypassing the factors (Gill 1925, 188–89). Many of these merchants were also bleachers, engaged in finishing the cloth prior to export. Finally, Liverpool began to replace London as the main port of destination for Irish linens, accounting for over 60 percent of the total by 1812 (Solar 1980, 64). Irish linen exports went through a prolonged depression in the late 1820s and early 1830s, followed by a strong recovery in the late 1830s and early 1840s (See figure 2.2) (Solar 1990).

Linen yarn exports followed a different trajectory from that of linen cloth. They increased steadily during most of the eighteenth century, growing quite substantially after 1750. From about 1780 onward, however, when linen cloth exports were growing by an average of nearly 12 percent per annum, yarn exports began to decrease, declining to below their 1700s level by 1820 (see Gill 1925, 339). By this time most Irish yarn was traded internally—between spinning and weaving districts. The linen yarn exported to Britain had been used primarily in the manufacture of cheap fabrics made from a mixture of linen and cotton and, until the introduction of machine-spun cotton in the 1770s, as the warp in cotton cloth, because hand-spun cotton was too weak for this purpose. Mill-spun yarn began to displace hand-spun yarn in Irish linen industry in the 1830s. Nonetheless, Geary (1998, 523) showed that as late as 1839, hand spinners supplied more than half the yarn absorbed by the weaving sector. Yarn and cloth made its way from dispersed rural households to Britain and America through a system of marketing that persisted through the early years of industrialization.

MARKETS: MERCHANTS, DRAPERS, JOBBERS, AND HAWKERS

As we have seen, Irish linen was exported by Dublin merchants who sold it through English factors. Much of the cloth was bought on commission for merchants in London, and this trend increased during the eighteenth century. Irish merchants, through lack of capital, were heavily dependent on English credit (Cullen 1968, 96–98). At the local level the cloth was purchased by drapers—small-scale merchants who had the cloth bleached before carrying it to Dublin for sale. Even lower in the hierarchy of trade were the jobbers—petty traders who bought yarn and cloth at local fairs in remoter parts of the countryside, and sold them again at the larger markets attended by drapers.

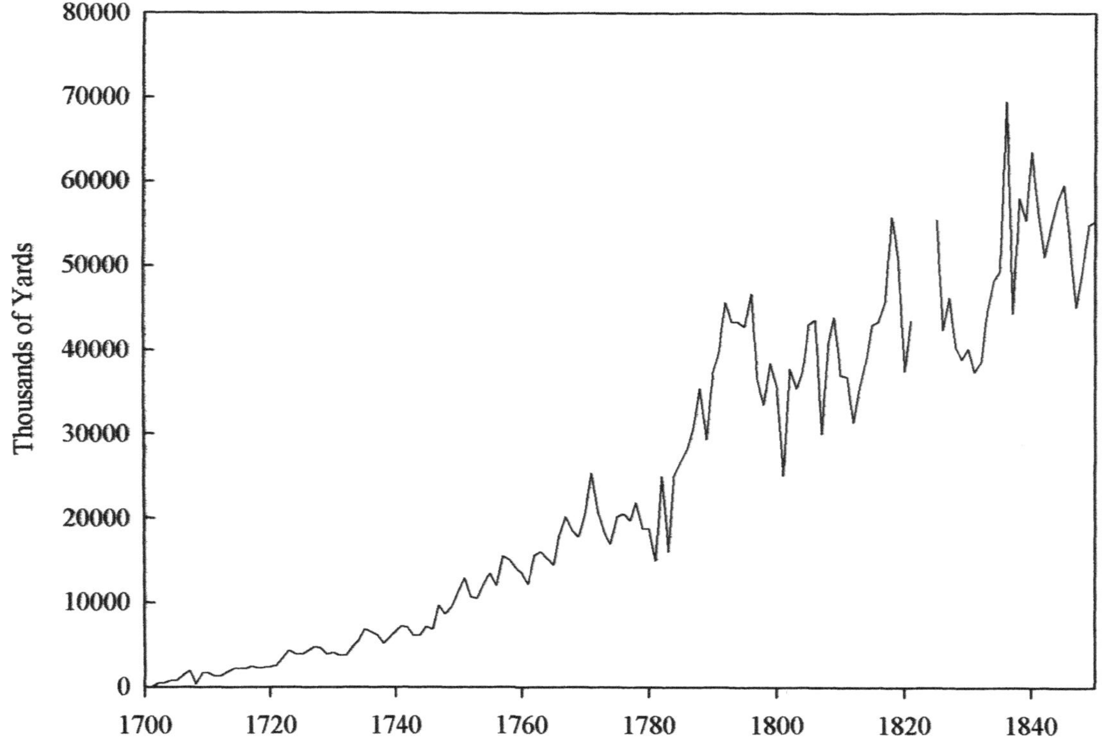

Figure 2.2. Plain Linens Exported from Ireland, 1700 to 1850
Sources: Gill 1925, pp. 341-342; Solar 1980, p. 64.

Yarn jobbers were also the crucial trading link between spinning and weaving districts.

The main sites of interaction between weaver and trader throughout most of the eighteenth century were the markets for "brown," unbleached linens. In 1776 Arthur Young observed the proceedings at the weekly market of Lurgan, Co. Armagh, where over one hundred thousand pounds worth of linen cloth was sold annually.

> When the clock strikes eleven the drapers jump upon stone standings, and the weavers instantly flock about them with their pieces: the bargains are not struck at a word, but there is a little altercation, whether the price shall be one halfpenny or a penny a yard more or less, which appeared to me useless. The draper's clerk stands by him, and writes his master's name on the pieces he buys, with the price; and giving it back to the seller, he goes to the draper's quarters and waits his coming. At twelve it ends; then there is an hour for measuring the pieces, and paying the money; for nothing but ready money is taken. (Young 1892, 128–29)

Despite their tumultuous appearance, the brown linen markets were governed by a complex set of regulations and supervised by a number of paid officials. The body with overall responsibility for regulating and promoting the industry was the Linen Board, established by the Irish Parliament in 1711.[1] The board consisted "almost entirely of members of one or other of the Irish houses of parliament and (included) representatives of the great officers of state, the judiciary, the episcopacy and the landed gentry" (Gribbon 1997, 77). In addition to managing the funds allocated for promoting the industry, the board and its officials performed the function of mediating between the various conflicting interests in the trade. Each link in the marketing chain would attempt to pass any losses associated with deficiencies in the cloth back to the preceding link—and ultimately to the producer—so that the Linen Board was inundated with demands for greater regulation of its sale. In 1763, for example, the board received a petition from several "Merchants, Factors, and Drapers of London"

> to lay before this Hon'ble Board the many Inconveniences we suffer . . . by the Frauds and Impositions of some Manufacturers, in lapping their Linen with conceal'd Holes, Rents, fine Laps and other Frauds and Damages, beside sometimes being tender or unsound, and frequently stamp'd a greater Length than they contain. (P.R.O.N.I. D562/1577)

The signatories suggested that the board purchase the deficient cloth and punish the "original proprietors."

From early in the eighteenth century, bleached, or "white" linens were subject to inspection by "lappers," officials appointed by the Linen Board, who charged a fee for stamping, or sealing, the pieces fit for sale. Such regulation was intended to standardize the pieces by length and breadth according to type, and to guarantee the quality of Irish linens. In 1733, provision was made for the appointment of lappers to stamp brown linens, but the regulations surrounding the presentation for sale of unbleached pieces were not enforced by the Linen Board until 1764, when public sealmasters were appointed. This initiative occurred in the wake of drapers' efforts to enforce the regulations at a number of markets in the northeast, culminating in a confrontation between weavers and buyers at Lisburn in 1762 (McKernan 1997). In 1782, the system of sealing was brought under greater supervision with the appointment of county inspectors and inspector generals with responsibility for monitoring the brown linen markets (Gill 1925, 68–70, 108–13, 207–208).

Gribbon (1997, 83) has described the policies of the Linen Board as "a mixture of severity, consideration and compromise," while noting that, in the second half of the century, the trustees "used the stick rather than the carrot" with respect to weavers. Specific regulations also existed for the production and making up of saleable yarn, but the Linen Board adopted a comparatively indulgent stance toward spinners, and there was little official attempt to enforce the rules. During the first half of the eighteenth century, the board employed inspectors to ensure that yarn presented for sale was correctly reeled. From 1723, it was an offense to possess "unstatutable" yarn. However, according to Gill (1925, 39, 68, 78), neither spinners nor merchants observed the regulations, and in 1757 all the yarn inspectors were dismissed. Early in the nineteenth century the Linen Board received new complaints from factors about unstatutable yarn reaching Dublin from a number of counties in Connaught and Leinster. However, Peter Besnard, Inspector General for the southern provinces, attributed the problem to the poverty of spinners in remote districts, and in 1818 the board established an annual fund for the purchase and distribution of reels in the southern provinces (Gribbon 1997, 81–82).

Table 2.2 gives an indication of the value of linen cloth sales at the major linen markets in Ulster in 1783, 1803, and 1821. I have included only those markets where sales exceeded £30,000 per annum in at least one of those years. Following Crawford (1988, 48–50), I have organized the markets by region, according to type of cloth sold. The most notable trend is the decline in value contributed by markets within the linen triangle,[2] the traditional heartland of fine yard-wide linens and cambrics, relative to the increase in value contributed by west Ulster, where narrower linens ("seven eights") suitable for shirting were manufactured, and relative to the spectacular rise of the

Table 2.2. Value of Sales in Thousands of Pounds by Region at Major Ulster Linen Markets, 1783, 1803, and 1821

	1783		1803		1821		1783–1821
Market	*Value*	*% Total*	*Value*	*% Total*	*Value*	*% Total*	*% Share Growth*
Linen Triangle							
Belfast	52	4.2	156	7.2	93	4.5	4.9
Banbridge	26	2.1	52	2.4	61	3.0	4.2
Tanderagee	26	2.1	42	1.9	57	2.8	3.7
Lurgan	130	10.6	130	6.0	153	7.4	2.7
Newry	52	4.2	104	3.8	67	3.3	1.8
Lisburn	104	8.5	146	6.7	97	4.7	−0.8
Richhill	31	2.5	5	0.2	0	0.0	−3.7
North Antrim and East Down (Northeast)							
Downpatrick	16	1.3	78	3.6	49	2.4	4.0
Ballymena	52	4.2	62	2.9	84	4.1	3.8
Ballymoney	30	2.5	12	1.0	31	1.5	0.1
South Ulster							
Armagh	94	7.6	208	9.6	360	17.4	31.7
Ballybay	26	2.1	47	2.1	49	2.4	2.8
Cootehill	52	4.2	114	5.3	61	3.0	1.1
Monaghan	36	3.0	57	2.6	45	2.2	1.0
Clones	31	2.5	21	1.0	16	0.8	−1.8
West Ulster							
Coleraine	4	0.3	31	1.4	74	3.6	8.3
Omagh	0	0.0	0	0.0	51	2.5	6.0
Strabane	36	3.0	78	3.6	86	4.2	5.9
Cookstown	6	0.5	26	1.2	44	2.1	4.5
Londonderry	52	4.2	104	4.8	79	3.8	3.2
Ballynagh	0	0.0	31	1.4	21	1.0	2.5
Dungannon	78	6.4	182	8.4	88	4.3	1.2
Killeshandra	16	1.3	31	1.4	17	0.8	0.1
Newtownstewart	31	2.5	52	2.4	32	1.6	0.1
Stewartstown	26	2.1	52	2.4	33	1.6	0.8
Regions (Sum of Major Markets)							
Linen Triangle	421	34.2	635	28.2	528	25.7	12.8
North-East Ulster	98	8.0	152	7.5	164	8.0	7.9
South Ulster	239	19.4	447	20.6	531	25.8	34.8
West Ulster	249	20.3	587	27.0	525	25.4	32.6
Minor Markets	218	17.8	357	16.4	318	18.2	11.9
All Ulster Markets	1225	100	2178	100	2066	100	100

Source: Crawford 1994, 78–80.

Notes: Ranked by percent share growth, 1783 to 1821. Major market defined as one in which the value of sales exceeded £30,000 in one or more years. Percentages refer to all Ulster markets.

market of Armagh, which specialized in coarse, yard-wide linens. The figures for Armagh are probably inflated, since it acted as a clearing house for coarse linens, which had previously been sold at smaller markets and fairs throughout south Ulster (Corry 1816, 74).[3] Despite concerns about the accuracy of the figures, they do show the extent to which the huge growth in output achieved after about 1780 depended first, on the dispersal of weaving to the west and south of the core districts, and second, on increased demand for plain and coarse linens. Part of the overall trend may also be attributed to the introduction of cotton weaving to the northeast during this period. It may have attracted many linen weavers in the core districts because initially it provided relatively high earnings (Crawford 1994, 39; 1988, 48). Between 1803 and 1821, the rate of growth in linen sales slowed, and there was a trend toward recentralization, as sales at many outlying markets declined.

By 1824 sales had temporarily recovered in the northeast, but this peak was followed by a long recession, and most commentators agree that outlying markets never returned to the prosperity of the 1780s and 1790s (Kennedy 1985), despite some evidence of increasing activity during the late 1830s and early 1840s (Collins 1982). By this period, the proportion of all linens exposed for sale at public markets had begun to decline. Strictly comparable figures are unfortunately not available for markets outside Ulster. However, estimates of the value of sales by county show that the most dramatic increase in linen output was achieved in Mayo, which had become the second most important linen county outside Ulster by 1816 (after County Louth).[4] Map 2.1 shows the distribution of linen markets and annual volume of sales throughout Ireland in 1821.

During the long eighteenth century, there was little change in the *organization* of marketing in the Irish linen industry. Yarn and cloth produced in dispersed rural households made its way to British ports through a network of fairs and markets. While formal, "brown-linen" markets were established from the mid-eighteenth century, some linens and almost all yarn continued to be sold at customary fairs and markets for livestock and provisions, where weavers and spinners set their pitch alongside other hawkers (Gill 1925, 53). Crawford (1988, 39) concluded that "the structure of the brown-linen trade that had been endorsed by the 1764 act [governing the appointment of public sealmasters] operated so well that it continued to be accepted in principle by all parties, even if not enforced in detail, up until industrialization"—that is, until the introduction of mechanized spinning on a substantial scale in the 1830s.

Nonetheless, despite this continuity in the structure of marketing, the discussion above has identified some important changes in the Irish linen trade during the 1780s and 1790s. We have seen that there was an increase in the

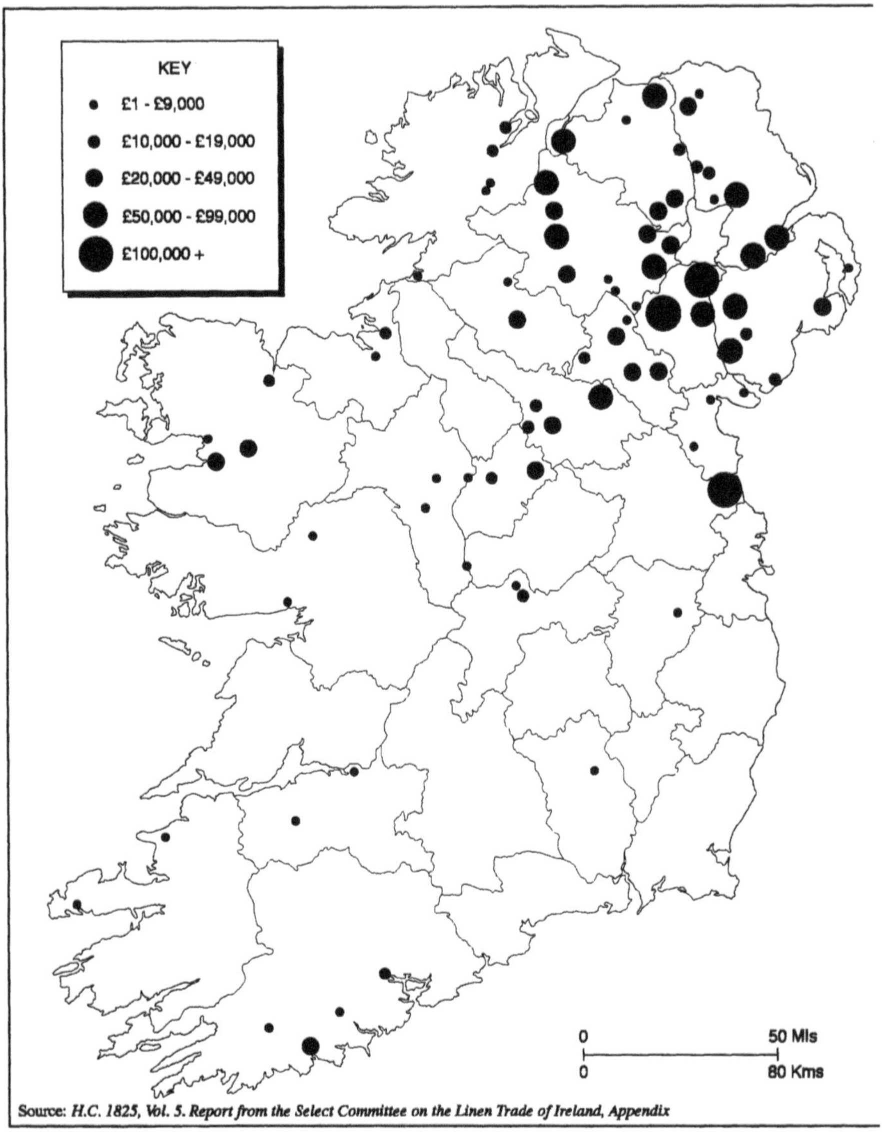

Map 2.1. Value of Sales at Irish Linen Markets, 1821

proportion of linens destined for the colonial market, together with an enormous increase in output during these decades. During the same period Belfast replaced Dublin as the main port of export, Liverpool replaced London as the main first port of destination, and Irish bleacher merchants accumulated sufficient capital to bypass the factors employed by English merchant houses.

Markets to the west and south of the original heartland of linen weaving accounted for an increased share of brown linen sales, while the coarse linen market of Armagh displaced the fine linen markets of Lisburn and Lurgan in preeminence. Meanwhile, exports of Irish yarn dwindled, as the demand from Irish weavers absorbed everything the spinners could produce, even as the demand from British cotton manufacturers dried up.

In England and Scotland, the last decades of the eighteenth century saw profound transformations in the organization of textile production, as mechanized spinning began to drive the development of both cotton and linen industries (Durie 1979; Harte 1973, 112).[5] In Ireland, while Belfast had a "brief flirtation" with mechanized cotton spinning, beginning in the 1780s, mechanization had little impact on the linen industry until the 1830s, when investment in mechanized flax spinning began to increase, and "capital and labor made a long run switch from cotton into linen" (Geary 1989, 267). The question of why the Irish market received the "wrong signal"—from the perspective of long-term development—to specialize in linen (Mokyr 1991, 189) will be pursued in chapter 6. In the next section, however, I explore the extent to which changes in the linen trade at the end of the eighteenth century were accompanied by changes in the organization of production (as opposed to marketing), despite the absence of technological innovation in the main branches of the industry.

PRODUCTION (1): FROM RURAL ARTISANS TO RURAL PROLETARIAT?

As well as governing the system of marketing yarns and linens, the Linen Board trustees were charged with enforcing regulations concerning the manufacturing process. A weaver was supposed to have served a five-year apprenticeship, followed by two years as a journeyman, before he set up as an independent master. The board did take action to enforce this legislation in County Down in 1722, but in general it seems to have been overlooked, and was repealed some time around the middle of the century (Gill 1925, 64–65; Gribbon 1997, 85). From 1758 onward, the board sponsored a number of laws directed against weavers' "combinations." These laws indicate that, at least in some sectors of the industry, weavers were working for others, rather than on their own behalf (Gribbon 1997). In 1816, in a request for more pay, Robert Fowler, a county inspector for Down mentioned that part of his time was spent "Settling disputes between Linen Manufacturers and their Weavers" (Corry 1816, 17). The extent to which linen weaving was characterized by a process of "proletarianization," whereby increasing numbers of weavers worked for putting out manufacturers over the course of the eighteenth century, has been the subject of some controversy in the literature.

Nineteenth-century accounts often looked back to an "ideal type" of rural artisan household believed to have prevailed in an earlier era. In such households, all parts of the production process were performed, from cultivation of the flax to sale of the woven and finished cloth. In the early part of the eighteenth century, according to Stephenson, writing in 1808:

> The farmers who had numerous families, committed the management of the land to one or two of their sons, and had weavers' shops erected, looms provided, and tradesmen engaged by the year, to teach the younger branches the art of weaving. The daughters spun flax; the good woman of the house, with the assistance of a girl, attended to the general affairs of the family and bleached the cloth which was spun and woven by her daughters and sons. . . . The land supplied the family with oats, potatoes, flax, and milk, and the rent was paid by the industry of the manufacture. (Quoted in Green 1949, 53)

This romantic picture of an artisan yeomanry may have approximated the Protestant Scots and English settler population of the northeast, amongst whom the export-oriented linen industry originated. However, it is unlikely that the self-contained household described by Stephenson could have remained the dominant form of manufacturing organization for long. Because of a technological bottleneck between spinning and weaving, at least four spinners were required to keep a full-time weaver supplied with yarn. Thus, as the time devoted to weaving increased, most families would have been obliged to purchase some yarn in the marketplace.[6] Moreover, the core linen weaving districts soon became densely populated, such that, according to Crawford (1982, 87), contemporaries noted their need to import flax, yarn, and food as early as the 1730s. Finally, responsibility for the process of bleaching was transferred at an early date from the "good woman of the house" to specialist bleachers. According to Gill (1925, 50), the evidence suggests that "a fair number" of bleachworks had been established, and that bleaching had "passed beyond the reach of the ordinary weaver" by 1725.

Bleaching and finishing were the main stages of the production process in which significant technological innovations were adopted during the eighteenth century. In the 1740s mechanized systems were introduced for washing, rubbering, and beetling the cloth (Crawford 1982, 90). After 1785, the use of chlorine greatly shortened the time necessary for bleaching (Green 1949, 69). Water power was also applied to the preparatory process of scutching flax, but according to Gill (1925, 264), much flax continued to be scutched by hand until the introduction of more efficient machinery in the early nineteenth century. Eighteenth-century innovations in the spinning and weaving phases were not widely adopted in the Irish linen industry. Two-handed spinning wheels were introduced to a number of European linen regions during the eighteenth century (Endrei and Maines 1995, 37–38), but there is little evidence of their use in Ireland.[7] Similarly, the flying shuttle, invented in 1733, was introduced only at the end of the eighteenth century, and did not become widely diffused until the nineteenth century (Crawford 1988, 41; McKernan 1995).

Outside east Ulster, at the beginning of the eighteenth century, linen weaving was carried on either by "bandle" weavers who supplied coarse narrow cloth to the peasantry, or by urban weavers who maintained traditional craft regulations. Linen weaving by private firms, who employed weavers in centers such as Drogheda, County Louth, and Mostrim, County Longford, accounted for most of the growth in cloth production outside Ulster in the mid-eighteenth century (Cullen 1972, 61). Sometimes landlords attempted to establish such concerns on their estates.[8] These efforts were clearly experimental, but "gentleman manufacturers" who exported their own cloth were also remarked on by Robert Stephenson in Sligo in 1762, while Besnard (1816, 13, 15, 22) noted that production by "Factory Masters" was typical of the midland counties of King's (now Offaly), Longford, and Westmeath, and of the northeastern county of Louth.

There is evidence, therefore, that whereas weaving for international markets took place in dispersed rural households in the northeastern countryside, in more southern counties it was relatively centralized. Cloth produced in this manner was sent directly to the Dublin Linen Hall and Cullen (1972, 62) argued that the extent of the weaving industry outside the northeast has been underestimated by considering only the amount of cloth sold at open markets. However, there is also evidence of a process of *decentralization* in the southern counties during the second half of the eighteenth century. In 1762, Robert Stephenson welcomed the establishment of public markets "throughout the Kingdom," on the grounds that:

> they will leave no Foundation for Combinations, and place every one concerned in the Manufacture, in a state of Independence of the other, and extend the trade with as much success, as it now spreads in several Counties in Ulster. (Stephenson 1762, 26)

In 1817, Peter Besnard echoed the theme in his remarks on the industry in County Longford:

> The trade of this County is at present very considerable, and in a very thriving state, and most strongly illustrates the value of public Markets for the sale of Linens, shewing in the clearest manner, the decided preference that should be

> given to encourage Weavers to bring their own Webs to Market, rather than to follow the plan formerly adopted here, of establishing large Factories dependent on one person, whose death or ill success may be attended with the most fatal consequences. (Besnard 1816, 15)

In the last two decades of the eighteenth century, growing numbers of rural households in north Connaught, especially in County Mayo began to weave coarse cloth on their own behalf for the export trade. As Cullen noted, the impetus for this development seems mainly to have come from within the rural population itself, but it was facilitated by the inmigration of several thousand Catholic weavers, fleeing from religious persecution in the northeast. In Mayo the spread of the weaving industry may have been partly due to the success of Lord Altamont's efforts to attract buyers to the Westport market (described by Young 1892, 255–56), but as in the southern and western counties of Ulster, a continued increase in demand for plain cloth was undoubtedly the most important reason for the proliferation of weaving in north Connaught.

While there was a decline in the significance of centralized manufactures in the more southern counties, in Ulster there is some evidence of a trend in the opposite direction over the course of the eighteenth century. In his classic study, Gill (1925, 138–162, 264–80) argued that, from the 1760s, drapers began to act as manufacturers, putting out yarn to a growing "weaving proletariat" which, he estimated, comprised more than 40 percent of all weavers by 1784, and two-thirds of the total by 1821. At that date, he argued, it was possible to distinguish three types of weaving district according to how fully "capitalism" had developed in each case. "Conservative" districts of "independent weavers" survived in "north Antrim, Tyrone, parts of Londonderry, and the outlying districts in general" (Gill 1925, 274). By contrast, the "bleaching districts" in the heartland of the industry—south Antrim, west Down, north Armagh, and east Londonderry—were characterized by "employment on a large scale" by a class of manufacturers that included enterprising bleachers (Gill 1925, 273–74). Finally, the district of south Armagh and north Monaghan was one of small employers (Gill 1925, 274–75).

Gill's analysis was driven by an implicit model of capitalist development as a linear process unfolding across a "correct" sequence of stages. Capitalism failed in the south because here, "leaders of enterprise were trying to take a short cut to the modern organization without the preliminary process of building up a market," in contrast to Ulster, where a class of manufacturing employers appeared "as a normal and healthy development, due to increasing trade" (Gill 1925, 133). In recent years, however, Gill's account has come under question. Crawford (1988, 36–37) concluded that Gill scrabbled about for evidence to support the unsustainable thesis that bleachers had become significant employers by the 1820s, and that even in relation to small manufacturers Gill overstated his case. Both Crawford (1988, 42) and McKernan (1997) claimed that, in his interpretation of the Lisburn riot of 1762, Gill drew unwarranted inferences about the emergence of class tensions between journeyman weavers and manufacturers. McKernan (1997, 95) convincingly argued that Reddy's (1984) concept of "market culture" provides a better theoretical framework for understanding this event as part of "an ongoing dialogue between producers and buyers over the terms by which the market would be supplied and controlled."

Gill's mechanistic understanding of the development of capitalism led him to overstate his case with respect to class differentiation in the weaving districts at the end of the eighteenth century. However, this should not blind us to the significance of "putting out" manufacturers, especially in south Ulster, where, as we have seen, production at the lower end of the market had increased rapidly. An oft-quoted description of these entrepreneurs was given by Sir Charles Coote, in his account of Armagh:

> Many of these farmers are master weavers, and are styled manufacturers; though they do not work at the loom they employ many weavers: their time is occupied at market chiefly in procuring yarn and disposing of their webs. Where a man of this description settles, and is so fortunate as to get a few acres, he soon establishes a manufacturing village around him, with those to which he gives employment. (1804, 138)

As Crawford (1988, 35) observed, such accounts "obscure many degrees of dependence, notably sons working for their fathers, or weavers taking yarn from jobbers either in hard times or until their own flax crop was harvested, scutched and spun." Young (1892, 130) referred to *drapers* advancing the yarn at the fine linen market of Waringstown, in County Down. However, relations of dependence between "master weavers" and "journeymen" were often superimposed on the traditional agrarian relationship between farmers and cottiers, especially in the western and southern weaving districts. Under the cottier system, a tenant farmer provided landless families with a cabin and small plot of land for cultivating potatoes (and sometimes flax), in exchange for labor on the farm. Grazing and turf-cutting rights were also sometimes included (Connolly 1998, 119). Entrepreneurial farmers adapted this system to the linen industry by substituting labor at the loom for labor in the fields.[9]

Instead of forming part of an inexorable process of class differentiation, many of these arrangements proved temporary. Landlords believed that farmer manufacturers were reaping profits from the land that rightfully belonged to them. In consequence, cottiers in the vicinity of the major linen markets were often able to outbid their former employers for tenancy on their small plots when leases came up for renewal (Crawford 1976, 197;

1983, 63). As more remote markets stagnated or declined in the first half of the nineteenth century, many manufacturers must have reverted to full-time farming. Nonetheless, a recognizable class of manufacturers was well established in Counties Antrim, Armagh, and Down by 1825, when it was reported to a Parliamentary Commission that up to 386 of them held brown linen seals. Despite employing relatively small numbers of weavers (from five to twenty), they were described as being of "as much worldly substance, as many to whom they sell their linens" (Crawford 1988, 44–45). These manufacturers remained a distinctive feature of the Irish linen industry, even after mill spinning had begun to obtain a foothold. According to a report dating from 1846:

> Among the Irish [mill] spinners, there are some who have cloth woven and even bleached on their own account, depending on the state of the market; these spinners are the most important. . . . Nevertheless, the larger share of yarn is sold by the spinners to manufacturers who give it out to weavers to be worked up at an agreed price. Among the manufacturers who buy yarn and give it out to be woven on their own account, there are some who sell it unfinished to the bleachers, and others who have it bleached for their own account and then ship it. The first sort is the most common; the bleachers in Ireland are at the same time, for the most part, first-class merchants; they have well established connections in all world markets, and it is for them and on their account that the greater share of exports are sent. (Solar 1988, 20)[10]

Thus the characteristic relationships between weaver, manufacturer, and bleacher merchant that had emerged in the late eighteenth century were not *transformed* by the mechanization of spinning, although they were concentrated within a smaller geographical area.

The system of manufacturing linen cloth that emerged during the late eighteenth century provided a flexible organizational environment for the introduction of mill-spun yarn to the weaving districts during the first half of the nineteenth century. According to Boyle (1997), manufacturers were at the core of organizational networks linking mill spinners to weavers in the Ulster linen industry during the first two decades of the industrialization process. With the introduction of power loom weaving from about 1850 onward, the manufacturers' role became obsolete, and the industry entered a phase of vertical integration.

PRODUCTION (2): GENDER AND THE SPINNING SECTOR

While the focus in the literature has been on class differentiation amongst weaving households, the gender division of labor between spinning and weaving households was of far greater consequence for the protoindustrial expansion and capitalist transformation of the linen industry. This relationship was slowly eliminated by the introduction of machine spinning, with devastating consequences for the great majority of rural industrial households, which depended on the manufacture of yarn, rather than cloth, for their survival.

Because of the bottleneck between spinning and weaving, the rapid growth in output of linens from the middle of the eighteenth century depended on the continued incorporation of new spinning households to the industry. It also depended on an increase in the area of land under flax. Unfortunately, we do not have statistics from Ireland's yarn markets comparable to those from the brown linen markets. However, in 1796, the Linen Board implemented an extraordinary scheme to promote flax cultivation by providing a spinning wheel in exchange for each rood (quarter acre) of flaxseed sown.

Map 2.2 shows the distribution of wheels claimed by county, normalized by number of households in 1791. It indicates that, at the end of the eighteenth century, the most important yarn counties were in northwest Ulster, followed by south Ulster, north Leinster, and north Connaught. The 1796 data also confirm that flax was cultivated in tiny quantities by numerous smallholders, and that the processes of flax cultivation and spinning tended to occur within the same households. During the era of protoindustrialization, the absence of commercial flax cultivation, and of putting out systems in spinning, remained a distinctive feature of the Irish linen industry.[11]

In the "yarn counties" the income derived from spinning in the households of smallholders was often crucial to their survival, and especially to the payment of rents (Collins 1979, 111). According to the Reverend William Henry, writing in 1739:

> The chief riches of this county (Donegal) arise from the advanced progress they have made in the linen manufacture. The farmer generally contents himself with no more land than is necessary to feed his family; which he diligently tills; and depends on the industry of his wife and daughters to pay by their spinning, the rent, and save up riches. (Quoted in Almquist 1977, 30–31)

Similarly, in County Mayo in 1776, Young (1892, 256) observed that "In their domestic economy, they reckon that the men feed the family with their labor in the field, and the women pay the rent by spinning."

Thus the Irish linen industry was characterized by a functional and regional division of labor between two forms of protoindustrial household, with different gendered relations to the marketplace. In the weaving districts men's labor provided most of the monetary income, and many households depended on the market for at least some of their provisions and raw materials. In such households, women's labor in spinning comprised an unremunerated input to the

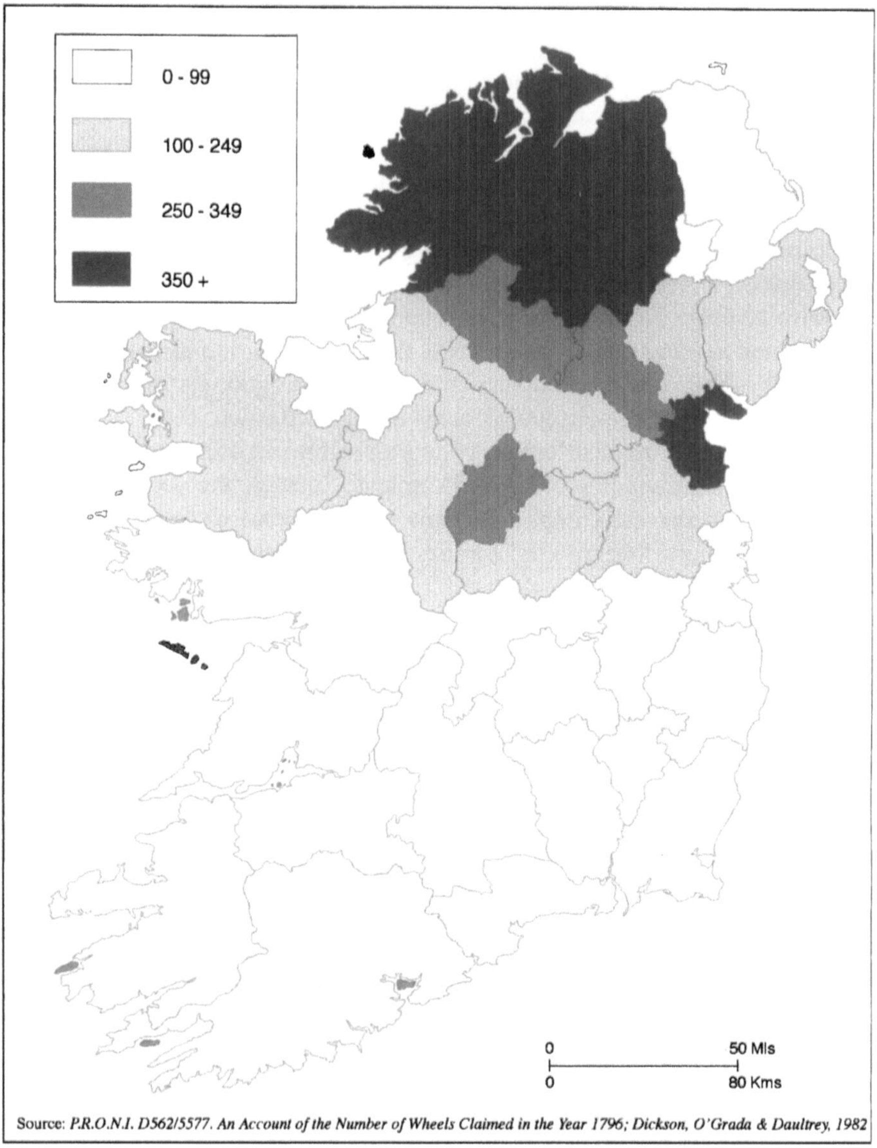

Map 2.2. Spinning Wheels Claimed per Thousand Households in Each County, 1796

end product which was sold in the marketplace, in addition to their contribution to the reproduction of the household through childcare, "housework," and labor in the fields. When weavers depended on outputters for their supply of yarn, women's labor in spinning may have been less essential to the household economy. Coote (1804, 253) reported that, in County Armagh, "Their earnings are generally spent on finery, as the men's labor procures them provisions." By contrast, in the spinning districts, women's labor was the main source of monetary income, and most household activities—including the cultivation of flax for spinning—remained largely outside the market.[12]

Given the bottleneck between spinning and weaving, and the absence of a functional division of labor between flax cultivation and spinning, the continued growth of the Irish linen industry depended on an exponential increase in the numbers of households within the second category described above. There were two ways in which this growth could occur: first, through the incorporation of new districts where the majority of households were poor and subsistence oriented, and second, through an increase in the population of such households within already incorporated districts. In the next chapter, I examine some of the evidence that both processes occurred in Ireland, through a dialogue with the theories of protoindustrialization.

CONCLUSION

In "The Penitent," James Orr described two different kinds of weaving household. The first might be described as "artisanal"—oriented primarily towards self-sufficiency and maintaining a customary standard of living. The second might be considered "protocapitalist"—oriented toward the market and accumulating wealth. Written in the climate of disenchantment surrounding the failure of the 1798 rebellion, Orr's poem expresses the hope that progress might be achieved through changing lifestyles rather than political transformation. I have discussed this aspect of his work in more detail elsewhere (Gray 1993c). For present purposes, it is important to note that while Orr, like Conrad Gill, represented progress in the form of a linear dichotomy, the reality of social change during the long eighteenth century was far more complex and uneven. Nonetheless, it is important to recognize that significant changes did occur in the Irish linen industry during the prefactory era. With the growth of the Atlantic economy, demand for plain and coarse linens increased in Britain and America. In this context, the dynamic core of the Irish linen industry shifted to Armagh and its hinterland, away from the fine weaving districts around Lisburn. Ulster's bleachers wrested control of the overseas trade from Dublin merchants, and manufacturers gained a foothold amongst the weaving households that supplied the brown linen markets.

These changes occurred without any fundamental alteration to the structure of marketing that channeled linens from the countryside to centers of finishing and trade. This resulted in a flexible organizational system that facilitated the introduction of mill spinning. However, this "modernization" of the weaving districts during the long eighteenth century depended on the continued incorporation of exponential numbers of relatively poor and "traditional" households in the spinning districts.

NOTES

1. More properly, the "Trustees of the Linen and Hempen Manufactures of Ireland."

2. Crawford (1988, 48–49) defines the linen triangle as the area between Belfast, Dungannon, and Newry, "where the finest yard-wide linens were produced." However, he describes Dungannon as "the greatest market" of the western district specializing in "seven-eights" linen, which suggests that most of the linens sold in that market originated outside the linen triangle.

3. See also the comments by Corry in the Linen Trade Report of 1825 (H.C. 1825, Vol. V., 851):

> In some cases it occurs that linens sold in one market are carried from thence by the purchasers, and sold in another, and are entered in both. . . . In other cases the public Sealmasters, who derive an income from the linens measured and stamped by themselves, but none other, confine their Returns to these linens only, and exclude all those that are brought to their markets with another's stamp on them; besides, there is reason to apprehend, that in some instances those Sealmasters . . . will understate the quantity sold, in order to understate the value of their own situations, and thus it happens, that the General Return, in some instances, makes the quantity *too much*, in others *too little* [emphasis in original].

4. See the estimates provided by Stephenson (1784) for 1770 and Besnard for 1816.

5. But see Berg (1994, 229), who argues that even in the linen and cotton sectors, "the break with older forms of work organization was not really so marked. As in the other textile manufactures, industrialization brought the intensification of a number of preexisting forms of work."

6. Collins (1982, 133–34) has pointed out that linen-manufacturing households also adopted strategies to increase the supply of female labor—by taking in relatives and employing itinerant spinners.

7. In the 1820s, a survey conducted by the North-West Society of Ireland in County Tyrone included a question on the diffusion of the two-handed spinning wheel. The responses were almost universally negative, except from the parish of Leckpatrick, where it was reported that: "The double wheel has made its way here: two or three of our most respectable farmers' daughters have got them, but there does not appear a general wish to adopt them or a conviction of their being better than the common wheel" (Day and McWilliams 1990, vol. 5, 126).

8. See Arthur Young's (1892, 225–26) account of the establishment in 1774 of such a "manufactory" in Ballymote, County Sligo, under the auspices of Lord Lucan.

9. Young (1892, 165) may have witnessed such an arrangement at Limavady, in County Derry: "Farms rise so high as 60 to 70 acres, and a few to 200, in general about

40 acres; many weavers' patches at 3 or 4; but the farmers themselves have yarn spun in their houses, which they give to the weavers to make into cloth: the farmer himself attending to nothing but the management of his land." See Sir Charles Coote's *Statistical Survey of the County of Armagh* (1802, 218–19) for a vivid description of the cottier weaver system in that county. His account suggests that cottiers could be employed to weave under both daily wage and piece-rate arrangements.

10. From Solar's translation of a pamphlet by Auguste Moxhet, published in 1849 and based on a letter to the Belgian Minister of Foreign Affairs. See Solar (1988), 16 and 24.

11. See chapter 6 for a thorough discussion of the implications of this feature of the Irish case, in comparison to those of Flanders and Scotland.

12. It should be noted, however, that Irish cultivators rarely saved flaxseed, so this did have to be purchased in the marketplace. In order to produce reasonably fine yarn, the flax stalk must be pulled before the seed is ripened. In order to save seed Irish producers would have had to set some of the stalks aside to dry before processing them for spinning coarse yarn. Gill (1925, 34) reckoned that, for Irish producers "It was doubtless cheaper to buy seed and produce flax at home than to save seed and buy a corresponding amount of imported flax." See also the discussion in Hood (2003) and Barker's (1917) fascinating account of why frontier agricultural conditions provided a more favorable environment for the production of flaxseed.

Chapter Three

Development

Och! mo bhean as mo chlann as mo thúirnín lín,
Mo chúpla punt go deo gan sníomh;
Tobac ar a bais as píopa len' ais,
'S is cuma san domhan ca ngabhann an cíos.

[Och! my wife and my family and my flax spinning wheel,
My couple of pounds forever unspun;
Tobacco at her hand and a pipe at her side,
And no care in the world where the rent comes from.]

The anonymous song, "An Túirnín Lín" [The Flax Spinning Wheel] (Ní Ógáin 1921, 24) humorously depicts the plight of a man who thought he had married a choice woman when she brought six pounds of flax as a dowry, but then found she took three months to spin just one pound. From the middle of the eighteenth century in Ireland, there was a steady increase in the number of poor households that maintained a precarious grip on the land through their women's labor in spinning. While such households were subsistence oriented, in the sense that their economy was one of "minimum consumption" (Scally 1995, 29), their fortunes were linked to the developing world economy through their production of linen yarn, and their consumption of purchased goods, including the addictive stimulant tobacco. Large tracts of the poorest counties in west Ulster and north Connacht were populated by spinning households, but similar districts formed pockets in the most prosperous counties touched by the linen industry.

I argued in chapter 2 that a sustained increase in the territories and households specializing in flax cultivation and spinning was an essential feature of the Irish linen industry. There was a dynamic interplay between economic growth, population increase, and the incorporation of new districts to the capitalist world economy.[1] This chapter examines this process of uneven development from about 1780, when both the economy and population of Ireland entered a period of rapid growth, to the years immediately preceding the crisis of the Great Famine that ravaged the country between 1845 and 1850. It does so through a dialogue with the theories of protoindustrialization, and their application to the Irish case.

THE DYNAMICS OF PROTOINDUSTRIALIZATION

Two main variants of protoindustrialization theory may be distinguished: a set of hypotheses first proposed by Mendels (see chapter 1), and the more elaborate demoeconomic model subsequently developed by Medick (1976, 1981a and b). I will focus particularly on the second variant, since it adds theoretical richness to the first, and has greater affinities with sociological (rather than economic) models of social change and development.

At the heart of Medick's model is the notion of a dynamic interplay between the micro strategies of rural industrial families, and macro transformations within the broader socioeconomic system. "It was a question of explaining the great developments encompassing the economy and population of whole regions and countries in terms of the life cycles and family strategies of individual persons and families" (Schlumbohm 1996a, 14). Medick argued that rural industrialization disrupted the demoeconomic balance characteristic of the European peasant family, and led to the emergence of a new type of family economy, with its own internal logic and contradictions. Whereas in the peasant model, marriage and household formation were tied to the inheritance of land, or other economic resources, in the protoindustrial model this link was broken, because young couples could expect to support a family through their labor in cottage industry.[2] Moreover, they had a positive incentive to marry early, since their earning capacity was greatest when they themselves were young, and since children could contribute to household production from a relatively early age.

In addition to expanding the labor supply through population increase, the protoindustrial family economy contributed to macroeconomic growth by enabling merchant capitalists to realize a "differential profit." As long as protoindustrial households retained access to small plots of land, they could produce commodities at significantly lower cost than either urban artisans restricted by guild regulations, or capitalist manufacturers employing wage laborers. Rural industrial producers supplied some of their own means of subsistence, and in many cases raw materials and equipment as well. Because they worked as a family unit, and received payment for the finished product, rather than for labor time expended, women's and children's contribution to the total labor input was not proportionally remunerated. Finally, protoindustrial producers absorbed much of the risk associated with fluctuations in market demand.

The logic of this model depends on the assumption that rural industrial households were oriented primarily toward achieving customary levels of subsistence, rather than toward accumulating surplus. "The family functioned objectively as an internal engine of growth precisely because subjectively it remained tied to the norms and rules of behavior of the traditional familial subsistence economy" (Medick 1981a, 52). This characteristic also proved to be the Achilles' heel of protoindustrialization. When demand increased rapidly and prices rose, rural industrial producers *reduced* their labor input, diverting free time and additional income to leisure consumption. In the short run, merchants could overcome this problem by extending their activities into more remote rural districts, but this increased transaction costs. In the long run the contradiction could only be overcome by investment in mechanization and the employment of wage laborers (Medick 1981a, 54).

The protoindustrialization model developed by Medick implies a trend toward social homogenization (rather than class differentiation) within rural industrial communities. Because the prosperity of household production units no longer depended entirely on access to land, the size of holdings tended to diminish over time, either through land subdivision, or as income from cottage industry enabled landless and land-poor groups to purchase or rent small farms (Medick 1981a, 47–50). Another strand of research on protoindustrialization has explored the extent to which the diminution of land holdings contributed to the "pauperization" of rural industrial communities, especially after the onset of deindustrialization (Levine 1976, 1977). The logic of the protoindustrial family economy meant that, just as household members tended to withdraw their labor when times were good, they were also willing to continuously increase their labor input when times were bad in an effort to achieve their subsistence target, often to a point that would be unsustainable in a profit-oriented enterprise. Especially where their tiny plots made it impossible to revert to agriculture for their survival, rural industrial producers continued to manufacture products under conditions of extreme poverty in competition with mechanized systems, contributing thus to the protracted and uneven nature of European industrialization (Kriedte, 1981b, 135–60).

Since the publication of *Industrialization before Industrialization*, protoindustrialization hypotheses have encountered sustained criticism on the grounds that many rural industrial regions did not follow the path predicted by the model. The evidence has been well summarized in Kriedte, Medick, and Schlumbohm (1993), and in Ogilvie and Cerman (1996). Some scholars have responded to the ambivalent balance sheet on protoindustrialization by calling for a simple rejection of the theory (Coleman 1983; Vandenbroeke 1996), or its replacement by another (De Vries 1993), while others have sought to identify specific local factors that might explain why the theory did not apply in a given region. Some candidates include:

1. *Differences in forms of agriculture and traditions of landholding*. This builds on an earlier body of scholarship that found rural industries to be more prevalent in areas characterized by less fertile soil, where waste land was available for reclamation, and where restrictions on inmigration and land subdivision were limited (Thirsk 1961; Jones 1968). Hudson (1981) showed how differences in forms of landholding and the quality of land were linked to differences in organization, finance and entrepreneurship in the Yorkshire woolen and worsted industries.
2. *The relative significance of agriculture for making a living*. A number of studies have suggested that where protoindustrialization occurred in regions characterized by commercial farming, the predictions of the theory do not seem to have been borne out (Gullickson 1983; Hendrickx 1993; Mastboom 1996). More recently, Hendricx (2003, 66) argued that wherever "a tie to agriculture was a natural and encouraged way of securing an additional income (whether in kind or in money), there was no existential need for early marriages and large numbers of children per family." He thus implied that the relative significance of agriculture in rural household strategies was governed by social and cultural, as well as purely economic factors.
3. *The extent to which families operated as production units*. Medick's model of the protoindustrial family economy assumes that all the members of a household were engaged in a cooperative enterprise to manufacture a given commodity and meet the subsistence requirements of the family—in other words, that they operated as a work unit. However, this was not always the case. Gullickson (1986) found, in her study of the Pays de Caux, that in many households women were engaged in spinning linen yarn, while their menfolk found employment as agricultural laborers. In some protoindustrial regions, family members worked side by side producing separate commodities for different outputters (Pfister 1995).
4. *The particular characteristics of the industry that developed in a given region*. In a trenchant critique, Mager (1993) argued that the focus on the linen industry in the classic studies of protoindustrialization distorted the overall picture. Linen was unique insofar as smallholders were able to supply their own raw material, and thus the "laws" of the family economy found full ex-

pression. In other industries however, different patterns emerged, because the raw materials had to be supplied by outputters or manufacturers.

5. *Variations in the institutional context.* According to Ogilvie (1996), a great deal of the divergence amongst rural industrial regions can be explained by "profound and enduring differences" in the "sets of established rules and practices through which people organized their economic, social, demographic, political and cultural activities" (p. 23). Related arguments have been made by Berg (1994) and by Sabel and Zeitlin (1985).

The original protoindustrialization hypotheses have proven extremely fruitful in generating a vast body of scholarship on the "regional dimension" in the demoeconomic transformation of Europe (Hudson 1989). In fact much of the variation had already been identified by the authors of *Industrialization before Industrialization*—something not often acknowledged by their critics. More recently, however, it has been argued that the models developed by both Mendels and Medick were vulnerable to the regional "exceptionalism" described above, because they remained embedded in "formalist" models of social change (Pfister 1996) conceived as a succession of "ideal types" (Gray 1993a; 1997). More dynamic models incorporate principles of variation at their conceptual and methodological core (Tilly 1984). Pfister (1996) has made an important contribution to protoindustrialization theory along these lines.

For Pfister, the coexistence of commercial and subsistence sectors is the central assumption at the heart of protoindustrialization theory. This dualism implies the existence of "underutilized factors." The path followed by a given protoindustrial region depended on "the relationship among factor productivity in the protoindustrial and subsistence sectors on the level of individual households." A long-term increase in the protoindustrial labor force could occur either through geographical extension, or through an increase in the application of labor to manufacturing within a given perimeter.

Geographical expansion was likely to be the dominant growth pattern where the productivity of labor in protoindustrial activities was not much greater than the productivity of labor in subsistence agriculture. Because the opportunity costs of abandoning subsistence production were relatively high, protoindustrial growth depended, under these circumstances, on the presence of structural unemployment (usually of women and children). Pfister argued that these kinds of protoindustries did not alter household dynamics fundamentally, and thus did not cause population growth, though they might penetrate regions subject to overpopulation for other reasons. By contrast, where the productivity of labor in protoindustrial activities was significantly higher than in subsistence agriculture, the rent derived from market activity exceeded the opportunity costs of forfeiting subsistence income. Where this was the case, protoindustrial growth did not depend on the existence of structural unemployment, and might lead to population increase for the reasons originally identified by Mendels and elaborated by Medick. Due to transaction costs, mature protoindustrial systems were often characterized by the first variant at their peripheries, and the second at their cores.

While most "second generation" scholarship on protoindustrialization has focused on the puzzle of regional variation, research by Hudson and King (2000) has demonstrated that aggregate shifts in demographic indicators can be caused by changes in the behavior of a *subgroup* of the population, or by changes in the *proportion* of the population experiencing extremes of behavior. In their study of two textile townships in Yorkshire they found that, for most people, rural industry promoted stability in demographic behavior by reducing out migration and increasing kinship density, thereby ensuring that they continued to be influenced by communal norms and practices. However, in both townships they found evidence of changing demographic behavior—earlier marriage, higher rates of illegitimacy and infant mortality, and increased marital fertility—amongst those people experiencing increasing economic insecurity due to proletarianization (increased dependence on outputters and the introduction of mechanized spinning).

Finally, it should be noted that several authors have rejected the idea, found in both Mendels's and Medick's models, that protoindustrial producers were subsistence oriented, in the sense that their participation in manufacturing was oriented toward maintaining a customary standard of living, rather than toward generating a surplus (Cohen 1990; Mokyr 1976; de Vries 1993). In direct contradiction to the original protoindustrialization hypotheses, de Vries (1993) proposed the idea of an "industrious revolution." Over an extended period of time, preindustrial households began to substitute labor for leisure, in order to purchase commodities in the marketplace, which they increasingly preferred to home-produced goods. Thus increased industrial output before the factory was driven less by external constraint, than by the emergence of new tastes and preferences.

How well does the evidence from Ireland fit protoindustrial models? In the next section of this chapter, I evaluate the existing evidence relating to the linen industry under the following three headings. First, I examine the regional dimension, focusing on the institutional and environmental contexts in which different patterns of protoindustrialization occurred. Second, I discuss the limited evidence available on the relationship between protoindustrialization and demographic change. Third, I explore the evidence on the relationship between protoindustrialization and social homogenization and pauperization in the Irish countryside.

PROTOINDUSTRIALIZATION AND THE IRISH CASE

The Regional Dimension

Kevin Whelan (1997, 70–85) distinguished five major regions in eighteenth-century Ireland with "well defined cores and more ambiguous edges," namely: dairying, cattle fattening, tillage, protoindustrial, and small farm. These regions emerged in the context of two key processes of incorporation to the developing world system: "[T]he initial subjugation, subsequent colonization and final integration of Ireland into the expanding English state, and the concurrent enhancement of Ireland's location within the North Atlantic commercial world" (Whelan 1997, 67). The colonial upheavals of the seventeenth century left Ireland with a unique pattern of commercial landed estates, owned by a small, predominantly Protestant elite, and operated according to a universally applied leasing system (Whelan 1997, 68). A multifarious population of tenants, cottiers, laborers, and squatters worked the land, their circumstances and composition varying greatly by region. Until 1778 Catholic tenants were precluded from holding leases for more than thirty-one years, or for lives. The establishment of the colonial estate system in Ireland meant that "[T]he rural lower classes became subject to the same broad body of property law as in England, but with none of the multiple accretions of use rights and customary entitlements that offered the population there and elsewhere a measure of protection from the pressures of a rapidly developing market economy" (Connolly 1992, 55).

The three main agricultural regions in eighteenth century Ireland were concentrated in the east and south of the country—commercial dairying in south Munster, tillage in much of Leinster and east Munster, and cattle grazing in northeast Leinster, parts of north Munster, and inner Connacht (see Whelan 1997, figure 9, p.70). Ulster had been the province least affected by commercial agriculture during the seventeenth century (Cullen 1972, 24). During the 1690s, however, significant numbers of Scottish colonists settled in the northeast where they were granted leases over the native Irish, many of whom became undertenants or cottiers. Landlords required the settlers to introduce "British" husbandry practices in place of the Irish pastoral system: the terms of their leases included, for example, such items as building a dwelling to certain specifications, planting an orchard, and fencing the boundaries of their holdings (Crawford 1976, 194). In return they benefited from what became known as "Ulster tenant right": they were considered entitled to sell their leases to other individuals without interference from the landlord. It was in this northeastern district that the domestic linen industry was first established and carried on most intensively throughout the prefactory era.

Whelan distinguished the protoindustrial zone of east Ulster from a "small farm" region spread along the western Atlantic fringe, from Donegal to Kerry, and including parts of the midlands. However, it is important to point out that these districts were in fact "protoindustrial," insofar as spinning represented an important source of income in many households, especially in the northwest.[3] Along the Atlantic seaboard, from Donegal to Galway, more than half of all occupied women in each county were spinners in 1841. It might be argued that the 1841 data give a distorted impression of the spatial distribution of spinning, since by that date mill spinning had begun to make inroads on the market for hand-spun yarn. However, Leister's (1962) map of the distribution of textile manufacturing in Ireland, based on Arthur Young's observations, suggests that spinning was already prevalent in much of the small-farm region at the end of the eighteenth century, as do the flax-premium data from 1796 (see map 2.2).[4] The significance of protoindustrial activity outside central and east Ulster has often been underestimated, because the quantity, and monetary value of the yarn produced in the small-farm region was relatively small. However, from the "subsistence" perspective of small farmers on the Atlantic fringe, the income from flax cultivation and spinning represented a vital input to their household economy.

Throughout the small-farm region land was often held in the manner known as "rundale." Under this system, small communities allocated arable land in usufruct shares and held grazing land and access to peat and seaweed (for fertilizer) in common. A permanently cultivated "infield," divided into unenclosed strips, was separated from the "outfield," which might be periodically reclaimed. Sometimes cattle were moved away from arable lands to highland grazing during the summer in a practice known as "booleying" (McCourt 1981, 120). The arable land was divided in such a way as to ensure that each family had the use of some good soil, so that individual holdings consisted of a number of widely dispersed, unfenced plots. Under a practice similar to the English "gavelkind" (or "changedale") land was transmitted, not through inheritance but by the periodic reallocation of land to the whole community. The landholders' houses clustered in villages (or "clachans") and the whole area was rented jointly by the community.

There has been some debate as to whether or not the small farm region is best thought of as a precapitalist economy, with rundale representing an archaic, or primitive form of agricultural organization. In 1960, Lynch and Vaizey first proposed the thesis that there were "two Irelands" at the end of the eighteenth century, corresponding to an east-west regional divide: a modern cash economy linked to Britain through trade, credit and travel, and a traditional subsistence economy that remained largely outside the market until after the Great Famine of the mid-nineteenth century. In his classic study of

Why Ireland Starved, Mokyr (1985) accepted the thesis of economic dualism, but argued that the two Irelands were not geographically separate, but were instead "living alongside each other, intertwined and mutually interdependent though entirely different in their degrees of commercialization, economic attitudes, agricultural techniques and so on" (p. 20). For Mokyr, the numerous class of cottiers and landless laborers, more characteristic of the eastern tillage and grazing zones than of the small-farm region, was also part of the subsistence sector because the use of money was not widespread among its members.

In one of the first applications of historical sociology to the Irish case, Clark (1979) argued that the subsistence sector was not the residue of an earlier period, but was instead a *product* of socioeconomic processes occurring during the eighteenth and early nineteenth centuries. In a similar vein Whelan (1994, 68–69) rejected the thesis that rundale villages represented a survival from precolonial or even neolithic times:

> They are not the degraded relics of an archaic, aboriginal settlement form, practicing primitive agriculture in 'refuge' areas. They are instead a sophisticated solution to specific ecological, environmental and social problems, which maximised the carrying capacity of a meagre environment in an expanding demographic regime.

Thus while scholars like Almquist (1977) and McCourt (1981) argued that the "elasticity" of traditional rundale settlements *facilitated* high rates of population increase, Whelan suggests that eighteenth and early nineteenth century rundale settlements were, in effect, *caused* by population growth.

Slater and McDonough (1994) made the strongest claim for the survival of precapitalist relations in nineteenth century Ireland. Whereas Lynch and Vaizey distinguished between "traditional" subsistence and "modern" cash sectors within the Irish economy, Slater and McDonough distinguished between the extraction of "absolute" and "relative" rental value under a "feudal mode of production" which, they argued, persisted in Ireland up to the 1880s, when the process of transferring land ownership from landlords to farmers began.

Absolute rental value was extracted simply by increasing rents, or by increasing the number of tenants on the land. Because all profits were channeled to the landlord under this system, farmers relied on customary, labor-intensive production techniques since they had neither capital to improve productivity nor incentive to do so in the first place. Slater and McDonough refer to the labor-intensive process within the absolute rental value regime as "spade husbandry." Farmers drew primarily on family labor. Additional labor requirements were met by the mobilization of a wider kinship or community based cooperative work team—a "meitheal." More substantial farmers might also draw on the labor of cottiers, resorting only in the last instance to employing waged laborers (Slater and McDonough 1994, 88). For Slater (1988), waged labor under spade husbandry was "living in the pores" of customary intensive processes. The labor-intensive character of spade husbandry, combined with reliance on family labor and the meitheal, favored smaller farms (Slater and McDonough 1994. 87). From the landlords' point of view, the extraction of absolute rental value had the advantage of not requiring any supervision of their estates. In the long run, however, the system tended to collapse, as rack renting, population increase, and the subdivision of land undermined the capacity of rent payers to meet their own survival needs.

Relative rental value was extracted by increasing the productivity of individual tenant farmers. This system entailed landlords restricting the number of people who could survive on the land in order to consolidate holdings and prevent subdivision. It thus encouraged the adoption of labor-saving technology—plough husbandry.[5] Farmers continued to rely primarily on family labor, but additional seasonal requirements were met by employing wage laborers. Kinfolk and neighbors sometimes pooled the technical means of production—horses, for example, might be joined to form a plough team. According to Slater and McDonough, the development of plough husbandry was stunted in Ireland because of the absence of tenurial security. Thus Irish farmers invested in purchased seeds and fertilizer, but not in the construction of outbuildings.

Slater and McDonough make the distinction between spade and plough husbandry in chronological terms—before and after the famine, with a transitional period between 1815 and 1850—but it seems reasonable to infer a spatial dimension as well, since the transition from absolute to relative rental regimes was an uneven process (Slater and McDonough 1994, 87). Just as spade husbandry continued in parts of the small farm region after the famine, so elements of plough husbandry were clearly present in the economy of late eighteenth and early nineteenth century Ireland. The authors place their argument firmly within a "modes of production" perspective that, following Brenner (1977), they believe to be fundamentally contrary to world-systems hypotheses. This is not the place to review the debate.[6] For my present purposes, Slater and McDonough's "spade" and "plough husbandry" represent useful orienting concepts for understanding the rural labor processes underpinning the development of the linen industry. This theme will be pursued in more detail in chapter 4.

To summarize, from the end of the seventeenth century, the linen industry developed in those regions of Ireland least fully integrated to the evolving,

British-dominated world economy. However, there were some important institutional differences between those districts in east Ulster that eventually formed the core of the protoindustrial zone, and those districts within the small farm region that formed its periphery. East Ulster was characterized by the presence of a Protestant settler tenantry that enjoyed a measure of customary security on the land, and that attempted to introduce "English style 'civility' in tidy enclosed landscapes with arable predominating over pasture" (Duffy 1995, 32). By contrast, the peripheral districts were characterized by "untidy," open-field farming, often on joint holdings operated under the rundale system. All parts of the protoindustrial zone were, by definition, integrated to the capitalist world economy. However, especially in the peripheral districts, production was oriented toward maintaining a minimum standard of living using customary labor processes.

The Demoeconomic Regime

From the middle of the eighteenth century to about 1820, Irish population growth was unusually fast, relative to other European countries (Guinnane 1997, 80). The total population is estimated to have tripled between 1740 and 1821 (Ó'Gráda 1994, 6). Dickson, Ó'Gráda, and Daultrey (1982) showed that between about 1750 and 1790, the most rapid growth occurred in Ulster, where population grew by between 1.8 and 2.2 percent per annum. After 1790 population grew most rapidly in Connacht, by about 2 percent per annum, while the rate of growth in Ulster slowed to 1.1 percent per annum. According to Ó'Gráda (1994, 6), "The surprise here is not so much Connacht's headlong population growth, as the relatively slow growth in Ulster after 1790, where modern industry was making greatest headway."

Unfortunately, because of the scarcity and poor quality of sources pertaining to demographic behavior during this period (Guinnane 1997, 125–28), it is difficult to draw any conclusions about the demoeconomic processes giving rise to general patterns of population change. Almquist (1979) made the only systematic attempt to test protoindustrialization hypotheses with respect to demographic variables in Ireland, using aggregate data from the 1841 census. He found that the percentage of spinners by county was correlated with high proportions of young women married, and with high proportions of children under fifteen years in the population. Using multiple regression models, Almquist (1979, 714) demonstrated that 64 percent of young female nuptiality was "explained" by the availability of waste land and the presence of high proportions of spinners. Almquist's research thus provides the best evidence we have in support of the protoindustrial model, given the absence of the kinds of historical records that would allow us to reconstruct demographic behavior at the level of individuals and households. However, the findings are compromised by the fact that, by 1841, mechanized spinning had already made substantial inroads on the protoindustrial system in Ireland. Moreover, Almquist found that *female* nuptiality was not significantly correlated with *weaving,* nor was it negatively associated with distance from Belfast.

Mokyr (1985, 63) concluded that the relationship between rural industry and propensity to marry was overdrawn in Almquist's analysis. Moreover, "[It] is not possible to leap merrily from 'marriage age' to 'fertility' to 'birth rates' to 'population growth.'" Mokyr's own analyses of data from the 1841 census yielded results that are not inconsistent with Almquist's findings, but are ambivalent from the perspective of protoindustrialization theory: cottage industry affected male propensity to marry, but not that of females (Mokyr 1985, 55). However, Mokyr measured "cottage industry" as the proportion of rural men and women employed in "occupations ministering to clothing" in the 1841 census, thus obscuring the different effects of spinning and weaving revealed by Almquist's analysis.

Most general accounts of Ireland's demographic regime before the Great Famine of 1845 to 1850 begin with the now classic arguments put forward by Kenneth H. Connell, in his *The Population of Ireland* (1950). According to Connell, the availability of land—either through partible inheritance, or the reclamation of waste—together with the possibility of relying on potato cultivation for survival, meant that Irish people were not subject to the constraints on marriage inherent in the European peasant system. However, in contrast to Medick's model of the protoindustrial family economy, where cottage industry provided an *incentive* to marry early, Connell argued that the Irish married young because of the *absence* of any prospect of improving their material well-being. Marriage was an "inferior good" in the context of Irish poverty (Ó'Gráda 1994, 7). Clarkson (1996, 72) implicitly reiterated Connell's thesis when he argued that:

> It is unnecessary to invoke protoindustrialization to explain the growth of the Irish population during the eighteenth century . . . when more obvious explanations are readily to hand. . . . Although the presence of rural industry stimulated the growth of population, for example in south Ulster, the most important influences were the peculiarities of a land system that permitted continual subdivision, and the widespread adoption of a diet dominated by potatoes that sustained a healthy and fertile population. Inasmuch as youthful and fertile marriages required an economic base, in Ireland it was amply supplied by the ubiquitous potato.

However, other recent research in Irish demographic history demonstrated that some aspects of Connell's argument clearly cannot be sustained. Most importantly, there is little evidence to support the thesis that the Irish married at an unusually young age (Guinnane 1997, 82). Calculations from the 1841 census suggest an average age at marriage for women of about twenty-six years (see Fitzpatrick 1985, table 2; Mokyr 1985, table 3.3).

Most commentators accept that early marriage may have been common among some social groups. While rejecting Connell's thesis that age at marriage was not responsive to trends in living standards, Ó'Gráda (1994, 10) agreed that the controls on marriage and household formation associated with the European peasant model "held little appeal" for "the poor who eked out a living on the margins of cultivation." According to Connolly (1985) farmers were more likely to postpone marriage than were laborers and other land-poor groups. However, O'Neill (1984, 181) concluded from an analysis of the 1841 census manuscripts for Killashandra, in County Cavan, that:

> The evidence . . . affords no reason for supposing that laborers as a group married considerably younger than farmers, but rather every indication that laborer's wives married later than farmers' wives throughout the prefamine period.

Nonetheless, O'Neill (1984, 182–83) found that the age at marriage for laboring women declined steeply between about 1795 and 1825. He argued that the achievement of near "equality of opportunity" for marriage by laboring women might have been sufficient to explain the overall increase in population. O'Neill attributed this decline to an increase in the demand for labor in the context of commercializing agriculture.

Unfortunately, O'Neill failed to consider the possible effects of protoindustrialization on age at marriage. This is disappointing given the dynamism of the linen market at Killashandra during this period (see chapter 2, table 2.2). Age at marriage for *both* farmers' and laborers' wives appears to have been lower in Killashandra (about twenty-two years) than in Ireland as a whole (about twenty-six years), and Guinnane (1997, 82) suggested the availability of income from rural industry might explain this difference. Morgan and Macafee (1984) provided further evidence of a link between the linen industry and relatively early marriage in their analysis of some surviving 1851 census enumerator's returns from County Antrim. They found that both male and female linen workers married younger than farmers and their wives, although the difference was less marked for women. These studies thus hint at a possible link between the linen industry and early marriage.

Population increase can have causes other than a decline in marriage age among women. In Swiss protoindustrial regions, population growth appears to have been caused by declining mortality, rather than by a lowering of the age at marriage. Householders invested their savings from rural industrial activity in agriculture, leading to improved nutrition and greater resistance to mortality crises through crop differentiation, including the introduction of potatoes (Pfister 1992; Pfister 1996, 146–47).[7] The evidence on mortality is particularly sparse in the Irish case (Guinnane 1997, 81). Inoculation against smallpox may have had a small effect (Ó'Gráda 1994, 12). There is tentative evidence in favor of relatively low child mortality (Ó'Gráda 1993, 43–46). Anthropometric research on average heights, and estimates of calorific intake, suggest that the nutritional status of Irish people was relatively good (Ó'Gráda 1994, 17–23 and 85–97). However this was not achieved by diversification of the nutritional base, but rather by near total dependence on the potato for food.[8] Almquist (1977) pointed to the relationship between flax and potatoes in crop rotations on smallholdings in County Mayo. However, outside the main zones of flax-cultivation smallholders, cottiers and laborers were equally dependent on potato consumption, so no simple connection between protoindustrialization and declining mortality may be inferred.

Guinnane (1997, 84–85) concluded that high rates of marital fertility most likely account for Ireland's population growth—that is, Irish women had unusually large numbers of children once they married. Calculations from the 1841 census imply very high rates of marital fertility relative to other European countries (Mokyr 1985, 36). High marital fertility is consistent with Medick's model of the protoindustrial family economy, since the labor of each additional child added an important marginal input to the overall prosperity of the household. However, Vandenbroeke (1996, 109) found that in Flanders, at the end of the eighteenth century, fertility in rural industrial areas was lower than in purely agrarian districts:

> The reasons behind these regional contrasts have to do with nursing habits and women's position in the production process. A high degree of domestic industry implies home saving, and a long lactation process (twelve months or more). In most cases, lactation causes temporary sterility, with the result that there are longer intervals between births. A side effect of this long and frequent nursing is lower infant mortality.

In the Irish case Schellekens (1993) argued that the demand for female labor in potato cultivation could have reduced the amount of time they spent breast feeding, leading to narrower birth intervals. As I will show in chapter 6, in Ireland, flax cultivation and processing also drew on vast amounts of female labor. Thus in the Irish case, protoindustrial activity could have had the opposite effect on birth intervals than in Flanders, where spinners bought their flax in the marketplace, rather than cultivating and processing it themselves (see chapter 6). Mokyr (1985, 57) found that "cottage industry" had a positive effect on total birth and fertility rates, but no apparent effect on marital fertility.

In summary, I cannot agree with Clarkson (1996, 72) that "[It] is unnecessary to invoke protoindustrialization to explain the growth of the Irish population . . . when more obvious explanations are readily to hand." On the contrary, in the absence of any convincing explanation for the dramatic increase in Ireland's population from the middle of the eighteenth century, it remains plausible that the availability of income from protoindustrial activity was one of the determining factors. However, the sparse evidence available includes a number of paradoxes indicating that—as in other parts of Europe—the relationship between protoindustrialization and demographic change was more complex than the original models suggested. Those paradoxes include: (1) the relatively slow rate of population increase in Ulster after 1791, when linen markets were booming; (2) findings that weaving and proximity to Belfast were not associated with young *female* nuptiality at the middle of the nineteenth century. In sum, the evidence suggests that from the end of the eighteenth century onward, "protoindustrial" demographic trends were more pronounced at the margins of Ireland's linen-manufacturing zone, than at its core.

Impoverishment and proletarianization

On the eve of the Great Famine more than half of all farms in Ireland were less than ten acres in size (Mokyr 1985, 19). However, there were distinct regional differences in the distribution of farm sizes:

In Connacht and Ulster farms were smaller than in Munster and in Leinster, but in the latter two the proportions of very small farms was larger. In Ulster and Connacht a single-peaked distribution of farms existed, whereas in Munster and Leinster the distribution of farms was bimodal, with large numbers of both very small and very large farms (Mokyr 1985, 19). In his analysis of the effects of land and saving markets on the distribution of landholdings, McGregor (1992, 490) found that: "Domestic industry was of particular importance in the reduction of inequality though it had little discernible effect on median holding size."[9]

Thus in Ireland, protoindustrialization does seem to have been associated with the homogenization of landholdings, as Medick's model implied. The precise mechanisms of the process are unknown, but partible inheritance and the reclamation of marginal land must have played a part. There is also evidence that cottiers' and farmers' sons used their earnings from linen manufacturing to bid for tenancies when leases came up for renewal (Crawford 1994, 51; 1983, 1976). Under the "absolute rental regime" described by McDonough and Slater (1994; see above), landlords were happy to subdivide tenancies in order to maximize their rental income.[10]

An overall tendency toward a reduction of inequality in landholding size does not exclude the possibility of class differentiation between manufacturers and cottier journeyman. As I described in chapter 2, this pattern was often remarked on by contemporary observers. Medick (1976, 308) argued that such arrangements "should be considered as specific variants or mutations of the substantial farmer's or craftsman's family and they must be distinguished from the main type of extended family to be found among the landless or land-poor protoindustrial producers." However, Cohen (1990) argued that the existence of petty manufacturers undermined the protoindustrialization thesis by showing that rural industrial producers were not just "passive victims whose 'traditional family subsistence economy' enabled merchants and putters out to realize a 'differential profit.'" At least some were motivated to accumulate profit and to employ others as wage laborers in order to do so. The question of "subsistence orientation" as a distinct mode of household economic behavior is pursued in some depth in chapter 4.

Did protoindustrialization in Ireland lead to impoverishment and proletarianization (or immiseration) by reducing the size of landholdings to the point where households were unable to revert to agriculture during the transition to mechanized industry? There is evidence for and against. We have already seen that McGregor (1992) found domestic industry to have had little effect on median landholding size. In her study of the fine linen-weaving district of Richhill, in County Armagh, McKernan (1990) found that most tenants leased plots of land sufficient in size to ensure independence. From Rathfriland, in County Down it was reported in 1840 that:

> The weavers who now work for employers are a different class from those who formerly worked on their own account. The farmers were formerly the manufacturing weavers, and divided their attention between the loom and their farm. The class who now work for employers formerly composed those who worked occasionally as day labourers for hire for the farmers, either on their land or on their looms. All those farmers who held from 10 to 20 acres and upwards have left off weaving, and only those who have from four to ten acres of land now attempt to carry on the manufacture of linen on their own account for the brown markets. (H.C. 1840, Vol. 23, 636)

On the other hand many commentators have observed that population densities in the weaving districts, especially in north County Armagh, were amongst the highest in Ireland (Crawford 1994, 26). According to the Devon Commission, eight acres was the minimum holding size necessary to support a family "in comfort" (quoted in McGregor 1992, 480). Poor Law Union data show that the highest proportions of holdings between one and ten acres were found in the provinces of Connacht (54.4 percent) and Ulster (42.6 percent) in the 1830s. However, in Ulster, more of those farms were greater than five acres than in Connacht (Mokyr 1985, p.19). Almquist (1979, 711) found that spinning—but not weaving—was significantly correlated with landholdings of more than one, but less than five acres.[11] In his dissertation he argued that flax cultivation and spinning interacted with the rundale system of landholding and inheritance to create a pattern of "involution" in County Mayo (Almquist 1977).

According to Medick's model of the protoindustrial family economy, rural industrial producers were likely to engage in "self-exploitation" as demand for their product declined. That is, they continuously increased the amount of labor devoted to industrial activity in order to glean an income. In Ireland, there is some evidence that spinners followed this path during the 1830s and 1840s, as mill-spun yarn began to substitute for the hand-spun product, pushing down prices. Contemporaries observed that women spent long hours at the wheel, even though their yarn sold for little more than the price of raw flax.[12] However, not all commentators accept that this represented a process of immiseration. Instead, they suggest that women continued to spin given the absence of other employment opportunities (Geary 1998, 535–36). Collins (1982, 141–42) argued that, in the outer weaving districts of north-central Ireland, rural industrial households remained viable by alternating the intensity they devoted to flax production and weaving, according to fluctuations in demand. In this context, spinning served to meet short-term cash requirements. "Although spinning was regarded merely as an alternative to idleness its production continued because the family labour which produced it was an invariable overhead cost" (Collins 1982, 142). I pursue this question in more detail in chapter 4, where I argue that women's willingness to engage in this kind of "self-exploitation" depended on the extent to which spinning was embedded in the family economy of their households.

Evidence that many rural households in the linen districts sought alternative sources of income in the 1850s and 1860s provides the strongest argument in favor of impoverishment. Collins (1988, 242) calculated that, in every county in Ulster, between one in four and one in nine women was employed in embroidery, sewing, or dressmaking in each decade from 1850 to 1914. In a study of six townlands in the Lagan valley—"just too far away [from Lisburn] for folk to walk to work in that town's spinning mills and weaving factories"—Collins found that most farms were too small for agriculture to provide the main means of a livelihood in the 1860s (1997, 230 and 233). Here, families supplemented their income through handloom weaving of fine linens and cambrics using mill-spun yarn under the putting-out system. In Connacht, the loss of income from spinning led many households to fall back on seasonal migration, illicit distillation, and begging.

Mokyr (1980, 450) remarked that "Ireland industrialized, but unfortunately for the Irish, its industrialization took place outside its borders: in northwest England, the Scottish Lowlands, and New England." Ulster's spinning mills absorbed only a small proportion of those who had depended on handspinning to maintain their access to the means of subsistence. Emigration provided an alternative to "industrial involution" for some families in the yarn districts—especially in Donegal, Londonderry, Tyrone, and Sligo (Ó'Gráda 1994, 74). Similarly, while some weaving households from the outer districts moved to Belfast and its environs, most migrants sought work overseas. Collins (1982, 144) demonstrated that weaving households from north-central Ireland were able to transfer their skills to textile centers in England, Scotland, and France. By contrast, emigrants from west Ulster "were treated as unskilled laborers by the countries which received them" (Collins 1982, 143). Families in other parts of the yarn districts—especially in west Donegal and Mayo—were more likely to resort to seasonal migration as agricultural laborers both within Ireland and to Britain. Why such families were so much more determined to retain their grip on Irish soil remains a matter of debate. However, it is likely that they had fewer resources—not just financially, but also in terms of literacy, English language, and kinship networks overseas—than those who emigrated permanently from west Ulster (Ó'Gráda 1994, 74–74).

In an analysis consistent with the immiseration thesis, Almquist (1977) suggested that "industrial involution," together with the decline of hand spinning in the 1830s, help to account for the severity of the Great Famine in County Mayo in the 1840s. However, the extent to which rural industry mediated the effects of the famine remains uncertain. In County Donegal, for example, the proportion of women who were hand spinners was greater than in County Mayo, yet the impact of the famine was far less severe. Regional data show that "mortality was highest in the extreme west, high in Munster and south Ulster, and very low in Dublin and in east Ulster" (Ó'Gráda 1994, 185). This seems to suggest that the core weaving districts were relatively insulated. In his attempt to explain county-level variation in famine mortality, Mokyr (1985, 274) was unable to determine the effect of rural industry: "In some specifications the relation seems to be negative, in others positive." However, using different mortality estimates, Ó'Gráda found that domestic industry "shielded people from death." Cohen (1997, 148–55) argued that vulnerability to the famine was differentiated by gender in core weaving districts. She found that in Lurgan workhouse the proportion of inmates who were women was greater in most years "due to the elimination of handspinning, greater economic expendability and desertion by husbands" (Cohen 1997, 151). However it is not clear that admission to the workhouse can be taken as evidence of greater vulnerability. Indeed Fitzpatrick (1997) suggested that their overrepresentation in workhouse admissions may *explain* women's lower mortality levels overall. Thus, to date, there is little evidence to support Almquist's hypothesis of a relationship between protoindustrialization, immiseration and vulnerability to the Great Famine. Instead, the preponderance of evidence suggests that rural industry ameliorated its effects.

In summary, there is evidence that the Irish linen industry was associated with the diminution of landholdings, but that the process was clearly mediated by geographical and institutional factors. On well-managed estates where landlords attempted to prevent subdivision, or where the transaction costs associated with distance from the marketplace made it difficult for landless weavers to purchase leases, rural industrial activity did not necessarily lead to impoverishment in land. By contrast, in the proximity of major linen markets, and on poorly managed land, especially in remote and marginal districts, many households were unable to fall back on full-time farming once the process of rural deindustrialization had begun. Under these circumstances, some households attempted to survive by allocating increasing amounts of women's labor time to spinning.

In the long run, the extent to which impoverishment led to immiseration depended both on distance from the major industrial centers, and on the skills base of different households and communities. At the core of the protoindustrial zone, where the "habit, knowledge and language of the loom" (quoted in Collins 1997, 240) was part of daily, lived experience, households could survive by weaving for outputters of mill-spun yarn. In the outer weaving districts, at least some families were able to transfer their skills to centers of textile production in Ireland, Britain, or further afield. Households in the yarn districts resorted to new commercial outlets for women's traditional skills, including sewing, embroidery and poultry keeping. Male seasonal migration provided an additional source of income in Connacht and west Donegal. Testimonies to the Poor Law Commission of the 1830s leave no doubt about the hardship caused by the loss of income from hand spinning. However, there was no simple relationship between protoindustrialization and immiseration in Ireland.

DISCUSSION

Research on the Irish case has added to the ambivalent balance sheet on the theories of protoindustrialization. Superficially, the high rates of population growth and diminution of landholdings in Ulster and Connacht seem to support the main hypotheses. However, more detailed studies have failed to provide convincing evidence that the household dynamics posited by Medick lay behind those trends. Instead, they have yielded a set of paradoxical findings suggesting that, at least by the nineteenth century, protoindustrial trends were more pronounced at the periphery of the Irish linen manufacturing zone, than at its core. This appears directly contrary to Pfister's (1996) model, although we cannot exclude the possibility that factors other than an alteration in household dynamics lay behind population increase and land impoverishment in the yarn districts. Neither can we exclude the possibility that such districts would have been characterized by high rates of population growth, even in the absence of protoindustrial activity.

However, the applicability of Pfister's model to the Irish case is limited by his treatment of gender as an exogenous factor. Superficially, the core/periphery structure of Ireland's protoindustrial zone conforms to Pfister's account. Relative to weaving, spinning was a low value-added activity. Therefore, we should not be surprised to find it extending to remote districts characterized by marginal land, and by landholding and inheritance practices that facilitated population increase. But spinning and weaving are not simply different activities; they are stages in a subdivided labor-saving process. The gender division of labor that restricted spinning to women had the potential to create labor-saving imbalances within individual protoindustrial households, especially given the labor-intensive nature of spinning (Collins 1982, 132–34). Weaving households could make up the difference by taking in female relatives and spinning servants, but in the long run increases in weaving output depended on the geographical extension of spinning, and thus on the emergence of a core/periphery structure in the protoindustrial zone. There was nothing "natural" or inevitable about this process, however. Weaving households displayed great flexibility in their efforts to expand labor supply, but *not* in the way they allocated men's and women's labor to different protoindustrial activities. In principle they could have allocated labor to different protoindustrial tasks according to overall household requirements rather than by sex; they did not. The causes and implications of this phenomenon are the subject of chapter 5.

In chapter 6 I show how other European protoindustrial regions developed different "solutions" to the bottleneck created by the gender division of labor between spinning and weaving. In Ireland, as we have seen, the solution was an almost infinite increase in the supply of cheap labor to spinning, through a combination of geographical extension and population growth. Why did the emergence of a functional division of intensive between spinning and weaving districts apparently lead to a decline in the rate of population growth, and of young female nuptiality in the latter?

It is possible that the declining significance of women's and children's spinning *within* weaving households reduced the positive incentive to marry early and have many children, especially given the degree of population pressure already existing on the land. Coote (1804, 253) observed of the women in County Armagh that "Their earnings are generally spent on finery, as the men's labour procures them provisions." So long as the earnings from weaving remained high, women's income had the status of pin money, given that most of the yarn absorbed by the household was purchased in the marketplace or put out by manufacturers. Once the process of deindustrialization began, that balance shifted once again, and spinning acquired new significance in the economic strategies of households under pressure (Collins 1982; see chapter 4).

What of the yarn districts? Pfister argued that protoindustrial activities in such places conformed to a "vent for surplus" model. They provided an outlet for the otherwise unemployed labor of women and children, but were not sufficiently remunerative to divert men from subsistence production. Under these circumstances there was no positive incentive for earlier marriage and increased fertility. But spinning was much more than a vent for surplus in Ireland's yarn districts: it paid the rent and thus enabled many families to gain access to land who would otherwise have been unable to do so. In a famous passage, Sligo landlord Charles O'Hara argued that the "villagers" in that county turned to spinning having been displaced from the better land by graziers:

> Such of the cottagers as remained . . . saw the necessity of an increase of industry but what to turn themselves to they know not. But what they themselves could not discover the Linen Board pointed out to them. The flax seed, wheels and reels given on public account, pointed out to them a branch of industry which they had never before considered but a saving in their own wear. They now solicited for flax seed and their women manufactured the produce into yarn. (P.R.O.N.I. T2812/19/1)

In good times, spinning not only provided the rent; it enabled families to purchase small luxuries and thus "save up riches" (Kirkham 1988). Scally (1995, 32) eloquently described the range of goods sold by itinerant peddlers in the west of Ireland:

> [Hats] were part of the flotsam and jetsam of the rag trade flowing from east to west circuitously seeking its lowest market, where the final drops of profit could be wrung out. . . . Shoes travelled the same silent routes, along with sundry other manufactured and processed items from within the industrial core of western Europe, and some, like cotton cloth, tea, or tobacco, from distances beyond the cognizance of the townlanders. This was one of the markets of last

> resort in Europe, where commodities of the lowest and most exhausted quality found their last buyer.

The important point here is that it was a *market*. The commodity chains that linked smallholders in the northwest to the world economy through the production of yarn also linked them through the consumption of those exotic luxuries that traveled along the chains in the opposite direction. Just as the relatively low value of the yarn they spun should not blind us to its economic significance, so the poor profits garnered by the pedlars should not blind us to the cultural significance of trinkets and stimulants from far-off places to those who lived on the edges of the protoindustrial zone. Thus spinning may have provided a positive incentive for earlier marriage, insofar as it ensured access to land, and enabled smallholders to purchase small luxuries that symbolized prosperity.[13]

It is a central argument of this book that there is no sense in which the households of the yarn districts were residual. Scholars have tended to underestimate their significance in the overall development of the industry because the value of what they produced was small in monetary terms, and because the producers were women and children. This, in turn, has led to an underestimation of the significance of spinning in the demoeconomic development of the yarn districts themselves. By contrast, the anonymous poem with which this chapter began highlights the significance of women's work in the small-farm economy of the yarn districts: it paid the rent that ensured continued access to the means of subsistence, and permitted the consumption of such small "luxuries" as tobacco. But the poem also reveals an interesting feature of spinning, namely, the extent to which it formed part of the everyday round of housekeeping. In the final stanza, the narrator tells us that his wife tries to fool him into believing that she is working hard all day:

> Nuair airigheann sí mé féin ag teacht chun an tighe,
> Teine mhaith mhóna cuireann sí síos,
> Stiúruigheann na leinbh ar fuaid an tighe,
> Agus scaoileann ar siubhal an túirnín lín.
>
> [When she notices me coming toward the house,
> She sets a good turf fire,
> Organizes the children around the house,
> And puts the flax spinning wheel in motion.]

Because it was carried on alongside, and constantly interrupted by their other household duties, women's labor input to manufacturing was difficult to measure, and therefore liable to be undervalued, both by their own contemporaries, and by modern economic historians. Chapter 5 examines the implications of this characteristic of women's work, both for the overall development of the Irish linen industry, and for the evolution of gender relations over time. First, however, in chapter 4, the broad regional differentiation between spinning and weaving districts identified thus far, is subjected to more detailed analysis at the level of an individual county.

NOTES

1. Incorporation is here understood as an "iterative" process (O'Hearn 2001). I do not mean to imply that these territories were somehow isolated, or without market links before.

2. Fertig (2003, 131) recently drew attention to the problems inherent in treating the "niche mechanism" thought to regulate population under the European peasant system as an "adequate model for understanding entire societies in past times." In particular, he observed that: "The rhetoric of balance is . . . of limited help for understanding biographical inequality among the rich and poor in preindustrial times." Fertig's critique has potentially serious implications for the demoeconomic system posited by Medick because it suggests that his model of the protoindustrial family economy is built on a false or incomplete understanding of peasant family economies.

3. In the southern parts of the "small-farm" zone, wool spinning may have been more important than flax spinning. See the discussion in Clarkson (1996). There was, however, a substantial linen industry centered in West Cork. In the 1820s, according to Bielenberg (1991, 10), "The total number of people employed in the cultivation of flax and the manufacture and finishing of linen in the Cork region was about sixty thousand." Donnelly (1975, 19) estimated that the decline of the industry in the late 1820s and 1830s "must have added several thousand displaced hand-loom weavers to the already overcrowded agricultural labour market."

4. See also the maps in Clarkson (1996) and Ó'Gráda (1989) showing proportions of individuals and households engaged in manufacturing in 1841 and 1821.

5. The difference in terms of labor requirements was immense. Ó'Gráda (1994: 92–93) cites evidence to suggest that spade husbandry required the equivalent of about fifteen days work per acre, compared to just two days under plough husbandry.

6. But see the discussion in Chase-Dunn (1989, 20–47).

7. The opposite appears to have been true in England where "protoindustrial areas bucked the national trend to falling mortality in the later eighteenth century" (King 2003, 27).

8. McGregor (1992, 479) pointed out that this does not mean that smallholders practiced potato monoculture. Oats were grown for the market in many districts. According to Ó'Gráda, (1994, 91), cabbages probably played an important subsidiary role in the Irish diet.

9. McGregor measured domestic industry as the percentage of men and women "ministering to clothing" by barony, in the 1841 census.

10. In an argument consistent with the protoindustrialization thesis, Miller (1983) suggested that in County Armagh, the removal of the traditional constraints associated with land inheritance on the behavior of young men partly explains the eruption of sectarian violence known as the "Armagh troubles" in the 1780s and 1790s.

11. These data are from the 1841 census, and may refer to Irish or Plantation acres, which were larger than English statute acres.

12. See, for example, the testimonies to the Poor Inquiry on women's and children's earnings (H.C. 1836, vol. 31, Appendix D).

13. Scally (1995, 32) argues that imported commodities functioned as symbols of "microstatus," and that excessive display could lead to community disapproval. However, he provides little evidence for this interpretation. It should be noted that spinning was apparently not widespread in the townland studied by Scally (1995, 163).

Chapter Four

Local Contexts

> [In] industry, unfortunately, they are very defective; spring time and harvest; turf and hay making revolve in perpetual succession, giving timely intimation of their approach and departure; and still the labours of the husbandmen are continually in arrear; a fair or market, a wake or wedding, will arrest industry in the most critical season; and expose to uncertainty the most pressing demands of subsistence or the liquidation of rent. (Day and McWilliams, 1998, vol. 40, 22)

Even though the once vibrant linen industry was almost extinct in the parish of Drung, in County Cavan, its inhabitants seem to have taken a cavalier approach to the cultivation of their tiny holdings, diminished by the pervasive practice of subdivision. How should we interpret this observation by a British army officer, in the mid-1830s?[1] Should it be dismissed as a prejudiced misrepresentation, or treated seriously as evidence of the plebian habits of behavior that had developed under protoindustrialization?

In this chapter I argue that this apparently feckless behavior on the part of small holders in Drung can be explained by the uneven nature of deindustrialization in County Cavan from the beginning of the nineteenth century. Uneven deindustrialization was in turn the result of locally differentiated and uneven patterns of incorporation to the world economy through the linen industry from the beginning of the eighteenth century. I argue that the trajectory of protoindustrialization depended on the timing of incorporation, and on local differences in patterns of settlement and the quality of land. Most importantly, the dynamics of protoindustrialization and deindustrialization depended on how spinning was embedded in the family economies of small farmers and farmer weavers. While weaving had died out in Drung by the 1830s, spinning remained widespread, despite rapidly decreasing prices for hand-spun yarn.

The chapter begins with a narrative account of the development of the linen industry in County Cavan. I then present a statistical portrait of the rural industrial population of the county in 1821. The portrait is based on a sample of households from the 1821 census manuscripts that survive for fifteen parishes in County Cavan.[2] I show that the rural industrial population was differentiated by class, household life cycle and locality, and I link these differences to divergent paths of demoeconomic change within the study area.

THE LINEN INDUSTRY IN COUNTY CAVAN TO 1821

Cavan is a mainly lowland county in south Ulster, characterized by numerous drumlins (map 4.1). Under the seventeenth-century plantation and subsequent Cromwellian land settlement, landed property was transferred from Catholic, Gaelic lords to British undertakers and speculators, who attracted Protestant immigrants from England and Scotland. From this period onward, County Cavan underwent a prolonged and uneven process of colonization and settlement. According to Duffy (1995, 32), "There was a two-fold process throughout south Ulster of Protestant consolidation on the good lands and withdrawal from poorer lands, to which the Catholic population was gradually displaced." By the 1800s, Protestants were concentrated in the northern parishes of County Cavan on the border with County Monaghan (see map 4.2), and along the banks of the River Erne, where "they attempted to achieve their objective of introducing English style 'civility' in tidy enclosed landscapes with arable predominating over pasture" (Duffy 1995, 32). By contrast, the inhabitants of poorer areas, such as the mountainous barony of Tullyhaw, in the northwest of the county, still seemed part of a different world to an Anglo-Irish observer at this time: "Their markets are distant and discouraging, but they rely on themselves chiefly for their necessaries, and are in a great degree independent, and confined to their own peculiar concerns" (Coote 1802, 95).

Duffy (1995, 25–26) provided a rich description of the "landscapes" of modernization and underdevelopment that had emerged in Cavan by the second half of the nineteenth century, linking them to earlier patterns of colonization and settlement:

> [The] landscapes in Cavan in which the forces of modernisation were most extensive ran from Cootehill to Cavan and Belturbet, with another district adjoining the Longford-Meath border. In addition to houses and demesnes, these areas also supported a suite of towns and villages which originated in the conditions of the Ulster plantation. With the county town of Cavan on the Farnham estate, all of these towns were associated with strong estate cores. On the other hand, the poor barony of Tullyhaw, and comparatively poor lands of Clankee were

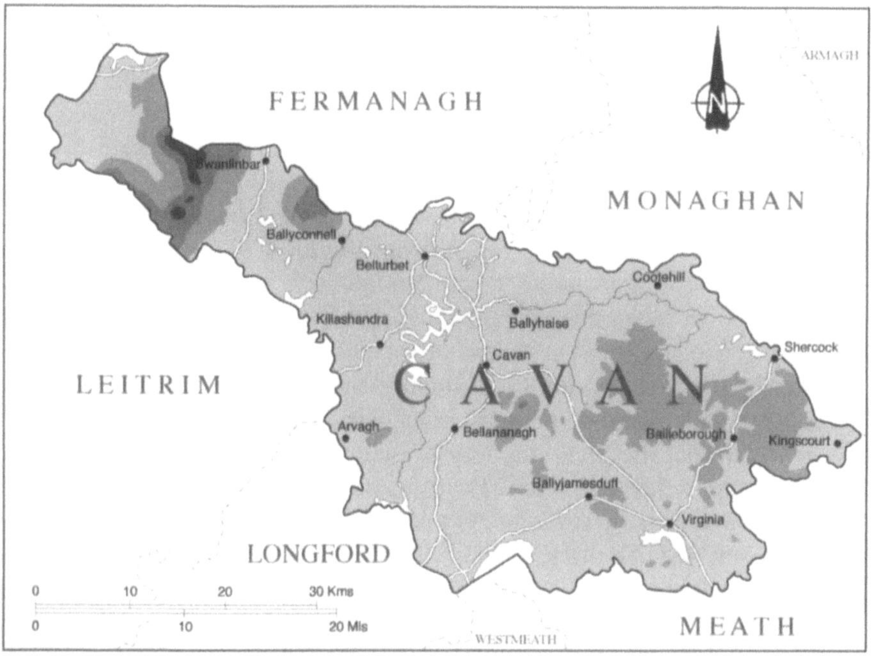

Map 4.1. Topographical Map of County Cavan

> characterised by a high degree of absenteeism among landowners. In these poor areas, and also in districts running westwards from Shercock to the Leitrim border, nonresident fragments of property were accompanied by wide variations in leasing arrangements, rental valuations and general levels of estate management to produce what has been called more 'haphazard, unregulated and protracted processes of colonisation and settlement.

This detailed account provides an orienting framework for my discussion of the uneven development of the linen industry in County Cavan, and will be referred to throughout the remainder of the chapter.

The spread of linen manufacturing throughout south Ulster illustrates the complex relationship between the processes of colonization and uneven incorporation to the world economy. During the first half of the eighteenth century, this region went through a phase of agricultural improvement, stimulated by demand from the dynamic, core linen manufacturing district to the northeast (Crawford 1975, 245). As we have seen, because of the bottleneck between the processes of spinning and weaving, the linen triangle also began to import yarn from outlying districts, so it seems probable that agricultural improvement in County Cavan was accompanied by an increased investment of women's time in spinning. Early in the century Cavan was said to be exclusively a yarn county (Connolly 1992, 52). As late as 1776, Arthur Young (1892, 211) noted that in this area the linen industry consisted mainly in spinning, and that "They do not raise enough [flax] for supplying their wheels, for much is brought from Dublin." In the early decades of the nineteenth century, Cavan was still "a very great yarn county" (Corry 1817, 62).

Approximately 16 percent of all households in County Cavan claimed spinning wheels as premiums for growing flax in 1796 (see map 2.2). The published "List of Persons to whom Premiums . . . have been adjudged" (1796) gives an indication of the spatial distribution of flax cultivation and spinning in County Cavan at the end of the eighteenth century (table 4.1). Unfortunately it is not possible to normalize the claims by number of households, as the latter data do not exist at the parish level for the 1790s. As elsewhere in Ireland, the great majority of claims in County Cavan (almost 90 percent) were for just one wheel. Focusing on those parishes where more than a hundred wheels were awarded, two zones of flax cultivation and spinning may be identified. The first stretches from Annagh to Drumgoon along the border with County Monaghan where Protestant settlers were concentrated. The second zone comprises a southwestern arc, stretching from Killashandra to Munter Connaught. It is noticeable that in the latter set of parishes, the proportion of claims for two or more wheels tended to be slightly higher than in the former. For example, the ratio of claimants to wheels in Kildrumsherdan was 1:1.06, whereas in Kilbride, at the other extreme, it was 1:1.08. Those parishes claiming smaller numbers of wheels comprised a third zone, stretching across the center of the county from Kilmore to Enniskeen (the exception is Bailieborough). There appear to have been no claims from parishes in the northwestern barony of Tullyhaw, which may therefore be described as a fourth zone. The spinning zones correspond remarkably well to Duffy's landscapes of modernization and underdevelopment.

Weaving linen cloth for sale was first introduced to south Ulster early in the eighteenth century by landlords who attracted groups of Protestant weavers from the core manufacturing districts of east Ulster to settle in their towns (Crawford 1975, 246). In 1739, the town of Belturbet was described as the most important market for linen from Counties Cavan, and Fermanagh (Crawford 1975, 246). The principal yarn market in County Cavan was at Cavan town. However, after about 1745, weaving spread throughout the religious and social hierarchy in the counties of Armagh, Cavan, and Monaghan, in response both to widespread crop failure and cattle losses at that time, and to the growing overseas demand fostered by the bounty system (see chapter 2.). In 1783, the most important market for linen cloth in Cavan was at Cootehill, on the northern border with County Monaghan.

Table 4.1. Persons Awarded Spinning Wheels under the Flax Premium Scheme in County Cavan in 1796, by Parish

	Number of Wheels Awarded					
Parish[a]	*Four*	*Three*	*Two*	*One*	*Total Wheels*	*Total Persons*
Kildrumsherdan	0	2	16	248	286	266
Killashandra	2	2	14	176	218	194
Kilbride	4	12	40	110	242	166
Annagh	1	1	10	152	179	164
Crosserlough	0	1	17	146	183	164
Drung	2	2	6	135	161	145
Drumgoon	2	3	9	106	141	120
Ballintemple	0	1	16	102	137	119
Munterconnaught	3	4	25	73	147	105
Drumlumman	0	3	8	78	103	89
Bailieborough	1	4	13	59	101	77
Kilmore	1	2	2	66	80	71
Ballymachugh	1	0	12	56	84	69
Enniskeen	2	1	10	56	87	69
Castlerahan	0	4	17	41	87	62
Denn	2	0	4	54	70	60
Larah	0	2	3	54	66	59
Drumlane	1	1	5	51	68	58
Castletarra	0	0	4	53	61	57
Knockbride	0	0	1	47	49	48
Lavey	0	0	1	47	49	48
Killinkere	3	0	9	33	63	45
Annagelliff	0	0	3	35	41	38
Killan (Shercock)	0	0	3	35	41	38
Kildallan	0	0	3	29	35	32
Mallycoram[b]	0	0	8	23	39	31
Urney	0	0	1	26	28	27
Collumkill[c]	0	0	2	15	19	17
Lurgan	0	0	1	6	8	7
Total	25	45	263	2,112	2,873	2,445

Source: County of Cavan. A List of Persons to whom Premiums for sowing Flax-seed in the year 1796 have been adjudged by the Trustees of the Linen Manufacture. 1796.
Notes: Ranked by number of persons awarded. (a) For convenience, I have altered the eighteenth-century spelling of parish names to conform to the standard spelling adopted in the mid-nineteenth century, except where it was not possible to identify the parish in question. (b) I have not been able to identify this parish. (c) The civil parish of Collumkill is in County Longford. It is possible that here it refers to the adjacent parish of Scrabby, in County Cavan.

This was a well-established weaving district: in 1754 Stephenson remarked that a good linen market had existed at Cootehill for some years.[3] There was a secondary linen market at Killashandra in the west of the county. Cootehill and Killashandra were embedded in different zones of specialization in the industry (see table 2.2; Crawford 1988, 48–49). Cootehill, (famous for its sheetings), was part of the southern region centered on the town of Armagh which specialized in the production of yard-wide coarse linens. Killashandra, on the other hand, was part of the western region stretching northwards to Inishowen, in County Donegal, and specializing in the production of narrower "seven-eights" cloth intended for shirting. Even within this zone, according to Crawford (1988, 48–49), Cavan "represented a world of its own," its markets attended by local buyers, rather than, as elswhere, by bleachers from Tyrone.

The 1780s and 1790s saw unprecedented increases in Irish linen exports (see figure 2.2). Sales at Cavan's linen markets more than doubled in this period (Crawford 1994, 78), which also saw the beginning of a new wave of agricultural commercialization in response to high wartime prices for corn (O'Neill 1984, 72–78). When Sir Charles Coote (1802, 71) surveyed the county at the beginning of the nineteenth century, he claimed to have found one or more weavers in every house. As we will see, this was almost certainly a gross overstatement of the case. By 1803, sales at Cavan's linen markets accounted for 8 percent of all sales in Ulster. They declined slowly thereafter, but Cavan still accounted for about 6 percent of the value of sales in Ulster in 1821. Data compiled by the secretary of the Linen Board suggest no real decline in the average number of weavers attending linen markets in Cavan between 1816 and 1820 (Crawford 1988, 47). There was a change, however, in the spatial distribution of the industry. Not only did sales at Killashandra decline more slowly than those at Cootehill, but the smaller markets of Arvagh and Bellananagh (or Ballynagh) to the south accounted for an increased proportion of all sales. Cootehill remained by far the most important linen market in Cavan, but there was a relative shift toward the west and south.

By the 1820s, then, there were two mini "linen triangles" within County Cavan. The first and older triangle centered on Cootehill in the northeast, but stretched westwards along the border with County Monaghan to the older markets of Belturbet and Ballyhaise, and as far south as Cavan town. It coincided with the northern spinning zone identified in table 4.1. The second triangle was located to the west of the river Erne. Centered on Killashandra, it stretched southwards to Arvagh in the west, and Bellananagh in the east, and coincided with the southwestern spinning zone.

In his account of Cavan, Coote (1802, 41) remarked on, and famously vilified, the prevalence of middle-man manufacturers who worked up to four looms in their own houses and employed their cottiers as journeymen. His concerns reflected those of landlords who were anxious to prevent the subdivision of their tenancies. However, after about 1800 landlords gave up trying to enforce clauses against subdivision in their tenants' leases, and instead let directly to the cottiers "at will" when leases came up for renewal (Crawford 1975, 255; O'Neill 1984, 35–36). In contrast to core linen-weaving counties like Armagh and Down, there were no remaining manufacturers authorized to seal brown linens in Cavan in 1821 (Crawford 1988, 44).

Emigration was another process likely to have contributed to the demise of manufacturers in the county. Coote (1802, 46) referred to an "extraordinary emigration of linen weavers" from Ulster in the year before he conducted his statistical survey and observed that:

> It is a well authenticated fact, that it was not the poorest class who left the country; for how could a poor man command six guineas for each of his family, which was the bare passage money only? And, although in former years their venture was linen cloth, yet it is well known they took out all they were worth, converted into specie; the interest of their farms, their stock on the farm, and in trade, was all sold for cash.

Mass emigration from Cavan began in the 1830s, but did not reach markedly high levels until the 1840s (Collins 1982). This emigration has been attributed both to the decline of the linen industry in south Ulster (Collins 1982), and to the economic difficulties experienced by laborers as their population began to exceed demand for their labor (O'Neill 1984).

In summary, the socioeconomic landscape of Cavan in 1821 was the outcome of an extended and uneven incorporation into the developing world economy through the interrelated processes of colonization, protoindustrialization and the commercialization of agriculture. Local and global factors combined to create an increased population, differentially exposed to the risks of deindustrialization, declining demand for agricultural labor, and the failure of the potato crop on which so many relied for subsistence. In the next section I draw on surviving census manuscripts to paint a statistical portrait of the rural population in fifteen Cavan parishes in 1821. In that year many rural households were under pressure due to falling agricultural prices and rising rents (O'Neill 1984, 76), and to an extended period of stagnation in linen exports (see figure 2.2). Throughout Ireland there is evidence of an overall decline in living standards between 1815 and 1835 (Mokyr 1985, 11–14). However, while circumstances were difficult in 1821, the economy had not yet entered a period of sustained crisis leading inexorably to the disaster of the Great Famine (O'Grada 1994, 158–62). Linen sales entered a new period of dynamism in the 1820s, and earnings from hand spinning were not yet affected by mechanization. Thus the 1821 manuscripts provide a window on the rural industrial population in County Cavan before the onset of deindustrialization—albeit one that is narrow and partially obscured.

THE CAVAN STUDY AREA: A STATISTICAL PORTRAIT

Manuscript copies of the original 1821 census enumerators' schedules for fifteen parishes in County Cavan are held in the National Archives of Ireland (CEN 1821/1-15; see map 4.2). I collected two sets of data from these returns. The first consists of the *population* of households where at least one weaver was resident. The second consists of a systematic sample with a random start of every fifth household where no weaver was resident. The combined data file amounts to a stratified sample of the population of enumerated households in the surviving returns.[4] For each household I recorded the number of acres and number of children under twelve years. Within each household I recorded the following information for every individual aged twelve years or more: relationship to the head of household; sex; age; occupation. The strengths and weaknesses of the sample are discussed in detail in appendix A).

Table 4.2 shows the distribution of households in the Cavan study area according to head's occupation. Farmers accounted for over half of all households. One in five households was headed by a laborer. About 5 percent of all farmers had weavers resident. 8.6 percent of all households had at least one

Map 4.2. County Cavan: Baronies and Parishes, Showing Parishes in the Sample

Table 4.2. Cavan Study Area: Distribution of Households by Head's Occupation

Head's Occupation	*Sample N*	*Weighted N*	*% Total*
Farmer (No Weavers Resident)	1459	1459	52.1
Farmer (Weaver/s Resident)	408	82	2.9
Farmer-Artisan (Not Weaver)	62	57	2.0
Farmer-Weaver	372	74	2.7
Laborer	586	565	20.2
Weaver	341	68	2.4
Other Artisan	111	107	3.8
Spinner	123	113	4.0
Other	109	103	3.7
Unspecified	189	170	6.1
Total	3760	2798	100.0

Source: 1821 Cavan sample.
Note: Weighted Ns calculated by dividing the number of households with resident weavers in each category by five. See text for clarification.

weaver resident. It should be noted, however, that there were almost as many households headed by spinners as by weavers. Fifty-two percent of all households in the sample had at least one spinner resident.

The census enumerators dutifully recorded an occupation for heads of household and nonfamily household residents. However, there is significant variation by gender and parish in the extent to which other family members had occupations recorded. Women were far more likely than men *not* to have an occupation recorded; just 16 percent of men in the sample were without an occupational title, compared to 41.8 percent of women. Table 4.3 compares the distribution of occupations for men and women in the study area as a whole with that of the subset of parishes where almost all individuals had an occupation recorded. It can be seen that just two occupations accounted for most of the variation—that of laborer for men, and spinner for women. Thus the proportion of spinners in a given parish depended on the proportion of women for whom an occupation was recorded. This problem is discussed in more detail below, and in appendix A.

Table 4.3 yields an important insight into the nature of spinning as an occupation within the family economy. Spinning was embedded within the everyday reproductive activities of the household. Protoindustrialization occurred when traders began to draw on existing consumption-oriented production in order to supply regional and overseas markets. In this respect spinning differed from weaving as a protoindustrial activity. Weaving was a *trade*, and thus for the 1821 census enumerators a clearly defined male occupation, in contrast to laboring, which was a general title for sons and other male relatives assisting in the reproduction of the household—as spinning was for female relatives.

Table 4.3. Cavan Study Area: Distribution of Occupations for Men and Women Aged Fifteen Years or Older, 1821

	Cavan Sample		*Cavan Sub-Sample*	
Occupation	*N*[a]	%	*N*[a]	%
Men				
Farmer	1432	30.6	474	28.4
Labourer	1421	30.4	746	44.7
Weaver	299	6.4	106	6.4
Spinner	0	0.0	0	0.0
Oth. Artisan	252	5.4	107	6.4
Servant	394	8.4	152	9.1
Other	129	2.8	55	3.3
No Occ.	751	16.1	28	1.7
Total	4679	100.1	1668	100.0
Women				
Farmer	133	2.8	55	3.3
Labourer	12	0.3	7	0.4
Weaver	2	0.0	0	0.0
Spinner	2023	42.6	1323	78.7
Oth. Artisan	48	1.0	30	1.8
Servant	515	10.8	205	12.2
Other	31	0.7	13	0.8
No Occ.	1985	41.8	47	2.8
Total	4749	100.0	1682	100.0

Cavan sample and subsample of parishes where most individuals (> 95%) recorded an occupation.
Source: 1821 Cavan sample.
Note: a. Ns are weighted to take account of the overrepresentation of individuals residing in weaving households in the sample. See text for clarification. Columns may not sum due to weighting.

This distinction between spinning and weaving is further demonstrated in table 4.4, which shows that a substantial proportion of weavers—over 15 percent—could not clearly be identified as relatives of the head of household. Over 6 percent were identifiably *unrelated* to the household head. By contrast, only 7 percent of spinners could not clearly be identified as relatives. On the other hand 9 percent of all spinners were relatives outside the nuclear family, compared to just over 3 percent of weavers. This may indicate that households tended to draw on family and kinship networks for additional labor in spinning, whereas weaving households were more likely to employ unrelated tradesmen. Those enumerators who dutifully recorded an occupational title for all adults, therefore, did not necessarily perform a service for historical sociologists. All women span as part of their household duties, and spinners were almost all family members before they were employees.

Table 4.4. Cavan Study Area: Spinners and Weavers Aged Fifteen or More Years, by Relationship to Head of Household

	Spinners		*Weavers*	
Relationship to Head of Household	*N*[a]	*%*	*n*	*%*
Head	113	5.6	713	52.4
Spouse	882	43.5	2	0.1
Son/Daughter	704	34.7	501	33.3
Sibling	98	4.9	36	2.4
Other Relative	88	4.3	15	1.0
Other	80	3.9	93	6.2
Missing	64	3.1	145	9.6
Total	2028	100.0	1505	100.0

Source: 1821 Cavan sample.
Note: a. Spinner Ns weighted to take account of overrepresentation of weaving households in the sample. See text for clarification. Columns may not sum due to weighting.

The enumerators distinguished between households headed by "farmer weavers" and "weavers," and these appear to have been quite distinct groups. Moreover, farmers employing weavers were different from other farmers in some respects, and from other linen-weaving households. It can be seen from table 4.5 that most farmer weavers occupied smaller landholdings than farmers in general, whereas farmers employing weavers occupied, on the whole, larger holdings. The degree of landlessness has to be estimated from the *absence* of any acreage recorded by the enumerators. This seems to entail a fair amount of error, since about 5 percent of farmers and farmer artisans, and about 10 percent of farmer weavers, implausibly had no recorded acres. Nonetheless, the category of households headed by "weavers" appears to have been predominantly landless.[5]

Table 4.6 , showing mean household, and mean family characteristics by head's occupation, is consistent with this interpretation. As might be expected, the more substantial farmers employing weavers had larger households than any other group.[6] They were more likely to have unspecified "inmates" or relatives outside the nuclear family residing with them, and to employ servants. However, it should be noted that most households did not employ servants; even within this group 66 percent of all households had no servants, and the proportion was correspondingly higher in each of the other categories. As elsewhere in Europe, service was clearly a life-cycle occupation, especially for women. Twenty-two percent of all women, and 17 percent of all men between the ages of fifteen and twenty-four years of age were in service; servants accounted for just under 10 percent of the population as a whole. The smallest households were found amongst the three main landless groups—laborers, weavers, and other artisans.

Table 4.5. Cavan Study Area: Distribution of Landholding by Head's Occupation

		Percent of Households				
	N[a]	*No Acres Recorded*	*Less than 5 Acres*	*5-9 Acres*	*10-14 Acres*	*More than 15 Acres*
Farmer (Not Weaving)	1459	4.5	18.9	45.7	18.1	12.8
Farmer (Weaving)	82	3.9	7.8	41.4	27.2	19.6
Farmer-Weaver	74	10.2	27.7	41.9	14.5	5.6
Other Farmer-Artisan	57	5.2	30.1	45.1	12.6	7.0
Labourer	565	91.8	5.5	1.8	0.5	0.4
Weaver	68	90.3	6.7	1.5	0.6	0.9
Other Artisan	107	94.8	1.1	1.1	2.1	0.9
Spinner	113	97.2	0.9	1.1	0.0	0.9
All Households	2798	39.2	13.3	28.2	11.3	8.0

Source: 1821 Cavan sample

Note: a. Ns are weighted to take account of the overrepresentation of weaving households in the sample. See text for clarification. b. There were 103 households with miscellaneous other occupations, and 170 with no recorded occupations in the weighted sample. Ns do not sum due to weighting.

In table 4.6, one of the most interesting features is the higher mean number of children under twelve years in the households of farmer weavers compared to farmers not engaged in weaving.[7] Farmers employing weavers had a lower than average number of children under twelve per household, but this is easily accounted for by the higher age of the parents—both husbands and wives were on average at least ten years older than their counterparts in other households. In order to determine whether or not the relatively high mean number of children under twelve years amongst farmer weavers was determined by the age structure of their households, I separated the data by wife's age (table 4.7). It can be seen that the difference is accounted for by the higher median number of children under twelve in the households of farmer weavers whose wives were aged twenty to twenty-four years, or forty-five years or more.[8] The data thus hint at a possible higher rate of fertility within marriage, or a lower rate of infant mortality, for farmer weavers. If true, this would be supportive of the protoindustrialization model (see chapter 3), but more detailed, microlevel research is necessary to test this hypothesis.[9]

Finally, what of Coote's (1802) "rapacious" employers of journeyman weavers? There is little evidence that they constituted a sizable group in the study area in 1821. Coote described his "middlemen" as employing four looms in their own homes, in addition to their cottiers. Less than 1 percent of all weaving households in the study area had four or more resident weavers, although fifteen farmers employing weavers, and twenty-five farmer weavers had at least three.

Some of the differences amongst the three categories of weaving household may be attributed to the family life cycle. Table 4.8 shows that farmers employing weavers were more likely than any other group to have reached what I describe here as *Stage IV*, when there were no longer any children under the age of twelve years in the household. Farmer weavers and weavers, on the other hand, were more likely to be in *Stage II*, when no sons or daughters had yet reached the age of twelve years. (Laborers were more likely than farmers to be in *Stage II*, but their households were more evenly distributed throughout the life cycle than either farmer weavers or weavers). In 1821 it was observed of Raphoe, in County Donegal, that twenty years previously "It was usual . . . for the farming heads of families to put their younger sons into this employment [weaving], many of whom were enabled by proper economy and application in a few years to purchase farms, but this practice has been long discontinued" (quoted in Crawford 1994: 51). If the same strategy persisted later in County Cavan, the farmer weavers and weavers in the study area may have been the sons of farmers who had employed them to weave before they set up households of their own. However, as I illustrate below, the three categories were not evenly distributed across the parishes in the study area.

Table 4.6. Cavan Study Area: Mean Household Characteristics, by Head's Occupation

Head's Occupation	*Valid N*[1]	*Wife's Age*	*Children < 12 Years*	*Sons 12+ Years*	*Daughters 12+ Years*	*Other Relatives*	*Servants*	*Inmates*	*Household Size*
Farmer (Not Weaving)	1122	38.93(36)	1.87 (2)	0.82 (0)	0.74 (0)	0.24 (0)	0.48(0)	0.19(0)	6.10 (6)
Farmer (Weaving)[2]	272	48.38(50)	1.21 (1)	2.03 (2)	1.22 (1)	0.30 (0)	0.50(0)	0.53(0)	7.48 (7)
Farmer-Weaver[2]	333	35.90(35)	2.26 (2)	0.70 (0)	0.56 (0)	0.27 (0)	0.40(0)	0.37(0)	6.44 (6)
Other Farmer-Artisan[3]	52	35.71(31)	2.07 (2)	1.06 (0)	0.70 (0)	0.32 (0)	0.51(0)	0.09(0)	6.66 (6)
Weaver[2]	296	35.77(34)	1.79 (2)	0.43 (0)	0.38 (0)	0.18 (0)	0.08(0)	0.19(0)	4.99 (5)
Other Artisan[3]	82	36.87(35)	1.62 (1)	0.41 (0)	0.43 (0)	0.25 (0)	0.25(0)	0.21(0)	4.93 (5)
Laborer[3]	493	38.14(36)	1.79 (2)	0.43 (0)	0.39 (0)	0.18 (0)	0.06(0)	0.19(0)	4.92 (5)
Spinner[3]	112	N/A	0.85(0.5)	0.70 (0)	0.48 (0)	0.11 (0)	0.01(0)	0.18(0)	3.34 (3)
All Households[3]	2072	38.70(36)	1.75 (1)	0.72 (0)	0.63 (0)	0.22 (0)	0.35(0)	0.21(0)	5.61 (5)

Medians in parentheses.
Source: 1821 Cavan sample.
Notes: 1. Smallest N for which a mean was calculated in each category. 2. Calculations based on population data for these categories. 3. Calculations based on weighted Ns for these categories since they include some weaving households. See text for clarification. Ns do not sum because some households were omitted. See Table 4.5, note b.

Table 4.7. Cavan Study Area: Median Resident Children under Twelve Years, by Age of Spouse and Head's Occupation

Age of Spouse	*N*	*%*	*Children < 12 Years*	*n*	*%*	*Children < 12 Years*
		Farmers[1]			*Farmer-Weavers*[2]	
< 20	5	0.4	0	0	0	N/A
20-24	94	8.0	1	36	10.8	2
25-29	173	14.7	2	66	19.8	2
30-34	223	19.0	3	60	18.0	3
35-39	143	12.2	3	55	16.5	3
40-44	141	12.1	3	46	13.8	3
45-49	95	8.1	2	25	7.5	3
50-54	121	10.3	1	24	7.2	2
55-59	71	6.1	0	11	3.3	1
60+	108	9.2	0	10	3.0	0
		Laborers[1]			*Weavers*[2]	
< 20	1	0.2	N/A	1	0.3	N/A
20-24	33	6.7	1	37	12.8	1
25-29	78	15.9	2	59	19.9	2
30-34	107	21.7	3	53	18.2	3
35-39	68	13.9	2	42	14.2	2.5
40-44	69	13.9	2	40	13.5	2
45-49	40	8.2	2	17	5.7	2
50-54	36	7.4	1	24	8.1	1
55-59	25	5.1	0	8	2.7	0.5
60+	34	7.0	0	13	4.4	0

Source: 1821 Cavan sample.
Notes: 1. Weighted calculations since these categories include some households with resident weavers. See text for clarification. 2. Calculations based on population data.

UNEVEN PATTERNS OF RURAL INDUSTRIALIZATION

Table 4.9 shows the distribution of weaving households by parish, and by head's occupation in the Cavan sample. Crosserlough, in the southcentral part of the study area, had the highest proportion of weaving households.

Relatively high concentrations of weaving households occurred along an axis linking the primary market of Cootehill, in the northeast of the county, to the secondary markets of Killashandra and its satellites in the southwest. It is possible to differentiate amongst parishes where more than 5 percent of all households had at least one weaver present, by focusing on which category of weaving household accounted for more than a third of the total (table 4.10). (Only in the parish of Kilmore was it not possible to identify a main type.) There is a distinct pattern within the Cavan study area: farmer weavers

Table 4.8. Cavan Study Area: Households by Crude Life-Cycle Stage and Head's Occupation

		Percent Households in Stage[3]				
Head's Occupation	*N*	*I*	*II*	*III*	*IV*	*V*
Farmer (not weaving)	1388	5.0	35.3	38.5	20.1	1.1
Farmer (weaving)[1]	397	1.5	10.1	48.4	40.1	0.0
Farmer-Weaver[1]	361	6.6	46.8	37.1	8.9	0.6
Laborer[2]	538	5.5	46.6	30.5	14.0	3.3
Weaver[1]	325	8.9	50.8	27.4	11.4	1.5

Source: 1821 Cavan sample.
Notes: Only households with both spouses present were included in the calculations.
1. Calculations based on population data in these categories.
2. Calculation based on weighted N since this category includes some households with resident weavers. See text for clarification.
3. Crude life-cycle stages defined as follows: I. Wife under age fifty, no resident children under twelve years, or sons or daughters aged twelve years or more. II. Resident children under twelve years, no sons or daughters aged twelve years or more. III. Resident children under twelve years, at least one son or daughter aged twelve years or more. IV. No resident children under twelve years, at least one son or daughter aged twelve years or more. V. Wife aged fifty years or more, no resident children under twelve years, or sons or daughters aged twelve years or more.

predominated in the northern parishes which are closest to the Cootehill triangle; farmers predominated in the middle parishes which are closer to the Killashandra triangle; and landless weavers predominated in the south.

Table 4.11 shows the distribution of spinning by parish within the Cavan study area according to the 1821 census enumerators, and provides comparative material from the published census returns for 1841.

Both the percentage of women reporting the occupation "spinner," and percentage of households with at least one spinner resident, indicate that in 1821, spinning was concentrated in those parishes with poor quality land in the southeastern part of the study area, and in the northwestern parish of Kinawley. However, as discussed above and in appendix A, the percentage of spinners in a given parish was dependent on the percentage of women for whom an occupation was recorded in the 1821 census, and the distribution is highly skewed. I believe it is very unlikely that so few women were spinners in those parishes in the northern part of the study area where the farmer weaver pattern predominated, and the 1841 data tend to confirm this suspicion. It is possible that the enumerators were more likely to record occupations for women where spinning was perceived to be more essential to the household economy, and I explore this proposition in more detail below. When the two sets of census data are compared with the evidence from the Spinning Wheel Survey (see table 4.1), it seems reasonable to infer that parishes with poor quality land were incorporated to the linen industry through spinning between 1796 and 1821.

Table 4.9. Cavan Study Area: Distribution of Weaving Households by Parish and Head's Occupation

	Weaving Households		*Weaving Households by Head's Occupation(%)*			
Parish	*n*	*As % Total*	*Farmer*	*Farmer-Weaver*	*Weaver*	*Other*
Annagelliff	51	8.8	3.9	66.7	21.6	7.8
Ballymachugh	56	10.9	28.6	21.4	46.4	3.6
Castlerahan	67	7.0	29.9	13.4	38.8	17.9
Castletarra	61	6.2	27.9	36.1	31.1	4.9
Crosserlough	246	17.3	36.6	31.7	26.8	4.9
Denn	116	14.1	39.7	29.3	24.1	6.9
Drumlumman	117	9.5	41.9	20.5	27.4	10.3
Drung and Larah	204	9.9	44.1	37.3	14.7	3.9
Kilbride	10	1.5	(1)	(2)	(6)	(1)
Kilmore	105	8.9	31.4	29.5	28.6	10.5
Kinawley	33	6.8	18.2	48.5	30.3	3.0
Lavey	71	8.7	43.7	38.0	14.1	4.2
Lurgan	38	3.6	7.9	7.9	78.9	5.3
Mullagh	21	2.7	(4)	(4)	(12)	(1)
Munterconnaught	6	1.4	(0)	(0)	(5)	(1)

Source: 1821 Cavan sample.

Differences in the distribution of weaving and spinning households across the study area were embedded in differences in the wider social structure. Table 4.12 shows the distribution of landholding by parish. There are two distinct patterns within the study area (see table 4.13). In the central and northern parishes stretching to the east of Cavan town small farmers holding less than ten acres were more numerous than landless households, whereas the opposite was true in those parishes stretching along the southern border of the county. Table 4.14 shows the distribution of households by parish in "early" and "late" stages of the household life cycle. In most parishes the proportion of households in an early stage (that is, where any children in the household were under twelve years of age) was around 40 percent (see table 4.15), but in three parishes (Crosserlough, Kinawley and Lavey) the proportion was considerably higher at around 50 percent.

In order to assess the relationships between different patterns of rural industrialization and variations in the wider social structure across the study area, I adopted two distinct methodological strategies. First, following Almquist (1979), I used correlation analysis to estimate the extent to which the percentages of households engaged in weaving or spinning were linearly associated with a range of theoretically relevant variables. Then I used the configurational approach to formal comparative analysis developed by Ragin

Table 4.10. Predominant Weaving Household Pattern in Parishes Where Weaving Households Are 5 Percent or More of the Total

Parish	*n*	*Farmer*	*Farmer-Weaver*	*Weaver*
Crosserlough	246	X		
Denn	116	X		
Drumlumman	117	X		
Drung and Larah	204	X	X	
Lavey	71	X	X	
Annagelliff	51		X	
Castletarra	61		X	
Kinawley	33		X	
Ballymachugh	56			X
Castlerahan	67			X
Lurgan	38			X
Kilmore	105		No Pattern Predominant	

Source: Table 4.9.
Note: Predominant means more than 33 percent of all weaving households.

(1987, 1994) in order to identify the combinations of factors associated with different patterns of population change within the study area between 1821 and 1831. The raw data for both analyses are presented in table 4.16.

The variables are as follows:

- weaving: percent households with one or more weavers resident in 1821
- spinning 1821: percent households with one or more spinners present in 1821
- spinning 1841: percent women aged fifteen or more years who reported an occupation ministering to clothing in 1841
- laboring: percent households headed by a laborer in 1821
- landpoor: percent households with land holding less than the study area median of seven acres in 1821
- landvalue: valuation per acre in 1841
- nuptiality: percent women aged seventeen to twenty-five identified as spouses in 1821
- popchange: percent population change between 1821 and 1831 (calculated from published census data)

According to protoindustrialization theory, weaving and spinning should be associated positively with land poverty, early marriage, and population in-

Table 4.11. Cavan Study Area: Estimates of the Distribution of Spinning by Parish in 1821 and 1841

Parish[1]	*Households with spinner(s) resident in 1821 (%)*	*Women 15+ years occupied as spinners in 1821 (%)*	*Women 15+ years ministering to clothing in 1841 (%)*
Crosserlough	93.8	80.4	38.9
Castlerahan	90.5	77.3	34.6
Mullagh	90.4	85.8	18.1
Lurgan	90.1	79.1	31.5
Kinawley	87.0	72.4	56.4
Munterconnaught	83.1	73.5	40.3
Kilmore	68.4	50.7	35.0
Lavey	51.7	44.0	50.3
Denn	49.2	39.4	40.9
Drung and Larah	40.4	29.2	59.5
Annagelliff	12.4	9.6	55.0
Castletarra	9.4	9.9	42.8
Ballymachugh	3.5	1.8	29.7
Kilbride	0.7	0.4	23.8
Drumlumman	0.2	0.1	43.9

Sources: 1821 Cavan sample; County of Cavan, General Table. H. C. 1843, vol. 24, pp. 298-301.
Note: 1. Ranked by percent households with one or more spinners resident in 1821.

crease. An earlier body of research (Thirsk 1961; Jones 1968) suggested that rural industries were more likely to occur in areas of less fertile soil where wasteland was available for reclamation and where restrictions on inmigration and land subdivision were limited. Weaving and spinning should therefore be associated negatively with land valuation. In his analysis of county-level data for Ireland in 1841, Almquist confirmed these predictions for spinning, but not for weaving (see the discussion in chapter 3). However, O'Neill (1984) proposed an alternative explanation for population growth in County Cavan before the famine. In his analysis of data from the surviving 1841 census manuscripts for the parish of Killashandra, he found that there was sharp decline in the average age at marriage for laborers' wives between about 1790 and 1821, so that they achieved near "equality of opportunity" for marriage with farmers' wives. He attributed this decline to an increase in demand for labor generated by the commercialization of agriculture. If his "market impulsion" theory is correct, we might expect laboring to be associated positively with early marriage and with population increase.

A complete correlation matrix is presented for all the variables in table 4.17. From the perspective of protoindustrialization theory the results are mixed and difficult to explain. Weaving is associated positively with land poverty, but not

Table 4.12. Cavan Study Area: Distribution of Households by Landholding and Parish

Parish	*Landless[1] (%)*	*< 10 acres (%)*	*10+ acres (%)*
Annagelliff	27.7	49.4	22.9
Ballymachugh	48.1	39.5	12.4
Castlerahan	46.0	39.1	14.9
Castletarra	39.8	45.8	14.4
Crosserlough	37.4	46.5	16.1
Denn	31.2	42.3	26.6
Drumlumman	45.9	35.2	18.9
Drung & Larah	25.3	50.1	24.6
Kilbride	53.2	33.5	13.2
Kilmore	48.5	38.6	12.9
Kinawley	35.6	31.7	32.7
Lavey	30.9	49.4	19.7
Lurgan	46.7	36.3	17.0
Mullagh	40.8	38.1	21.1
Munterconnaught	47.7	21.4	30.9

Source: 1821 Cavan sample.
Note: 1. Households with no recorded land.

with either of the demographic variables. Spinning in 1821 is associated negatively with land valuation and positively with population increase, but there is no association between spinning and young female nuptiality. (Spinning in 1841 is associated positively with land subdivision. I discuss this relationship more fully in the section on deindustrialization, below). There is no association between laboring and either of the demographic variables.

There are a number of problems with using correlation analysis to test protoindustrialization hypotheses in this way. Apart from the problem of ecological fallacy, quantitative analysis cannot capture *combinatorial* explanations, especially with small Ns (see Ragin 1987, 58–67). As I described in chapter 3, recent research suggests that the demoeconomic trends predicted by protoindustrialization theory were sometimes absent where agriculture continued to be a viable source of income, irrespective of the presence of rural industries (Hendrickx 1993; Mastboom 1996; Pfister 1995, 1996b; Ogilvie 1997). Other analyses have suggested that demoeconomic trends varied according to the type of protoindustrial activity engaged in (Mager 1997; Pfister 1997) and according to the gender composition of the protoindustrial labor force (Gullickson 1986). Thus it is likely that there were multiple combinations of factors leading to different paths of development in protoindustrial districts.

The method of "Qualitative Comparative Analysis" (QCA) developed by Ragin (1987) provides a solution to the problem of identifying the combinations of factors associated with different patterns of demoeconomic change within the study area. QCA uses Boolean algebra to identify the minimal con-

Table 4.13. Landholding Pattern, by Parish

Parish	*N*[a]	*Small Farm Pattern*[b]	*Laborer Pattern*[c]
Annagelliff	116	X	
Castletarra	198	X	
Crosserlough	285	X	
Denn	164	X	
Drung and Larah	411	X	
Lavey	163	X	
Ballymachugh	103		X
Castlerahan	190		X
Drumlumman	246		X
Kilbride	136		X
Kilmore	237		X
Lurgan	209		X
Munter Connaught	84		X
Kinawley	97		
Mullagh	158	No Distinct Pattern	

Source: Table 4.12.
Notes: a. Ns weighted to correct for overrepresentation of weaving households in the sample. See text for clarification. b. Small Farm Pattern: Households with less than ten acres predominant. c. Laborer Pattern: Landless households predominant.

figurations associated with particular phenomena or outcomes. Because it assumes complexity, QCA is particularly useful for exploring diversity amongst cases, and for identifying types and subtypes (Ragin 1987, 168–80). It must be emphasized, however, that the analysis below cannot be considered a causal test of protoindustrialization hypotheses in County Cavan, since the relevant universe of cases cannot be included. Moreover, because the parishes in the study area are characterized by limited diversity, the minimization that can be achieved is small. Nonetheless, the analysis identifies some of the conditions under which the predictions of protoindustrialization theory were borne out, and others under which they were not. It helps to clarify the relationships amongst cross-sectional and spatial variation in the study area, and the development of the linen industry over time.

I used QCA to identify the minimal sets of combinations of weaving, spinning, laboring, land valuation, and young female nuptiality associated with relatively high and low rates of population increase between 1821 and 1831. The procedures for calculating these sets are explained in detail in note 10.[10] There were two distinct demoeconomic regimes associated with a relatively high rate of population increase. Both occurred on poor quality land. In one cluster of parishes, where spinning coexisted with a high proportion of landless laborers, population increased even though young female nuptiality was not high. However in a second cluster, population

Table 4.14. Cavan Study Area: Distribution of Households by Crude Life-Cycle Stage and Parish

	Household Life Cycle[1]				
Parish	*Stage I (%)*	*Stage II (%)*	*Stage III (%)*	*Stage IV (%)*	*Stage V (%)*
Annagelliff	6.5	34.2	44.2	14.9	0.2
Ballymachugh	5.3	36.0	43.4	14.0	1.2
Castlerahan	3.9	37.2	38.5	19.8	0.6
Castletarra	6.1	35.2	32.9	24.1	1.6
Crosserlough	6.6	42.9	30.8	17.8	1.9
Denn	4.6	36.7	36.1	21.2	1.4
Drumlumman	5.2	35.6	32.3	25.4	1.4
Drung and Larah	5.9	36.0	37.6	18.4	2.1
Kilbride	3.4	25.0	46.7	21.7	3.2
Kilmore	2.2	36.9	41.1	16.2	3.7
Kinawley	4.5	46.9	40.4	7.1	1.1
Lavey	4.9	47.0	29.4	17.5	1.3
Lurgan	8.7	38.4	32.8	19.5	0.5
Mullagh	1.5	37.6	36.2	22.7	2.1
Munterconnaught	5.2	38.2	33.2	20.8	2.6

Source: 1821 Cavan sample.
Note: (1) For an explanation of how the life cycle stages were calculated, see table 4.8. Percentages do not add to one hundred, because households with no wife present were not included in the calculations.

increase was associated with high young female nuptiality, where weaving coexisted with a low proportion of landless laborers. There were two main types of demoeconomic regime associated with a relatively low rate of population increase in the study area. Relatively low rates of spinning and young female nuptiality were common to both. However, one cluster was characterized by a high proportion of landless laborers on good quality land, while the other was characterized by the coexistence of weaving with low proportions of landless laborers.

Thus QCA identified four clusters of parishes in the study area with distinct demoeconomic patterns in 1821. Table 4.18 summarizes the results. Cluster 1 falls within the first landscape of modernization identified by Duffy (1995, see the discussion above). These parishes were characterized by a small-farm pattern of landholding, and by the farmer-weaver type of weaving household. Within the study area they were incorporated earliest to the linen industry, due to their relative proximity to the linen market at Cootehill and to the yarn market at Cavan town. It seems likely that the linen industry contributed to land subdivision in this district. Given that farmer weavers had high proportions of children under twelve years, it is possible that the household dynamics predicted by protoindustrialization theory played some part in this process. By 1821, however, linen sales at Cootehill

Table 4.15. Distribution of Households in Each Parish by Life-Cycle Pattern

Parish	*N*[a]	*Mature Pattern*[b]	*Transitional Pattern*	*Immature Pattern*[c]
Annagelliff	116	X		
Ballymachugh	103	X		
Castlerahan	190	X		
Castletarra	198	X		
Denn	164	X		
Drumlumman	246	X		
Drung and Larah	411	X		
Kilmore	237	X		
Mullagh	158	X		
Lurgan	209		X	
Munterconnaught	84		X	
Crosserlough	285			X
Kinawley	97			X
Lavey	163			X

Source: Table 4.14.
Note: The parish of Kilbride was characterized by an advanced lifecyle pattern with just 28.4 percent of households in stages 1 or 2. See table 4.8 for an explanation of how the household life-cycle stages were calculated. (a) Ns weighted to correct for overrepresentation of weaving households in the sample. See text for clarification. (b) Mature Pattern: circa 40 percent in stages 1 or 2. (c) Immature Pattern: circa 50 percent in stages 1 or 2.

were in decline, landlords were taking a more active approach to the management of their estates, and the increased demand for agricultural products provided an alternative source of income.[11] These conditions inhibited further land subdivision, so that young female nuptiality was not high in 1821, and population grew relatively slowly to 1831.

Clusters 2 and 3 fall largely within Duffy's second landscape of modernization. Both were characterized by the predominance of landless laborers over small farm households but they had distinct demoeconomic patterns in 1821. In the parishes within cluster 2, to the southwest of the study area, better quality land seems to have been associated with relatively low rates of young female nuptiality and population increase. This was true even though three of the parishes were characterized by the presence of weaving and the fourth (Kilbride) claimed a large number of spinning wheels in 1796 (see table 4.1). These parishes, adjacent to the secondary linen triangle centered on Killeshandra, were incorporated to the linen industry later than the parishes in cluster 1, at a time when demand for agricultural produce was also increasing. In line with recent research, it seems likely that protoindustrialization did not alter the dynamics of household formation under these circumstances. In cluster 3, however, where the quality of land was poorer, near universal reporting of the occupation spinner was associated with a relatively

Table 4.16. Cavan Study Area: 1821 to 1841

Parish	*Weaving*	*Spinning (1821)*	*Spinning (1841)*	*Laboring*	*Land Poor*	*Nuptiality*	*Land Value*	*Pop. change (1821–1831)*
Annagelliff	**8.8**	12.4	55.0	14.6	31.7	15.9	**0.60**	12.1
Ballymachugh	**10.9**	3.5	29.7	**23.4**	30.6	16.2	**0.73**	15.5
Castlerahan	**7.0**	**90.5**	34.6	**22.6**	24.6	9.8	0.57	**43.8**
Castletarra	**6.2**	9.4	42.8	13.8	34.2	16.4	**0.60**	15.9
Crosserlough	**17.3**	**93.8**	38.9	17.8	30.1	**23.7**	0.54	**22.2**
Denn	**14.1**	49.2	40.9	6.9	30.7	**25.7**	0.52	**28.8**
Drumlumman	**9.5**	0.2	43.9	**27.4**	23.1	15.4	**0.60**	10.1
Drung and Larah	**9.9**	40.4	59.5	9.2	34.0	14.0	0.56	13.7
Kilbride	1.5	0.7	23.8	**33.2**	19.4	12.5	**0.73**	12.2
Kilmore	**8.9**	68.4	35.0	**22.5**	25.6	16.1	**0.70**	0.8
Kinawley	**6.8**	**87.0**	56.4	13.5	19.5	**28.3**	0.17	**19.0**
Lavey	**8.7**	51.7	50.3	16.7	30.3	**27.0**	0.50	**41.2**
Lurgan	3.6	**90.1**	31.5	**26.1**	21.5	**27.4**	0.47	9.0
Mullagh	2.7	**90.4**	18.1	**22.8**	17.4	18.4	0.48	**39.1**
Munterconnaught	1.4	**83.1**	40.3	**35.6**	13.1	10.9	0.52	**19.6**

Data for comparative analysis.
Sources: 1821 Cavan sample; Abstract of the Population Returns, 1831. H. C. 1833, vol. 39. General Valuation of Ireland, County of Cavan. 1841. Newry: James Henderson. County of Cavan, General Table. H. C. 1843, vol. 24, 298–301.
Note: Cases highlighted in bold were coded positive for QCA. See text for explanation of variables and further clarification.

Table 4.17. Correlation Coefficients for Variables Included in the Comparative Analysis of Parishes

	Weaving	*Spinning21*	*Spinning41*	*Laboring*	*Landpoor*	*Valuation*	*Nuptiality*
Weaving							
Spinning21	−.111						
Spinning41	.300	−.207					
Laboring	−.486*	−.064	−.636**				
Landpoor	.636**	−.346	.479*	−.704**			
Valuation	.230	−.654**	−.197	.228	.325		
Nuptiality	.157	.279	.118	−.414	.086	−.609**	
Popchange	−.025	.479*	−.046	−.225	−.057	−.427	−.361

Sources: As for table 4.16.
Notes: * p >.05; **p >.01 (Spearman's rho, one-tailed test). See text for explanation of the variables.

Table 4.18. Typology of Rural Industrial Districts in the Cavan Study Area in 1821

Type of District	*Characteristics*	*Parishes*
Mature Protoindustrial	Weaving, small farm landholding pattern, low young female nuptiality, and low rate of population increase	Annagelliff Castletarra Drung and Larah
Developing Protoindustrial	Weaving and spinning, small farm landholding pattern, poor quality land, high young female nuptiality, and high rate of population increase	Crosserlough Denn Kinawley Lavey
Mature Agricultural	Some weaving and spinning, laborer landholding pattern, good quality land, low young female nuptiality, and low rate of population increase	Ballymachugh Drumlumman Kilbride Kilmore
Developing Agricultural	Universal spinning, laborer landholding pattern, poor quality land, low young female nuptiality, and high rate of population increase	Castlerahan Mullagh Munterconnaught

high rate of population increase—perhaps through inmigration, since the proportion of young women married was not high. It is possible that in these parishes spinning was taken up in order to provide an additional source of income given the pressures created by population increase, rather than the other way around.

Finally, the parishes in cluster 4 fall within Duffy's two landscapes of underdevelopment. In these parishes characterized by relatively poor quality land, low rates of landlessness, and inattentive estate management, weaving was associated with a high proportion of young women married and a high rate of population increase to 1831. It is reassuring that this cluster includes the two parishes in the study area with the highest proportions of weavers (Crosserlough and Denn), and that all of them had relatively high proportions of spinners (see table 4.11), even though just two were coded "present" for the purposes of QCA (see note 10 for clarification of this point). These parishes are at a distance from the primary linen triangle centered on Cootehill, and were incorporated later to the linen industry during the wave of expansion associated with the growing demand for plain and coarse linens from the end of the eighteenth century (see chapter 2).

The analysis above has suggested that divergent patterns of rural industrialization were linked to variations in the *timing* of incorporation to the linen industry, and in the socioeconomic context which received it. The classic pattern of protoindustrial household formation emerged when spinning and weaving provided a better living for land holders than commercial agricultural production, because the quality of their land was poor, or because of weak demand for agricultural produce, or for other reasons. (Remember that weaving first spread into south Ulster in the aftermath of an agricultural crisis created by widespread crop losses and cattle disease). These conditions fostered the development of a functionally integrated, "whole house" system of protoindustrial production. By contrast, household dynamics were not altered where agriculture continued to be a major source of income, either because the quality of land was good and demand for agricultural produce relatively strong, or because distance from markets made the returns to rural industry relatively small. In these contexts farmers might take up rural industry under favorable market conditions, but the restrictions inherent in the "peasant" model of household formation were not lifted. Similarly, laborers might welcome the additional income to be gleaned from their wives' spinning, especially where competition for their labor was high, but the dynamics of household formation were not altered because they lacked access to land. In the next section, divergent processes of deindustrialization are linked to these uneven patterns of incorporation to the linen industry. The analysis of deindustrialization highlights the ways in which the "classic" protoindustrial pattern was distinguished by the extent to which women's labor was embedded in the household economy.

UNEVEN PATTERNS OF DEINDUSTRIALIZATION

After about 1825 the linen industry began a process of recentralization in east Ulster as the introduction of mill-spun yarn slowly undermined the gendered regional division of labor that structured the industry from the middle of the eighteenth century (see chapter 2). In the 1830s Ordnance Survey Memoirs were returned from the parishes of Drumgoon, Drumlumman, Drung, Kildrumsherdan and Larah in County Cavan. The linen industry was reported to be in severe decline. While few looms were still in operation, "the noise of the spinning wheel" could still "frequently be heard," even though an "industrious spinner" could now earn no more than 2d. a day—compared to about 4d. a day in the 1770s (Young 1892).

As prices for their yarn declined, handspinners increased the intensity and duration of their labor, snatching more time for the wheel from the interstices of their daily routines, and working into the night. But deindustrialization was neither sudden nor unilinear. Geary (1998, 523) calculated that, in Ireland as a whole, "the process of replacement of hand-spun by mill-spun yarn to 1850 was less than half complete by 1839." In other words, the spinning mills could not have supplied sufficient yarn to produce the volume of cloth exported from Ireland. Who were the women who made up the difference, and why were they willing to work so hard at producing yarn that sold for little more than the price of raw flax?

Map 4.3 shows the percentage of women reporting an occupation "ministering to clothing" to the 1841 census in each parish in County Cavan. It shows that the highest proportions of spinners were found in two districts: first, in the cluster of parishes to the east of Cavan town which were characterized by land fragmentation and a 'farmer-weaver' pattern in the 1821 Cavan Sample, and second, in the mountainous, northwestern barony of Tullyhaw. Spinning appears to have declined in significance in those southeastern parishes with relatively poor quality land where the proportions of spinners were very high in 1821. This cluster of parishes was characterized by high proportions of households headed by landless laborers. O'Neill (1984, 148–49) argued that by the 1830s laborers were experiencing extreme poverty because of population growth and declining demand for their labor. He also found that in Killashandra in 1841, laborers' daughters were much less likely than farmers' daughters to operate unprofitable wheels. Thus "increasing "application to the wheel" in the context of declining prices occurred primarily in small-farm households.

These were concentrated in mature protoindustrial districts and in newly incorporated "yarn districts" on marginal lands.

Commentators often suggest that women continued to spin because of the absence of any other source of employment. Thus according to Collins (1982, 142), "Although spinning was regarded merely as an alternative to idleness its production continued because the family labor which produced it was an invariable overhead cost." Similarly, Geary (1998, 535–36) observed that "Hand spinners . . . did not receive a contractual wage; their earnings were realized when the household web was sold or when they sold their yarn. In this latter circumstance, constrained by a lack of alternative employment opportunities, they appear to have acted as price takers." No doubt if other sources of money income were available for women, spinning would have been more widely abandoned (or indeed might have been less widely taken up). But women were not "content to sit up in the evening without a light and charge little or nothing for it" because they literally had nothing to do. As laborers explained to the Poor Law commissioners, it was difficult for their wives to combine long hours of spinning with domestic responsibilities, and there is no reason to believe they differed from small farmers' wives in that respect.[12]

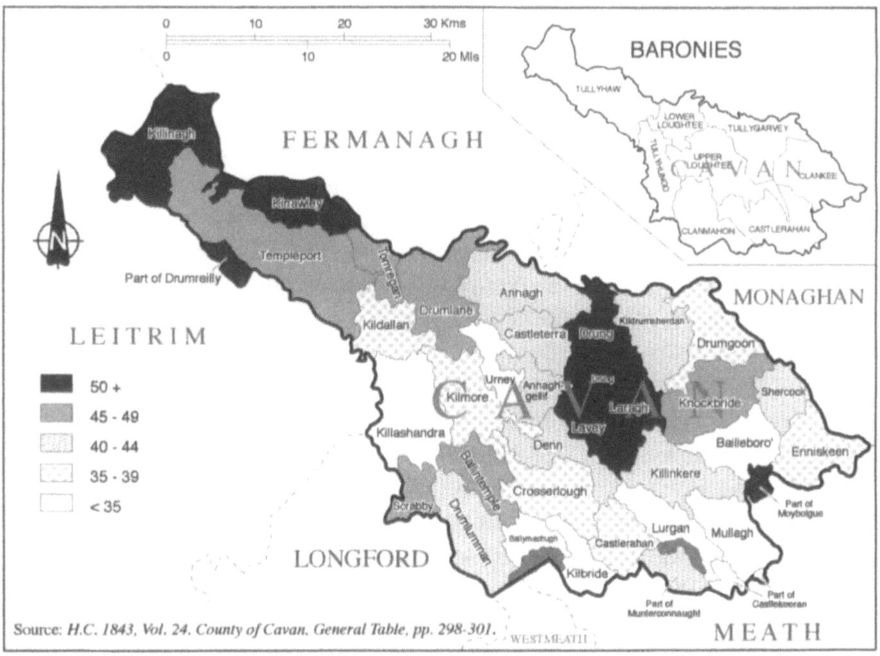

Source: *H.C. 1843, Vol. 24. County of Cavan, General Table, pp. 298-301.*

Map 4.3. County Cavan: Percent Women "Ministering to Clothing" in 1841

Women found themselves in the position Geary describes because the household division of labor consigned them to a low-productivity phase of the production process, and also—as I will argue in chapter 5—because in the prevailing ideology spinning was not distinguished from women's other household tasks, even when it was integrated into regional and international markets.

The following passage from the Ordnance Survey Memoir for Aghalurcher, in County Fermanagh, is a particularly good illustration of the gendered construction of work and leisure in protoindustrial households in the context of deindustrialization:

> In the leisure time intervening sowing and harvest time the more industrious among the young men apply themselves to weaving coarse linens. Weaving, however, is not carried on to any great extent in this parish.
>
> The female part of the community invariably spin and earn but a very scanty profit for their almost incessant application to the wheel. The women, however, are not excused from the labors of husbandry, and during the more busy periods of the year may be seen with their husbands or brothers assisting in the business of farming. It is to be lamented that there does not exist other employment to occupy the spare time of the agriculturalist, which sad to say is too often spent in idleness and drinking. *These remarks apply chiefly to the very small farmers, for to apply it generally would be doing injustice to a great proportion of steady, well-doing farmers*. (Day and McWilliams, 1990, 12, my emphasis)

That women's "spare time" was invariably occupied by spinning, whereas weaving had been generally abandoned and most men had leisure for drinking, can only be understood in terms of the unequal gender relations that were an underlying feature of the protoindustrial family economy. Women continued to spin because their application to this labor-intensive task was the decisive factor both in the overall growth of the linen industry under protoindustrialization, and in the labor-consumer balance of individual protoindustrial households.

The defining features of such households were first, that their economic activities—both agricultural and industrial—were rooted in the family labor strategies associated with "spade husbandry," (see chapter 3) and second, that they retained access to small plots of land enabling them to continue to pursue those strategies. Under deindustrialization, it made sense to suspend or abandon the more capital-intensive process of weaving, where in relative terms the loss of income was greater, in order to devote more labor to agriculture—both for domestic consumption and for the marketplace. Collins (1982, 141) suggested that such households alternated the intensity of labor devoted to weaving and flax cultivation in response to fluctuating prices.

However, the gender division of labor ensured that women (rather than men) responded by increasing their "self-exploitation"—that is, by continuously increasing their application to the labor-intensive process of spinning, in the face of declining prices.

By contrast, households in farming communities that were already more fully incorporated to the money economy might diversify into spinning and weaving under favorable market conditions, but because the underlying logic of household production was different, deindustrialization there had different consequences. Laboring women whose households felt the brunt of "over-population" and declining demand for agricultural labor ceased to spin, not so much because the cost of the equipment made spinning irrational (as O'Neill suggested), but because their lack of access to land made it so.

CONCLUSION

The central argument of this chapter has been that local differences in forms of protoindustrialization and rural deindustrialization during the transition to factory industry depended both on the timing of incorporation to the world economy, and on differences in patterns of landholding and the quality of land. The physical and social environment that received the linen industry was itself the product of earlier waves of incorporation through colonization and settlement.

The gender division of labor between spinning and weaving crosscut these processes in complex ways. On the one hand, as I argued in chapters 2 and 3, it ensured the continued spatial expansion of the linen industry, so that even the most remote and marginal districts in the county were incorporated through spinning by the early nineteenth century. On the other hand, the analysis in this chapter has added complexity to the broad distinctions between spinning and weaving districts described in chapter 3. There is tentative evidence to suggest that the demoeconomic trends hypothesized by the theories of protoindustrialization occurred at two "moments" in the overall development of the linen industry in County Cavan. The first phase occurred in districts that were incorporated relatively early to the linen industry, during a period when commercial agriculture did not provide a viable economic alternative. The second phase occurred in districts of poor quality land during a period of rapid growth in the market for both linens and agricultural products. Districts of relatively good quality land that were incorporated to the linen industry during the latter period did not manifest the demoeconomic trends associated with protoindustrialization because agricultural activity provided a significant alternative source of income at that time. Poorer lands with high proportions of landless laborers experienced population growth, but this increase does not appear to have been linked to young female nuptiality.

I have argued that, as a result of these differences in the timing and nature of incorporation to the world economy through linen manufacturing, spinning varied in its significance within the family economy, both across space and between social groups. This meant that, during the process of deindustrialization, small-farm rural industrial households adopted behaviors reminiscent of the subsistence-oriented strategies, and plebian patterns of work and leisure classically associated with the protoindustrial family economy, but those with larger farms, or who were landless, did not.

It is in this context that we must understand the behavior of small holders in Drung, described in the quotation at the beginning of the chapter. Differences in household behavior depended, in part, on how women's labor was mobilized within the family economy at different times and places, and amongst different social groups. The wives and daughters of more substantial farmers, and of landless laborers, added something to the common pot by spinning, but in contrast to the wives and daughters of farmer weavers and small or "subsistence" farmers, their labor in spinning did not form part of an integrated household economic strategy.[13] The next chapter shifts our focus from regions and social groups to the intimate sphere of the household, in order to examine the gender division of labor as an aspect of the personal, daily relationships between women and men.

NOTES

Some of the material in this chapter has been published in Gray 1999.

1. Probably 1834 or 1835.
2. In fact, data survive in the National Archives for sixteen parishes, but in the 1821 census the parishes of Drung and Larah were treated as a single unit, probably because a small part of Drung forms an island within the boundaries of Larah.
3. In 1740 it was reported that: "There is a great number of weavers and bleachers in this town and neighbourhood and no less than ten bleach yards the least of which bleaches a thousand pieces of cloth every year," quoted in Crawford (1971), 120.
4. In what follows, where data are reported for the combined sample, the weaving data are weighted by dividing them by five. This is explained where appropriate in the footnotes to the tables.
5. The acres reported in the 1821 manuscripts are probably not statute acres, but "Cunningham" or "Plantation" acres which were somewhat larger (Cunningham 1960). Because of this uncertainty, the data should be treated with caution. I am assuming that the reported values are sufficiently reliable to give an indication of variation amongst social groups in the Cavan Study Area. However, care should be taken

when making comparisons with other sources of information on landholding in prefamine Ireland.

6. I use the word "household" to refer to what Carney (1972) termed the "houseful" in his analysis of a sample drawn from the 1821 census manuscripts. His calculation of mean houseful size for County Cavan (5.69) corresponds well to my estimate of 5.61.

7. The 95 percent confidence interval for the mean number of children under twelve years in nonweaving households headed by farmers is 1.78 to 1.96, compared to the mean of 2.26 in the population of farmer-weaver households.

8. Amongst nonweaving, farmer-headed households where the spouse was aged twenty to twenty-four years, the mean number of children under twelve years was 1.32 (95 percent C.I. = 1.11−1.54), compared to the mean of 1.58 children under twelve years amongst the population of farmer-weaver households in this category. Where the spouse was aged forty-five to forty-nine, the mean number of children under twelve years was 2.01 (95 percent C.I. = 1.72−2.31) compared to 2.64 amongst farmer-weaver households.

9. Unfortunately, since the 1821 census enumerators did not gather data on marital status, it is virtually impossible to estimate the average age at marriage within the study area. If it is assumed that only those who were identified as spouses, or who were heads of households in the absence of a spouse were married, the singulate mean age at marriage (SMAM) for women can be calculated as 26.6 years (see Hajnal 1953). However, a significant proportion of household residents could not be identified in terms of their relationship to the household head, or were identified as lodgers or beggars. It is not possible to hazard a guess as to the marital status of such individuals. Assuming them to be married, the SMAM for women can be calculated at 25.6 years. While these estimates are high compared to the average ages at marriage in the parish of Killashandra (O'Neill 1984, 178), they are consistent with other estimates for prefamine Ireland (Guinnane 1997, 82).

10. The model may be expressed as follows (see the main text for an explanation of the variables):

$$\text{popchange} = \text{weaving} + \text{spinning 1821} + \text{laboring} + \text{landvalue} + \text{nuptiality}$$

Because QCA addresses dichotomous factors representing the "presence" or "absence" of a phenomenon, deciding where to "make the cut" in continuous data presents a dilemma. For example, what percentage of weaving households should be considered "high"? In general, I adopted the strategy of dividing the variables where there were clear gaps in the distribution of values, while also seeking to maximize complexity by choosing gaps that ensured relatively equal numbers of "present" and "absent" cases. The values coded "present" are highlighted in bold in table 4.17 (main text).

Weaving was the most problematic variable, because there were three clusters of cases: two parishes (Crosserlough and Denn) with notably higher percentages of households weaving; a middling cluster of eight parishes where the percentages of households weaving ranged from six to eleven percent; and a smaller cluster of four parishes where less than four percent of households had resident weavers. I decided to code all parishes where weaving was six percent or higher "present." This may seem generous, but it must be remembered that if weaving is expected to affect demoeconomic patterns at the level of whole parishes, it can only be on the assumption that the presence of weavers had an indirect effect on local household formation strategies by creating a demand for yarn. In the 1841 county-level data analysed by Almquist, Armagh had the highest proportion of occupied men weaving at 22 percent, and just seven out of thirty-two counties reported more than 6 percent of occupied men weaving.

Table 4.19 presents a Boolean truth table for the six conditions included in the analysis.

It can be observed that there were four configurations associated with a relatively high rate of population increase between 1821 and 1831. Using the convention of expressing the presence of a condition in uppercase letters and its absence in lowercase letters, these four conditions may be expressed as follows:

1. weaving.SPINNING21.LABOURING.value.nuptiality
2. WEAVING.SPINNING21.LABOURING.value.nuptiality
3. WEAVING.spinning21.laboring.value.NUPTIALITY
4. WEAVING.SPINNING21.laboring.value.NUPTIALITY

Boolean minimization proceeds by comparing configurations in a stepwise fashion (see Ragin 1987, 85–102). Where two configurations associated with the same outcome differ on only one condition, that condition may be considered irrelevant to the outcome and removed. Thus:

a. 1 + 2 = SPINNING21.LABOURING.value.nuptiality
b. 3 + 4 = WEAVING.laboring.value.NUPTIALITY

Table 4.19. Truth Table Showing Configurations Associated with High and Low Rates of Population Increase, 1821 to 1831

Row	*W*	*S21*	*L*	*V*	*N*	*P*	*Number of Parishes*
1.	0	1	1	0	0	1	2
2.	1	1	1	0	0	1	1
3.	1	0	0	0	1	1	2
4.	1	1	0	0	1	1	2
5.	1	0	0	0	0	0	1
6.	1	0	0	1	0	0	2
7.	0	0	1	1	0	0	1
8.	1	0	1	1	0	0	3
9.	0	1	1	0	1	0	1

Sources: As for table 4.16.
Notes: W = Weaving, S21 = Spinning21, L = Laboring, V = Valuation, N = Nuptiality, P = Popchange. See text for an explanation of the variables.

No further minimization is possible for the configurations associated with a relatively high rate of population increase. The result may be factored as follows:

POPCHANGE = value(SPINNING.LABORING.nuptiality) +
(WEAVING.laboring.NUPTIALITY)

There were five configurations associated with a relatively low rate of population increase. The first round of mimimization yielded the following four "prime implicants":

c. spinning21.LABOURING.VALUE.nuptiality
d. WEAVING.spinning21.VALUE.nuptiality
e. WEAVING.spinning21.laboring.nuptiality
f. weaving.SPINNING21.LABOURING.value.NUPTIALITY

However, table 4.20 shows that the original five "primitive expressions" are covered by prime implicants c, e, and f, so it is possible to minimize the solution further by dropping d.

The remaining prime implicants may be factored to give the following solution for a relatively low rate of population increase in the study area:

popchange = spinning.nuptiality (LABOURING.VALUE) +
(WEAVING.laboring) +
weaving.SPINNING21.LABOURING.value.NUPTIALITY.

Prime implicant f—which was not subject to any minimization—refers to the parish of Lurgan. This case was similar to its neighbors Mullagh and Munterconnaught insofar as it was characterized by a combination of spinning and laboring on relatively poor quality land. Strangely, however, unlike its neighbors, Lurgan was characterized by a relatively low rate of population increase despite a high proportion of young women married. This might be explained by the fact that population density was already quite high in Lurgan in 1821, possibly because, as indicated by the "Spinning

Table 4.20. Coverage of Prime Implicants for Parishes with a Low Rate of Population Increase between 1821 and 1831

	Prime Implicants			
Primitive Expressions	*s.L.V.n*	*W.s.V.n*	*W.s.l.n*	*w.S.L.v.N*
W.s.l.v.n			X	
W.s.l.V.n		X	X	
w.s.L.V.n	X			
W.s.L.V.n	X	X		
w.S.L.v.N				X

Wheel Survey" (see table 4.1) the parish was incorporated to the linen industry through spinning much earlier than the other two.

11. With the exception of Drung and Larah, each of the parishes within this cluster had relatively high land valuations. In fact the parish of Drung had a relatively high valuation (.63), while that of Larah was relatively low (.51). I suspect that if it had been possible to separate the two parishes for the analysis, Larah would have fallen within cluster b.

12. See the testimonies of Adam Finlay and John McCrome, laborers from the barony of Upper Iveagh in County Down and "universal opinion" in the barony of Lecale, County Down. House of Commons, "Reports from Commissioners, Poor Laws (Ireland), appendix D." British Parliamentary Papers, 1836, vol. 31, 93, 115.

13. In landless households spinning formed part of an "economy of expedients" (Hufton 1975) that may be distinguished from the household economies of those who had access to land.

Chapter Five

The Household Arena

The mountain lass, at her wee bit wheel,
        How blythe was her e'e, an' how rosy her cheek!
Her bosom was white, an' her heart was leal,
        Her mien it was modest, her manner was meek,
But now the pert maidens, wha ply in the mill,
        How wan is their visage,—how dim is their e'e
For the ban they maun bide is enough to chill
        The spring o' the heart an' to deaden their glee:
To toil for men that are hard to please,
In a hot-bed rank wi' vice an' disease.

An' when they speak, it maun be wi a squeal;
        They maun rise an' rin at the toll o' the bell,
An' brook the insult o' a tyrant an' de'il,
        An' the jargon they hear is the language o' hell
To breed a bit lassie in sic a vile place,
        Instead o' her ain father's cot on the green,
It puts the puir thing in a pitifu' case
        Ah! Black was the day when they made the machine.
It has added mair pelf to the hoards o' the great
And left those that were low in a far lower state.

In his poem, "The Auld Wife's Address to Her Spinning Wheel," Thomas Beggs framed his critique of proletarianization as the transfer of control over the labor of young women from fathers to mill owners. Thus in a sense the poem captures the central argument of this book: that unequal gender relations structured the development of the linen industry in Ireland. In earlier chapters I showed how the division of labor between spinning and weaving was implicated in Irish patterns of protoindustrialization. This chapter examines that division of labor as a dynamic process *within* the household arena. My portrayal differs from that of Beggs, insofar as I believe his poem, as a political intervention, exaggerated the meekness and loyalty of the daughter spinner. I argue that relations between fathers and daughters, and between husbands and wives, were characterized by tension as well as harmony, and that changing patterns of household production and consumption comprised a series of provisional bargains between the sexes. Along the way, I support my argument with evidence from contemporary upper-class observers, and from the weaver poets.

THE PRICE AND VALUE OF SPINNING

In 1825, a Parliamentary Commission of Inquiry investigated the regulations governing the Irish linen industry (H.C. 1825, Vol. 5). The Scottish Linen Board had been effectively abolished in 1823, with no obvious ill effects (Durie and Solar 1988, 214). Indeed, it was apparent to the commissioners that the Scottish industry was more developed, insofar as it was characterized by putting out systems in both spinning and weaving, and by investment in flax-spinning machinery. The leading questions addressed to their witnesses revealed the commissioners' belief that overregulation on the part of the Irish Linen Board had increased the cost of hand spinning in Ireland, making it unattractive to manufacturers.

As I will argue in the next chapter, with the wisdom of hindsight we can probably agree with the commissioners that the organization of spinning in Ireland contributed to the long-term underdevelopment of the linen industry. However, as their witnesses forcefully asserted, the problem could not be attributed to the high cost of female labor in Ireland. When asked about the feasibility of importing foreign yarn, the manufacturer George Grier remarked that: "I can scarcely conceive how any foreign yarn can be supplied much cheaper than the Irish yarn; the price of labor cannot be much cheaper on the continent than it is in the west of Ireland." The argument reached telling levels of absurdity when one of the commissioners argued with Peter Besnard, the Linen Board's inspector general for Connacht and Munster, over the meaning of the phrase "division of labor." Besnard used it to refer to a household's ability to draw on the expandable labor of all its members. "They have the article cheaper than it can be got in any other way," he insisted, "they set little value on their own labor." The commissioner retorted that "the principle of division of labor (would) be more accurately applied if one set of persons confined themselves to grow the flax, if another set of persons confined themselves to dress the flax, and if a third set of persons confined themselves to spinning the yarn."

Besnard had much to lose if the functions of the Linen Board were disbanded, so perhaps it is not surprising that the committee found it impossible to credit that "there are two prices for the labor; that there is one price for the work of the laborer hired, and a distinct price for the work done [by those who spin for themselves]." But was Besnard right? I contend that it is possible to demonstrate Besnard's point using data collected by Arthur Young in County Armagh in 1776. Table 5.1 shows that a small manufacturer who purchased flax in the marketplace, put it out to spinners, and then put the yarn out to weavers would make a loss—or a very small profit if the cost of spinning was at the low end of the range provided by Young—even with the omission of ancillary costs.

When the processes of spinning and weaving are disaggregated, it can be further demonstrated that the profitability of manufacturing linen cloth depended on the value of spinning. A manufacturer who purchased yarn in the marketplace, and put it out to weavers, could make a profit on the web, provided the price of yarn did not exceed 7d a hank. However, a manufacturer who purchased flax in the marketplace, and put it out to spinners, could not make a profit on the yarn *unless* it sold for more than 7d a hank.[1]

Unfortunately, Young does not give us a market price for yarn at Armagh, but he does tell us that yarn of the same quality—two and a half hanks to the

Table 5.1. Cost of Manufacturing Linen Yarn and Cloth about Armagh

A. Purchase Flax, Employ Spinners and Weavers, Sell Web	*B. Purchase Flax, Employ Spinners, Sell Yarn*	*C. Purchase Yarn, Employ Weavers, Sell Web*
1.5 Stone Flax @ 7s (84d) = 126d	1.5 Stone Flax @ 7s (84d) = 126d	7.5 Spangles (30 Hanks) @ 7d = 210d
Spinning 7.5 Spangles (30 Hanks) @ 1s (12d) = 90d	Spinning 7.5 Spangles (30 Hanks) @ 1s (12d) = 90d	
Weaving 25 Yards @ 2.5d = 62.5d		Weaving 25 Yards @ 2.5d = 62.5
Total Cost = 278.5d	Total Cost = 216d	Total Cost = 272.5d
Sell 25 Yards @ 11d = 275d	Sell 30 Hanks @ 5d = 150 @ 7d = 210 @ 8d = 240	Sell 25 Yards @ 11d = 275d

Source: Young 1896, vol. 1, 122.

pound of heckled flax—was sold to jobbers in Sligo at 5d a hank. Similar yarn sold for 7d a hank at Inishowen, in County Donegal, and at Westport, in County Mayo, although in both places, Young was informed that this was an unusually high price. Much finer yarn (six or more hanks to the pound) sold for 10d a hank near Randalstown, in County Antrim, 9d a hank at Hillsborough, and 8d a hank at Warrenstown, both in County Down. Thus in general, putting out flax to spinners would not have been a profitable enterprise, as Besnard contended.

While it is important not to make too much of these figures, I think it is reasonable to conclude that spinners contributed an unremunerated input to the overall value of the Irish linen trade, especially when it is remembered that, in general, they also cultivated and prepared the flax for their own wheels.[2] George Grier reckoned that spinning accounted for half the value of Irish linen, but that value was not reflected in the market price of yarn. Instead, it was captured when the woven piece of linen was sold in the marketplace. In a self-contained manufacturing household, where all stages of the production process were performed, women might reap the value of their work as members of the collective production unit.[3] However, as I have shown, few weaving households supplied all of their own yarn. Thus part of the value of the yarn produced in spinning households was garnered by the independent weavers and manufacturers who purchased it. Because, in Ireland, the gender division of labor between spinning and weaving was expressed as a regional division of labor between spinning and weaving districts, women's unpaid labor was at the heart of an unequal exchange between core and periphery.

In the language of world-systems analysis, the spinning and weaving districts comprised nodes on a "commodity chain." Commodity chains are "tree-shaped interconnections between processes of production, distribution and consumption" (Chase-Dunn 1989, 205). Many commodity chains are centripetal, linking peripheral zones of the world economy to its core. For Wallerstein (1983, 30–32) commodity chains channel surplus toward the core, at least partly because, at peripheral nodes on the chains, production is often carried out by semiproletarian workers whose households "subsidize" the cost of their labor (see chapter 1). Recently, Dunaway (2001) criticized world-systems scholars for failing to enter through the doorway of the household, where they would see women producing much of the surplus generated within commodity chains through their long hours of unpaid and underpaid labor. The remainder of this chapter examines why and how that process of gender exploitation functioned within the Irish linen industry. However, I also want to emphasize that the exploitation of women's labor was neither timeless nor undifferentiated. As Dunaway (2001) observed, women at "higher" nodes on a commodity chain may benefit from the labor of women at "lower" nodes. Moreover, while women's labor was undervalued throughout the protoindustrial and industrial periods, the extent and form of that undervaluation varied across time and space. I begin by discussing some explanations for the gender division of labor within linen-manufacturing households.

EXPLAINING THE GENDER DIVISION OF LABOR

Throughout the protoindustrial era in the Irish linen industry, spinning was exclusively women's work, while weaving was generally men's work. There is some evidence that the allocation of weaving to men was less rigidly adhered to. McKernan (1995) has presented evidence that some women took up weaving with the flying shuttle in the early 1800s, when male labor was in short supply because of the Napoleonic Wars. According to Crawford (1991, 261), "The absence of direct evidence for weaving by women throughout the eighteenth century probably has much to do with the fact that men were responsible for selling the webs as well as purchasing the yarn in the markets." Nonetheless, the preponderance of evidence shows that weaving was generally confined to men until the introduction of mill-spun yarn in the 1830s. As late as the 1841 census, just 13 percent of weavers in Ulster were female, even though contemporaries had begun to observe that women were taking up weaving as mill-spun yarn was introduced.

It might be argued that, in their division of labor by gender, Irish households were simply following custom. In Europe, spinning had been women's work for centuries. In a classic cross-cultural analysis Murdock and Provost (1973) found that spinning was a "quasifeminine" activity—that is, one usually, but not universally, assigned to women. According to Brown (1970, 1075), compatibility with childcare is the distinguishing feature of such activities:

> They do not require rapt concentration and are relatively dull and repetitive; they are easily interruptible and easily resumed once interrupted; they do not place the child in potential danger; and they do not require the participant to range very far from home.

However, while these characteristics may explain why Irish women span, they fail to explain why men did not do so, as spinning was no less *incompatible* than weaving with men's other activities.[4] Men did engage in spinning in other parts of Europe (Medick 1981, 62; Pfister 1992, 130; Vardi 1993, 127)). Clearly, the division of labor in the Irish linen industry cannot be explained simply by reference to custom, or to some universal difference between men and women. Instead, we have to examine the gender division of labor as an aspect of the *family strategies* adopted within protoindustrial households.

The concept of "family strategies" was most fully developed by Louise Tilly and Joan Scott (1978) in their classic study of industrialization and family change in England and France. According to Tilly (1987), family strategies comprised sets of implicit rules for making economic and social decisions affecting the family as a whole, and for devising solutions to everyday problems. The division of labor by gender can be seen as one aspect of a family's overall survival strategy. In preindustrial households, the demands on women's time were more complex than on men's (Tilly and Scott 1978, 50), because of their responsibility for childbearing and household management, responsibilities that were, in turn, rooted in biological difference:

> It is not entirely clear that a partnership of labor meant there existed a 'rough equality' between husband and wife in all areas of family life. It is clear, however, that the survival of the family depended on the work of both partners. The household division of labor reflected the biological differences between husband and wife. But tasks performed were complementary. The differentiation of work roles was based in part on the fact that women also had to bear children and manage the household, activities which were necessary too, to the family economy. (Tilly and Scott 1978, 53)

This way of understanding household economic behavior improves on Brown's (1970) cross-cultural argument because in principle it can also explain variations in the gender division of labor as strategic adaptations to different demographic, social, and economic circumstances.

Employing a similar model of the family economy, Medick (1981, 61–62) argued that the gender division of labor tended to be less well defined in protoindustrial households, where men spent more time within the domestic arena traditionally controlled by women. The survival of the protoindustrial family economy required a high degree of familial cooperation:

> This was achieved by optimally distributing and balancing the scarce labor power of the individual family members. Under certain market conditions and within certain industries this could go so far as to erase the traditional division of labor between the sexes and age groups. The domestic production process of the rural industrial workers was thus characterized by a greater flexibility in the role responsibilities of the family members than was customary among peasants, including smallholders and subpeasant classes. (Medick 1981, 61)

However, in many case studies, scholars have found little evidence to support the hypothesis that gender roles became more flexible under protoindustrialization (see for example Gullickson 1986; Liu 1994; Hudson 1996 and the discussion in Honeyman 2000, 242–24). In the Irish case, the maintenance of a gender division of labor between spinning and weaving throughout the protoindustrial era seems to contradict it fundamentally. As I argued in chapter 4, if Irish weaving households were primarily interested in an optimal distribution of labor power, they would have allocated some male labor time to spinning.

Both Tilly and Scott, and Medick, were influenced by Chayanov's theory of the peasant household economy, and assumed that protoindustrial households were oriented primarily toward meeting their subsistence needs.[5] Pfister (1992, 128–31) agreed that protoindustrial households were characterized by "continuous cooperative effort between spouses," but argued that their family strategies, including the gender division of labor, could be explained by neoclassical principles.

> Where several types of protoindustrial activities are available, individuals maximize their own labor productivity by engaging in the activity whose work pattern best suits the role they perform in the rest of the household economy. . . . This means, on the one hand, that women generally tend to engage in activities that provide continuous employment whereas men choose activities that can be performed as sideactivity with agriculture. As for women from different social strata, on the other hand, the wives of farmers, who have to perform a variety of tasks in the agricultural sector of the household economy, tend to engage in protoindustrial activities with flexible work patterns which can be performed as side activities. In contrast, women of lower-class origin and living in households with a small agricultural interest tend to engage in activities providing full-time employment. (Pfister 1992, 129)

Comparing the Pays de Caux to a village in the Canton of Zurich, Pfister suggested that women concentrated on spinning cotton in the first case because it provided continuous employment, whereas in the second case women concentrated on cotton weaving because a dense commercial network ensured a continuous supply of yarn. In each case, men engaged in discontinuous activities: temporary weaving in the Pays de Caux, and ancillary tasks, including spinning, in the Canton of Zurich.

In the Irish linen industry, contemporary observers emphasized the suitability of spinning to Irish women, given their other household responsibilities:

> Spinning by the hand, in a country like Ireland, where the sedentary occupation of the female must so often be interrupted, not only by domestic, but agricultural labors, is attended with one very striking advantage, namely, that it can be suspended and resumed without inconvenience, and thus small intervals of time are filled up that would otherwise be lost. (Wakefield 1812, vol. 2, 686)

It might be argued, therefore, that Irish women maximized their productivity by spinning, because it provided flexible employment that did not prevent them from completing their other household tasks.[6] Irish men could maximize their productivity by weaving, since they experienced more extended gaps in their labor time during the agricultural "slack" season.

However, this argument is not fully satisfactory. Where the supply of yarn was abundant, some women could have maximized their productivity by weaving, even if their earnings were lower than men's because of constant interruption. In New England, women took up weaving, in addition to spinning and their other household tasks, from early in the eighteenth century (Ulrich 1998). In Ulster by the end of the eighteenth century weaving had become a year round occupation in the core weaving districts, and many households had to purchase their yarn in the marketplace, or take it from outputters (chapter 2). Yet even under these circumstances weaving remained men's work. By contrast, in the second half of the nineteenth century, women wove machine-spun yarn alongside men, in rural households that continued to combine cottage industry with farming or seasonal agricultural labor. Women wove even though it was observed that: "The housewife can only afford to work six or seven hours because she has to look after the house" (quoted in Collins 1997, 240).

Women's adoption of weaving from the 1840s onward is usually attributed to technical changes. The more even quality of machine-spun yarn, together with use of the flying shuttle, meant that weaving was less physically demanding, and required less training and experience (Collins 1997, 238). However, the flying shuttle was invented in 1733, a century before it was adopted in the Irish linen industry. "There was strong prejudice against the flying shuttle because it was new and because the hand shuttle had done a long time and had made good weavers, far better, it was prophesied, than would ever be made by any other mode whatever" (quoted in Crawford 1994, 33). This failure to adopt the flying shuttle is not merely a curiosity. As Berg (1994, 181) wrote:

> Resistance to technology was an aspect of the very structure of industrialization; in the industrial sector, above all, this was marked by unevenness and division. Divisions in experience and reception at the regional and local level were not just about factors of environment and local economy—they were also about the social and economic structure of industry in different places and, equally significantly, about the differences in community structures and traditions.

Women's absence from weaving before the mechanization of spinning cannot be attributed simply to technological factors.

Throughout the eighteenth and early nineteenth centuries, weaving did require a significant investment in equipment and training. A loom cost up to five times more than a spinning wheel,[7] and as I described in chapter 2, weavers were required to undergo a period of apprenticeship, although the regulations were probably not always strictly adhered to. Because of the high entry costs to weaving during the protoindustrial era, the majority of households participated in the linen industry only through spinning. Why did men in such households not seek to maximize their productivity by spinning in their spare time?

In my view the evidence shows that the allocation of protoindustrial tasks by gender during the protoindustrial era was linked to—and served to reproduce—status differences between women and men within the household. The gender division of labor between spinning and weaving cannot be explained solely by reference to family *economic* strategies, whether those are conceived as oriented towards maintaining subsistence or maximizing income. Some scholars have concluded that family strategies were guided by the interaction of economic exigencies and cultural values (Hareven 1991; Moen and Wethington 1992, 237). According to Pfister (1995, 139), "gender-specific work roles" were "strongly influenced by normative forces." However, it is essential to avoid the pitfall of bringing culture back in as a "residual" factor to explain what cannot be accounted for with reference to economic calculation. Such an approach would severely diminish the overall explanatory power of the family strategies model.

Other scholars have argued that the family strategies approach, with its emphasis on partnership and collective well-being, obscures the reality of inequality between women and men within the household (Moch 1987). "Given traditional gender and age status systems in a society, it will typically be the husband's wishes that have the most impact on the family economic decision-making process, with consequent impact on the family's economic adaptation" (Moen and Wethington 1992, 239). In turn, some strategies may be more "adaptive" for the men of the household than for the women. The challenge, therefore, is to develop a model of family strategies that incorporates a formal understanding of the relationship between cultural and economic factors, and includes gender inequality at its core while also recognizing the salience of cooperation and tacit agreement amongst men and women.

FROM FAMILY STRATEGIES TO GENDER CONTRACTS

Rather than seeing the gender division of labor as part of a collective family *strategy*, it may be more useful to think of it as the outcome of a process of bargaining, in which one party has less "bargaining power" than the other. Amartya Sen (1990) argued that such an approach takes cognizance of the fact that gender relations within households are characterized both by cooperation and conflict:

> [The] members of the household face two different types of problems simultaneously, one involving cooperation (adding to total availabilities) and the other conflict (dividing the total availabilities among the members of the household). Social arrangements regarding who does what, who gets to consume what, and who takes what decisions can be seen as responses to this combined problem of cooperation and conflict. The sexual division of labor is one part of such a social arrangement, and it is important to see it in the context of the entire arrangement. (Sen 1990, 129)

Cooperation is essential for both husband and wife to prosper. Both would be worse off if the household unit of production and consumption were to disintegrate. However, because the wife's "breakdown position" is worse than her husband's—she would be even worse off than he if the household were to break down—she has less bargaining power than he does. As a consequence, the "family strategies" adopted within the household will be less favorable to her well being than to her husband's. (Of course the opposite would be true if the husband's "breakdown position" were worse than his wife's.) This is the *breakdown well-being response* (Sen 1990, 135).

Sen added complexity to this basic model by arguing that individuals do not have precise and unambiguous understandings of their personal "interests." Thus "perceptions" can affect bargaining power in two ways. First, if one partner attaches little value to his or her personal well-being, placing more value than the other on the well-being of the family as a whole, then that partner will have less bargaining power. This is the *perceived interest response* (Sen 1990. 136). Sen suggested that this was most likely to be true of women in traditional societies. Second, if one partner is perceived as making a greater contribution to the overall well-being of the household, then the family strategies adopted will be more favorable to that person. This is the *perceived contribution response* (Sen 1990, 136).

According to Sen, the asymmetrical "collusive solutions" to cooperative conflicts tend to reproduce themselves from one generation to the next, because the deal achieved by the "winners" in one round tends to place them in a better bargaining position for the next. Equally importantly, however, changing circumstances can alter the bargaining power of the weaker party. For example, the opportunity to earn income outside the household can improve a woman's bargaining position within it. "Outside earnings can give the woman in question (1) a better breakdown position, (2) possibly a clearer perception of her individuality and well-being, and (3) a higher 'perceived contribution' to the family's economic position" (Sen 1990, 144). Seccombe

(1992, 34) suggested that women's bargaining power depends on the extent to which their daily experience is "individuated" within marriage and the household. Using the language of Sen's argument, when women gain an increased opportunity to interact with one another outside the household, their "perceived interest response" improves.

Sen's model provides a powerful set of tools for understanding gender relations within Irish linen manufacturing households. I will argue that the availability of income from spinning improved women's "breakdown position," but that the increase in their bargaining power was limited by "perception bias" regarding the value of their contribution to the overall prosperity of the protoindustrial household. Women's improved bargaining position provided them with increased opportunities for consumption, and for interaction with other women outside the household. However they did not gain access to other kinds of employment—such as weaving—that would have improved their breakdown position still further. Thus protoindustrialization in Ireland altered gender roles within the household in ways that increased women's entitlement, but which also created a new form of gender exploitation.

Evidence that spinning enabled Irish women to survive independently of men would constitute strong evidence in favor of a significant improvement in their breakdown position. Collins (1982) cited evidence for the existence of a class of "itinerant spinners." However, in the Cavan Study Area (chapter 4), I found that most spinners were related to the household head (see also Gill 1925, 38). Nonetheless, the proportion of women aged fifteen to twenty-four years who were heads of household was positively correlated ($r = .64, > .01$) with the proportion of households engaged in spinning in the Cavan Study Area. This may indicate that young widows were able to continue longer on their own before remarrying. There is more convincing evidence that spinning increased women's opportunities for consumption. Anthropometric research by Oxley (2004) showed that, at the end of the eighteenth century, Protestant Ulster women were taller than women from Connaught and Munster. By the 1830s the heights of Catholic women in Ulster were converging with those of Protestant women, while elsewhere in Ireland women's heights stagnated or declined (Oxley 2004, 286–87). Intriguingly, Oxley (2004, 288) also found a negative relationship between women's marriage rates and their heights. She concluded that: "Ulster offered economic options to women that increased the opportunity cost of marriage while offering an alternative and underpinned superior living standards or at least access to nutrition" (Oxley 2004, 290). Clearly Oxley's evidence is consistent with the idea that spinning increased women's consumption entitlement in Ulster, and that it may also have improved their breakdown position. Moreover, references to Ulster women's consumption of tea and imported "finery" abound in the comments of contemporary observers and in the folk poetry. These will be discussed in detail in the next section.

There is also some evidence that the extension of flax cultivation and spinning provided women with new opportunities for socializing outside the household. Wakefield's (1812, II, 739) account of spinning gatherings has often been quoted. The Ordnance Survey Memoirs provide evidence of similar gatherings for the purpose of scutching.

> Any person wishing to get their flax scutched has only to give a day's notice to the females of their neighbourhood, or at least to as many as may be deemed necessary to perform the job in one day. They assemble in numbers from five to twenty, each taking their scutching stock and handle, and generally set to work in a barn, or if the day will permit in the open air. About the close of the day a number of young men of the neighbourhood repair to the "scutching" (generally favourites privately invited). Tea and punch are the indispensable requisites, and the whole concluded by a dance, or as it is more commonly called "a screech of the fiddle." (Day and McWilliams 1990, vol. 4, 69)

Such events always seem to have included an element of courtship. They were sometimes explicitly organized as competitions, or "camps," where women demonstrated their prowess at spinning to prospective suitors.[8]

Medick (1984, 332) argued that spinning bees reveal the extent to which protoindustrial producers were oriented towards the reproduction of the family economy, rather than towards maximizing their income: "Neither the demands of the market nor the demands of the rulers gave form of impetus to the rhythm of production of linen thread. What specified production in the Spinnstube was the nature of the village marriage market." Recently, however, Ogilvie (2004) described spinning bees as rival social networks to the formal institutions and "multiplex relationships" that tended to exclude women from access to social and economic resources in preindustrial communities. In southwest Germany, various community institutions attempted to regulate and prohibit spinning bees, partly because of their "tendency to create a social capital of information transmission and collective (albeit informal) sanctions" against the authorities and "respectable" people (Ogilvie 2004, 354–56). There is a humorous reference to this kind of gossip at *older* women's gatherings in one of the folk poems from Ulster described below.

As in southern Germany, the female work gatherings in Ireland's protoindustrial zone emphasized the centrality of marriage in women's lives. There appears to have been an interesting tension between the opportunity for female solidarity presented by working together, and the reinforcement of women's "individuation" through public competition. Of course many collective work gatherings were everyday, informal affairs. Even in such contexts, however, the connection between work and courtship limited the potential for women's work gatherings to increase their power within the community by reducing their members' solidarity. As Ogilvie (2004, 356) observed, informal networks of the powerless cannot compete with formal institutions that have the capacity to enforce network "closure." Nonetheless, by highlighting the importance of women's skills in flax cultivation and spinning, even the most competitive female work gatherings must have helped to increase women's bargaining power *within* marriage.

The existence of spinning competitions demonstrates that rural industrial producers recognized the existence of variations in women's skill, and that these variations affected the overall prosperity of their households. Nonetheless, women appear to have been unable to turn this recognition into a significant improvement in their breakdown position.[9] In my view this is because spinning—in direct contrast to weaving—was a skill all women were expected to master. Sonya Rose (1992, 28–29) observed that, under a later phase of industrialization:

> In structuring work employers exploited traditional definitions of what was skilled work and what kinds of machines required mechanical aptitude. They also accepted without question that formal apprenticeship or specific entry-level jobs were the only source of training. By conflating masculinity and skill, industrialists obscured and naturalized the training that women received for what were assumed to be their "natural" talents. Thus women's sewing, whether done by hand or machine, was assumed to be a "natural" talent because young girls presumably learned it as a part of growing up. Because it was a "natural" talent, it was not a skill. In contrast, the predominantly men's trade of tailoring was considered to be a skilled trade, and employers attempted to deskill it by contracting to have the work done by women.

Throughout preindustrial Europe, spinning was a normal part of women's household duties. Women spun flax and wool into yarn that they then paid a "customary weaver" to manufacture into cloth for the family's use. Especially in the more peripheral yarn districts of Ireland, the opportunity to earn a few pence by selling hanks of yarn rather than consuming them within the household must have seemed more like a windfall than a reason to look at women's economic contribution with new eyes. It is likely that this explains why spinning does not seem to have increased women's consumption entitlement in Connaught. Oxley (2004) found that Connaught women's heights consistently languished below those of other Irish women throughout the prefamine era. The Linen Board reinforced this perception by emphasizing the significance of apprenticeship in weaving, and by exercising a good deal more vigilance with respect to weaving regulations in general (chapter 2).[10]

The insight that women spun because it did not interfere with their other household duties takes on new meaning in light of the analysis above. Precisely because spinning was embedded in their everyday tasks—it was perceived to be something they "did anyway"—women failed to obtain an increase in their bargaining power commensurate with the value of their work to the family economy.[11] This perception bias created the conditions for the system of unequal exchange described above, and for the phenomenon of spinners' "self-exploitation" described in chapter 4. It should be noted, however, that the reproduction over time of this particular form of gender inequality in linen manufacturing households was contingent on the "limitless" supply of female labor in the Irish context (chapter 3). This theme is pursued in more detail in chapter 6.

Once the gender division of labor within households is understood in terms of "cooperative conflicts," it becomes easy to understand why women gained access to weaving as mill-spun yarn was introduced. The collapse in the market for handspun yarn, together with the downward spiral of earnings from weaving, weakened men's breakdown position *proportionally* more than women's, and threatened the very survival of the household. Under these circumstances there was no longer any "conflict" in the allocation of labor to weaving. That there once had been is revealed by one weaver's remarks about the relationship between women's entry to the trade and the decline in apprenticeship: "The old weavers were formerly bound as apprentices, generally for three years; at present there is no binding by indenture in this neighborhood. All girls of 13 to 15 years of age hereabout are weavers and have nothing else to do; their wheels are now thrown by" (John Duff, quoted in Crawford 1994, 63). Now all members of the household wove (from around the age of 14), and male and female wage rates were about the same (Collins 1997, 240).

Throughout this section I have referred to "conflict" and "bargaining" as though these were explicit occurrences in everyday household life. No doubt all husbands and wives engaged in some open conflict and bargaining. Over extended periods of time, however, family strategies must have been stabilized by shared understandings that guided men's and women's perceptions of interest and contribution within the household. I think it may be useful to think of these shared understandings as *gender contracts*. I have borrowed the concept from Hirdman's (1998) theory of gender and the welfare state, but I have modified it substantially for my present purposes. First, in Hirdman's work "gender contracts" represent changing political solutions to the tensions created in modern capitalist societies where women's social position is no longer determined exclusively within the private sphere of the household. In my usage, gender contracts refer to "collusive solutions" to the cooperative conflicts inherent in the household economy that were accepted amongst whole communities over extended periods of time.[12] Second, whereas according to Hirdman women were effectively excluded from the negotiations leading to the state policies she describes, I think women were agents in negotiating the kinds of gender contracts I have in mind, albeit from a weaker bargaining position than men.

Thinking about family strategies as "gender contracts" permits a more dynamic understanding of the interaction between cooperative conflicts at the microlevel of individual households, and historical trends in normative household behavior and gender role expectations at the macrolevel of whole communities. This approach also historicizes our understanding of the part played by culture in family strategies. While cultural values served to stabilize family strategies by providing shared perceptions of the interests, contributions, and entitlements of different family members, they were also subject to change, especially during periods of heightened gender "conflict" when changing material circumstances had the potential to alter men's and women's respective breakdown positions. The relationship between culture and material circumstances is thus explicitly stated, without reducing one to the other, or conflating the two. Because perceptions play a key part in determining the outcomes of cooperative conflicts, material change does not lead to a transformation in gender relations in any linear or mechanistic way. It is likely, however, to lead to struggles around the legitimacy of the existing gender contract within the cultural domain. Most of the time, this is how the material "conflict" generated by a change in women's breakdown position is articulated.[13] Thus cultural values are not simply determined by the material conditions of life, but neither are they unrelated to them.

I posit that the extended era of protoindustrialization and early industrialization was a period of intense gender conflict (in the sense described above) because it first challenged the traditional gender contract of peasant households by providing new income-earning opportunities to women, and then threatened to remove the foundations of that gender contract altogether through the process of proletarianzation. In the next section I explore how that conflict was articulated within a limited cultural domain through an examination of folk poems from Ulster. The strengths and weaknesses of this analytical strategy, including the limitations of the sources themselves, were discussed in detail in chapter 1.

"THE WEE DRAP TEA": GENDER CONFLICT AND PLEBIAN CULTURE

In his classic study of the protoindustrial family economy, Medick (1981a) argued that the conspicuous consumption of luxury goods was central to the cultural reproduction of a distinct, rural industrial "plebian public." Following E. P. Thompson (1974), he argued that in the long period of industrialization before the factory, commodity producers experienced growing independence in their daily working lives. The task-oriented nature of their work allowed them to develop an autonomous culture characterized by spontaneity and apparent disorderliness. Through the sociable consumption of luxury goods, rural artisans sought to distance themselves from the world of the peasant, and to develop a new "communal consciousness." The advent of the factory system led to the suppression of this disorderly culture and to the imposition of time discipline at work. It meant the adoption of more methodical habits in everyday life, a decline in the significance of festivals and holidays, and a movement toward sobriety and respectability that was to lay the foundation for organized class resistance (Thompson 1967).

Medick further argued that changes in the gender division of labor brought about by protoindustrialization led to increased participation by women in the public arena:

> [There] are indications that role behavior of the sexes in consumption among the rural artisans was by no means constantly tied to a division of labor in which men would function as privileged consumers 'symbolizing the role of breadwinner,' and were thus entrusted with status consumption in public, whereas women would be restricted to householding, to caring and preparing for the necessities of life. It is precisely in status consumption that an egalitarian role of both sexes came to be symbolized. This happened within the boundaries of the house as well as in the wider community. In the 'plebeian public' of the rural artisans both sexes frequently articulated their needs by drinking and smoking in common. (Medick 1976, 312–313)

As we have seen, other scholars have found that protoindustrialization was not always associated with more egalitarian gender relations, either in private or in public. There is evidence that Irish flax spinners did succeed in increasing their consumption of luxury commodities, but my interpretation of this is somewhat different from Medick's. As I argued above, women's conspicuous consumption reflected their increased bargaining power within the household, but it did not signify a fundamental change in the terms of the gender contract. Moreover, its treatment in the folk poetry suggests that it remained a source of ambivalence and contestation.[14]

Items of consumption from the mundane (potatoes and whiskey) to the luxurious and exotic (fine clothing and tea) were a favorite theme in the poetry of Ulster's rhyming weavers. The poets often used consumption items as symbolic vehicles through which they represented and organized their perceptions of the social environment and their sense of identity. Thus James Orr's earlier poems, dating from the late eighteenth century, celebrated the daily life of rural industrial producers in the form of "odes" to the potato, beer, and tea. By contrast, David Herbison's poems, dating from the mid-nineteenth century, use the device of lamenting a worn-out object—a hat, a teapot—to conjure up the sense of loss generated by the machine's destruction of a way of life. Thomas Beggs's poem, quoted above, also falls within this category.

Tea is of particular interest for my purposes, since it early acquired a particular association with women. Still a luxury item in Ireland at the end of the eighteenth century, its consumption in the weaving districts increased from about 1780 onward (Lysaght 1987). The folk poets' treatments of tea reveal a good deal about the shared understandings—and anxieties—surrounding gender relations in their communities. By carefully linking references to women's consumption in the poems, to observations by contemporary upper-class observers, it is possible to track changes in the cultural construction of gender over time, and to relate those changes to the gender division of labor and the overall development of the linen industry.

In 1776, traveling from Newry to Armagh, Young noted that "the manufacturers' wives drink tea for breakfast." He observed patterns of work and leisure fitting Thompson's and Medick's depiction of "plebian culture." Weavers were "licentious and disorderly," and worked only for subsistence, choosing leisure over work whenever possible. "The men do not work more than half what they might do," he noted in Warrenstown, County Down, "owing to the cheapness of provisions making them idle, as they think of nothing more than the present necessity." Their leisure activities were public and crowded, and they included the classic "plebian" amusements of cock fighting and bull baiting. Young men were particularly fond of hunting hares. In Maghan, Young was amazed by the sight of weavers abandoning their looms at the sound of the hounds' cry, but was assured that this was "very common" (Young 1892, 127, 132).

Tea drinking was indispensable at women's collective work gatherings, and in this sense, perhaps, it formed part of the rural industrial "plebian public." In his humorous poem "Tea," James Orr wrote that "At breakin' clovin', kirn, an' quiltin', / 'Tis ay the base that bliss is built on." Similarly, at fairs, young girls clustered around the fortune teller who read "the story of their future match" in the tealeaves. At older women's gatherings, tea helped to deflect the malignancy of their gossip:

> Losh! how they rauner, rail an' ripple
> Their nybers names, an' mumph an' sipple!
> But, conscience! if the auld delft nipple
> Nae ooze wad bring,
> The priest, an' parish, king, an' people,
> Might tak their swing.

Within the household arena, tea kept "peace about the poor man's cot" by making wives more tolerant of their husband's indulgence in alcohol. In his ode to "The Potato," Orr associated tea directly with harmonious domestic relations:

> Sweet in the morning, after dashlin',
> Thy daigh is, pouther't owre wi' mashlin;
> Creesh't scons stan' pil't on plates, or brislin'
> Aroun' the ingle,
> While a fand Wifie fast is fislin',
> An tea-cups jingle.

In "Tea," however, the beverage provided a vehicle for articulating anxieties about women's reliability within the household economy:

> The L-d leuk on her wretched bield,
> Whase pence are out, and hank unreel'd!
> Nae griddle's het, nae pratoe peel'd,
> To mak' a bap o't;
> Nor weed nor head-ach tak's the field
> Without a drap o't.

Tea's role in this situation is ambiguous: on the one hand, it helps the family get down to work; on the other, its absence may be the source of the woman's negligence in the first place. Orr condemned "the smuggler, fause an' fell, / wha brews't in tinfu's by hersel';" behind the back of her children's "drudgin' daddy." In this poem, the problem of a woman's "smuggling" was lightly tossed aside—its worst consequence would be her husband's inconveniently coming in just when the tea was made—and tea's addictive qualities were explicitly rejected: "Tea mak's man a nerveless wrig, / The doctor says-p-x on the prig!" However, in Orr's later, serious poem, "The Penitent," his addicted wife's smuggling contributed to the overall collapse of the farmer weaver's household:

Mary ne'er min't the house—mair like a byre,
    But clash'd wi' nyber wives. Unkent to him
For tea, an' snuff, the troubled dames desire,
    She'd smuggled meal an' seeds; tho' hunger grim
Devour'd the duddy weans, now in a wretched trim.

Throughout the poem "Tea," there is an implicit contrast between the domestic world of women, and the male world of public sociability associated with alcohol, which, Orr hinted at the end of his poem, he would have preferred to offer his guests. While tea did form part of the cultural reproduction of the local community at festivals and collective work gatherings, it also symbolized sobriety and domesticity, curing men of their hangovers, and helping all members of the family to get back to work. In this respect, Orr's poem drew on an association between women and the *respectability* of household production, contrasted with the public, disorderly world of men and leisure.

In County Sligo, where "in their domestic economy they reckon that the men feed their families by their labor in the fields, and the women pay the rent by spinning," Young observed with satisfaction: "no tea drinking here." Curiously, in the weaving districts, women's conspicuous consumption appears to have increased as their real contribution to the household economy through spinning declined (chapter 2). In County Armagh Coote (1804, 264) remarked that women's earnings were spent on "finery" because "the men's labor procures them provisions." In this context, women's consumption symbolized the independence and prosperity of their households by providing proof of their "industriousness."

The "plebian" cultural association between "independence" and public status consumption was emphasized in an observation from Cappagh, County Tyrone, in the 1820s:

> In proportion to their success in life they generally extend their comforts. Those who become independent like to have their families well dressed and comfortable, and usually give evidence of their prosperity by the smartness of their appearance. A greater taste for dress displays itself amongst the lower classes than for domestic comforts. More money is expended on their backs than on their dwellings. The one requires regular care, attention and steady habits of order, which as yet have made but a moderate progress here, so far as relates to their domestic arrangements, whilst the Saturday night's labor cuts a great figure on the Sunday morning. (Day and McWilliams 1990, 124)

Throughout the protoindustrial zone contemporary upper-class observers found that women dressed better than men in public, although they were more likely to go without shoes in private. Such observers may have thought the white cotton gowns that were fashionable amongst women in the core weaving districts to be "flaunting and tawdry looking" (Gamble 1813, 114), but they tended toward an indulgent interpretation: "The women might be thought too well dressed for their station, was it not known to be the fruits of their industry, and to procure it, often an incitement to exertions" (Dubourdieu 1812, 498).

Sarah Leech, the only "rhyming spinner" amongst the folk poets, offered a different interpretation. In her humorous "Address to Bachelors," she gave a detailed description of a fashionable young woman's attire:

> Ilk lass maun ha'e a snaw-white goun
> Wi' span-lang flounces wavin' roun',
> Some weel-plait straw upon her croun,
> And ribbons gay,
> While hose weel starched an' right-left shoon
> Her feet display.

However, Leech presented her poem as a warning to gullible bachelors who might be duped by a girl's appearance into believing that marrying her will make them wealthy. In fact, "sic dames o' fashion" are shrewish, violently dominant over their husbands, and addicted to tea and "the barley bree":

> Too late you may have cause to wail,
> For should the tea or whiskey fail,
> She, vixen like, will you assail,
> Or chide and snap,
> And swear, should you be dragged to jail,
> She'll have her drap.

In the final stanza, she hinted coyly that young men would be more likely to find happiness with a hard-working spinner like herself:

> But hark! the clock is striking two,
> And time goes rinning,
> So I'm obliged to bid adieu,
> And join my spinning.

But the old life pattern, in which a woman's spinning ability determined the prosperity of her household, was already under threat amongst those core weaving communities that were dependent on purchased and put-out yarn. Within a few years the spinning mills would begin to have devastating consequences for hand spinners' earnings. Thus, in hindsight, Leech's poem serves to highlight the extent to which women's conspicuous consumption represented a cultural "bluff," a declaration of household independence that disguised a real and imminent loss of independence.

In the early 1800s, upper-class observers began to comment on an increase in "industry and sobriety" amongst the rural industrial population of east Ulster. Coote (1804, 264) contrasted the inhabitants of County Armagh with those of "the poorer counties," in respect to their greater time discipline: "In this county, a steady industry affords a sufficiency for the moderate comforts of life, and will admit of a redundancy for other purposes, without exhausting nature at such a sedentary business as the loom." In County Down: "It seems to be the received opinion that the inhabitants are growing daily more sober, and return from the fairs and markets at earlier hours than formerly" (Dubourdieu 1802, 260). From Seagoe, County Armagh, it was reported that weavers still abandoned their looms when they heard the hounds' cry, but that "they rarely fail to make up by redoubled exertions for any time lost on an indulgence of this nature" (Blacker 1816, II, 528). By the 1830s, the Ordnance Survey memorialists were usually able to report that such pastimes as cockfighting, bull baiting, and card playing were no longer popular (see Connolly 1983).

In the folk poems, this turn away from public disorderliness is associated both with greater happiness in the domestic sphere, and with the preservation of an independent way of life. In his "Address to Beer" Orr contrasted its virtues with whiskey's vices. Whereas whisky might detain male "spen'thrifts" in the "house of pleasure" for a week, tenpence worth of beer would send them homewards to "hain their treasure." There is a sense in which beer is an honest workingman's drink, in contrast to whiskey, which impoverishes its crazed victims, and punch, which is favored "mang nice tea parties." Thus Orr's poem posited a social identity below polite society but above those who desperately sought to forget their poverty and misery in drink.

The reasons for this turn away from "plebian culture" toward the celebration of respectable domesticity are complex, and I have explored them in detail elsewhere (Gray 1993c; 1996). They include the traumatic experience of failed rebellion in 1798 and the influence of evangelical Protestantism, including Methodism (see Hempton and Hill 1992, 20–46). It can also be understood as part of the widespread adoption throughout Europe of the middle-class ideology of "separate spheres" (Frader and Rose 1996, 12), and of a new "individualistic" (rather than "corporate") ideology of work that tended to obscure women's labor within the image of a "dependent family"(Honeyman 2000, 30–32). In Ulster, the adoption of these ideas by rural industrial producers can be understood as a strategy of resistance to the loss of household independence associated with changing gender relations and creeping proletarianization.[15]

In his poem, "The Auld Wife's Lament for her Teapot," David Herbison was openly nostalgic for a way of life that had been destroyed by "that machine that spins the yarn," and was symbolized by the broken teapot. The "auld wife's" spinning wheel "now sits silently / aboon the bed." She describes the course of her life through the history of the teapot, beginning when she bought it herself for a half crown and when "At every party it was down, / Throughout Dunclug." However, the teapot faced its first challenge when her daughters "a' got spruce, / And wanted men":

> Whene'er their wooers cam' to see them,
> A wee drap tea they be to gie them,
> For fear, as I thought, they would lea' them,
> Alone to rove,
> They never fail'd wi' sweets to free them
> Frae ithers love.

This courtship strategy almost destroyed the teapot, which was finally broken when "my daughters a' are wed, / And health and peace frae me are fled."

Thus Herbison linked the destruction of the rural industrial way of life with women's increased status consumption. Whereas the "auld wife" had used her *earnings* to participate in collective festivities, her daughters used the *consumption* of "sweets" to attract marriage partners. It is in this context that we must read Beggs' idealized representation of gender relations before the factory. As we have seen, throughout the protoindustrial era women's increased earning power, and their access to status consumption, led to cultural anxiety about the proper relations between men and women, as well as cultural celebration of the increased prosperity of their households and communities. Beggs' image of hand spinners as innocent, modest creatures under the protection of their fathers and husbands is belied by earlier images, such as that given by Orr in his account of the faction fight at Ballycarry Fair: "Ilk maid and matron hands her dear, / The baulder that he's hauden, O." Thus the idealized protoindustrial household invoked by Beggs was, at least in part, a form of cultural resistance to the transformation in gender and class relations wrought by the factory system.

CONCLUSION

It is now widely accepted that the Marxist-feminist scholarship of the 1970s and 1980s foundered on the attempt to link gender inequality to capitalism. Even the most sophisticated versions of these theories were limited by their insistence that "the origins of and changes in gender systems [are] found outside the sexual division of labor" (Scott 1988, 35). Evidence that household based production was characterized by "partnership" between women and men (Hamilton 1978; Tilly and Scott 1978; Segalen 1983) provided a useful corrective, both to the sociological assumption that women's status improved inexorably as societies modernized (Tilly, Scott and Cohen 1976), and to the radical feminist suggestion that patriarchal power has continued unchanged throughout history (Scott 1988, 34). However, the idea that gender inequality originated with capitalism was clearly unsustainable, especially as scholars began to demonstrate the significance of continuities in gender relations throughout the industrialization process (Berg 1994; Rose 1987, 1992). By linking gender inequality so closely to the separation of home from workplace under capitalism, Marxist feminists failed to challenge the conventional understanding of what counts as "real" production (Seccombe 1992, 14). More generally, they reproduced the notion of public and private "separate spheres" that—as we have seen—formed part of an ideology intimately linked to gender and class struggles in the eighteenth and nineteenth centuries (Frader and Rose 1996, 11–19; Honeyman 2000, 95–114).

In response to these shortcomings of Marxist-feminist theory, feminist scholars of the 1990s began to emphasize the cultural and ideological aspects of gender. Thus, Frader and Rose (1996, 16) defined gender as "the cultural meanings associated with perceptions of sexual difference, and the ways in which sexual difference forms the basis for social exclusions and inclusions and constitutes inequality in power, authority, rights, and privileges." However, this way of understanding gender may be too restrictive. I believe the concept of gender must encompass, not just the set of meanings that legitimates inequalities in the distribution of power, but also the systematic *patterns* of inequality between men and women in society. Throughout this book, I have argued that the gender division of labor *structured* the development of the linen industry over time. In this chapter I have proposed a model of gender inequality that allows us to understand both changes and continuities in the gender division of labor. Using this model, the historical relationship between cultural constructions of gender and the gender division of labor can be analyzed without reducing one to the other, or conflating the two. Beggs's poem formed part of a changing cultural construction of gender that, as Marilyn Cohen has shown, structured the gender division of labor under the factory system (Cohen 1997, esp. 119–33 and 209–59). However, it also constituted a cultural *response* to changing gender and class relations. In the next chapter I will argue that differences in the gender division of labor can help us to understand variations in the transition to capitalism amongst European linen manufacturing regions.

NOTES

1. Contemporary demonstrations of the unprofitability of putting out may be found in Young (1892) and Thompson (1802). However, in these accounts it is difficult to disaggregate the costs at each stage of the production process. The detailed information gathered by Young at Armagh is therefore more useful for my purposes.

2. The cultivation and preparation of flax was extremely labor intensive, and is discussed in more detail in chapter 6. A similar argument could be made with respect to children's work. Children were often responsible for the task of winding yarn onto "pirns" or bobbins to be inserted in the shuttle. Weavers' testimonies to the Handloom Weavers Commission in 1840 emphasized the value of winding. "As a single man, I paid to one of these farmers and weavers £8 a year for my board and lodging; I had my own loom and for the £8 in addition to the board, lodging, and washing, the farmer's family did my winding besides. . . . I bought my own materials and sold my own web" (Robert Hammond, quoted in Crawford 1994, 63).

3. Even under these circumstances, the members of a weaving household earned less, collectively, than if they had each been regularly employed as agricultural laborers (see chapter 6).

4. Ogilvie (2003, 323) argued that women's concentration in domestic locations has been overstated. In Wurrtemberg "less than half of all observed work by females occurred in domestic locations, hardly greater than the proportion for men." Marriage seems to have led to greater domesticity for both women and men.

5. See Emigh (2001) for an elaboration of some of the theoretical perspectives underpinning the family strategies concept. As she pointed out, authors using the idea of family strategies often fail to specify or articulate any underlying theoretical perspective on the household economy.

6. Spinning did not provide continuous, year-round employment, unless the smallholder's own supply was supplemented with bought flax. (See the "Account of Kilmactige" in Mason 1816, 387. It was considered "scarcely worth a woman's while to sit down to spin bought flax, as she will not earn more than twopence a day by so doing.")

7. This estimate is based on the amount the linen board paid for the wheels (10 to 12 shillings) and looms (50 shillings) distributed under the 1796 flax premium scheme (P.R.O.N.I. D562/5577).

8. See for example the account of spinning contests from the Ordnance Survey Memoir of the parishes of Aghaderg in County Down (Day and McWilliams 1992, Vol. 12, 7) and Magilligan in County Londonderry (Day and McWilliams 1991, Vol. 11, 140).

9. Klasen (1998, 457–58) argued that in Germany participation in protoindustry reduced excess mortality amongst rural women in the eighteenth and early nineteenth centuries because their households were characterized by a less pronounced sexual division of labor than exclusively agricultural households. Using Sen's model of household bargaining, Klasen showed that an increase in excess female mortality during this period was linked to differences in men's and women's "breakdown position" and in their perceived interests, in the context of changes in agriculture. My argument that

spinning did not lead to a significant improvement in Irish women's breakdown position does not contradict the hypothesis that women in protoindustrial households gained increased access to resources relative to their counterparts in agricultural households. Indeed the evidence on consumption behavior by women in the linen districts supports it.

10. The board did establish spinning schools in an effort to teach girls to spin fine yarn, and with the hope of extending flax spinning in the provinces of Leinster and Munster. However, the policy seems to have been inconsistent and ineffective, with many of the schools existing only "on paper" (Gill 1922, 75–76).

11. Their situation was therefore similar to the Indian lacemakers studied by Maria Mies (1982), and discussed by Sen (1990, 144–45). However, in contrast to the lacemakers of Narsapur, Irish spinners' contribution does appear to have increased their "extended exchange entitlement." Perhaps the spinners' attendance at public markets to sell their yarn meant that their perceived contribution was somewhat greater than that of the lacemakers, who were contracted to work for employers through their husbands.

12. Even in preindustrial societies gender contracts were affected by the actions of merchants, states, and other regulatory institutions, as Ogilvie's (1994, 1997) work demonstrates.

13. Alternative responses include a pattern of women opting out of marriage in different ways, and the formation of organized women's movements. I am convinced that, in principle, both can be explained using the logic of cooperative conflicts, but the linkages are likely to be highly complex, and the question is, in any case, outside the scope of this study.

14. See Maynes (2004, 59) for a discussion of evidence that "the 'industrious revolution' may have had the effect of moving some forms of material wealth toward women" in France and Germany.

15. There has been considerable research on the significance of "respectability" in English class politics of the nineteenth century. For a comprehensive discussion see Honeyman 2000, especially chapter 6, 95–114.

Chapter Six

Paths to Industrial Capitalism: Ireland, Scotland, and Flanders

The linen industry has had a poor reputation among scholars of the transition to industrial capitalism. Crouzet (quoted in Mokyr 1976, 71) described linen as "an archaic industry, doomed anyway." O'Hearn (1997, 2001) argued that the Irish linen industry was intrinsically "semiperipheral," insofar as it was characterized by low wages, slow rates of change in technology and productive organization, and was largely disarticulated from other economic sectors. During the transition to capitalist factory production, "the existing level of linen output was simply concentrated from an Ulster-wide industry to the Lagan valley"(O'Hearn 1997, 185).

Elsewhere, linen has enjoyed a better reputation. In the Scottish historiography, according to Devine (1983, 15), the linen industry has been regarded as "the source of enterprise, capital and labor for cotton, the 'leading sector,' which ushered in the age of industrialization and future prosperity." Mixed claims have been made for the Flemish linen industry. Whereas Mokyr (1976) and Mendels (1972) argued (in different ways), that linen paved the way for Belgium's relatively early industrial transition, Vandenbroeke (1987) and Van Der Wee (1996) depicted linen as a source of delay and irregularity in the process.

This chapter explores the problem of regional differentiation in linen-manufacturing regions during the transition to modern capitalist industry, through a comparison between the Irish case, and those of Scotland and Flanders. Building on the argument developed throughout this book, I suggest that differences in how men's and women's labor was mobilized in the production of linen, (from the cultivation of flax to the manufacture of woven cloth), contributed to regional differentiation in the development of linen-producing regions, and thereby to differences in the transition to factory industry.

Before proceeding, a word of caution is in order regarding the status of the "industrial revolution" in sociological theory. Conventionally, the transition to industrial capitalism has been treated as the "great divide" separating modernity from traditional society (Sanderson 1995, 244). However, world-systems scholars have tended to displace the industrial revolution from its preeminent position. For Wallerstein (1991, 47), the set of interconnected changes that began in northwest Europe at the end of the eighteenth century was just one of a series of similar phases that have occurred at cyclical intervals throughout the history of the modern-world system. As Sanderson (1995, 250) argued, it is possible to accept the merit of Wallerstein's argument in its broadest outlines, while also acknowledging the significance of the industrial revolution:

> It is quite true that a good deal of industrialization had already occurred throughout Europe by 1760. . . . However, it is also true that after 1760 technology evolved, the factory system expanded, and the productivity of labor increased on a scale and with a rapidity never before seen in the history of capitalism. The Industrial Revolution was not something that emerged out of the blue in societies that had previously known only agriculture. But it was a revolution in the sense that some rather dramatic technological and economic changes occurred within a short period of time.

According to Sanderson, industrialization is best understood as a process of mechanization within capitalism that was accelerated by a "major burst" at the end of the eighteenth century.

In this chapter I adopt Sanderson's position that the industrial transition marked the beginning of a new phase of development within capitalism. However, there are important aspects of the transition that are not captured by his treatment of protoindustrialization as a "technoeconomic stage of development [that] preceded and prepared the way for full-scale industrialization" (Sanderson 1995, 253). It ignores the gendered relations of household production that structured the mobilization of growing amounts of labor in manufacturing before the factory. In turn, the factory system did not just increase the productivity of labor, it opened up new ways of mobilizing men's and women's labor within capitalism (see chapter 5). The central argument of this chapter is that differences in the gender division of labor under protoindustrialization explain differences in the transition to the factory system.

ABUNDANT LABOR AND THE INDUSTRIAL REVOLUTION

All of the major theoretical strands agree that protoindustrialization occurred through an increase in the supply of labor to market-oriented manufacturing, by tapping into previously underemployed labor, and/or by fostering population growth. Thus, in principle, mature rural industrial regions were characterized by an abundance of labor that could be mobilized by the factory system, either because high population densities inhibited a return to agriculture for many families, or because cottage producers had accumulated useful craft skills and experience. But what role did abundant labor play in the nature and timing of industrial transition?

Mokyr (1993, 85) observed that "there are two competing and apparently incompatible views." According to one view, technological innovation is more likely to occur where labor costs are high. An abundance of cheap labor acts as a disincentive to capital investment and technological change. Thus according to Vandenbroeke (1987), lower wage costs *delayed* the industrial take off in Flanders relative to England. O'Hearn (1997, 185) argued that, "Because [Ireland's] wages were low, it was rational to compete by 'adaptive response' (extending the use of labor and intensifying its exploitation) rather than by introducing new technologies, labor relations, and forms of productive organization."

According to the second view, industrialization should occur faster and earlier in low wage economies. Thus Mokyr (1976) argued that the linen industry in Flanders generated a pool of low-wage labor that provided the technologically innovative cotton industry with a "quasirent," facilitating continuous reinvestment in the modern industrial sector, during the "growing up" period when traditional, or protoindustrial manufacturing coexisted with modernizing industry.

Ireland represents a problem case for this second model, since despite the existence of a substantial "traditional" sector based on linen manufacturing, and wages that were amongst the lowest in Europe, the industrial revolution there was late, slow, and regionally circumscribed. Furthermore, in Ireland, the transfer of capital from a declining cotton industry facilitated the modernization of the linen industry, whereas in Belgium this process took the form of capital flows from one modernizing industry to another. When profits fell in the cotton industry, retained earnings were invested in linen, but this did not lead to the demise of cotton manufacturing (Mokyr 1991, 183; 1976, 74.) This difference is important because cotton was the "leading sector" in the phase of industrialization centered on textile production (O'Hearn 1994, 596–98). Where the transition to factory industry was based on linen alone—as in the Irish case—it was "underdeveloping," insofar as it was characterized by relatively low wages and profits, few linkages to other regional industries, and market stagnation (O'Hearn 2001, chapter 4). In Scotland, the coexistence of modernizing cotton and linen industries took the form of regional specialization. The fine-linen industry in the west of the country was rapidly displaced by cotton at the end of the eighteenth century (Durie 1979, 95). Cotton spinning mills were also established in the eastern districts which specialized in the production of coarse linens, but they seem to have disappeared as the number of flax spinning mills multiplied (Warden 1864, 598–99). Of the three regional *linen* industries, Scotland's was the first to undergo mechanization. As early as 1815, spinning mills accounted for half the yarn produced in Scotland (Durie 1979, 98). Similar developments did not occur in Ireland (Geary 1998, 523) and Flanders (Mokyr 1976, 72) until the late 1830s.

Mokyr has proposed two explanations for the apparently contradictory Irish case. First, he noted that Ireland was the only country in Europe to experience large-scale out migration in the first half of the nineteenth century, and that the province of Ulster (where the linen industry was concentrated), was overrepresented in the emigrant flow (Mokyr 1980, 450). Second, Mokyr (1991, 184–89) argued, Irish workers were "inherently" less productive, and therefore expensive in real terms. Under these circumstances cheap, but inefficient Irish labor led to the failure of the Belfast cotton industry, and sent the "wrong signal" to specialize in the linen industry. Thus the implication of Mokyr's argument is that where protoindustrialization created an abundant pool of skilled, productive labor, it facilitated rapid industrialization during the "growing up period," but where it created abundant unskilled or unproductive labor the industrialization process was inhibited.

The collapse of the Irish cotton industry has been the subject of much debate. According to the traditional view (see Monaghan 1942), the Irish industry was undercapitalized, and survived only as long as protective duties insulated it from English and Scottish competition.[1] However Geary (1989, 1981) argued that there is no evidence to support the contention that the Belfast cotton industry suffered from a shortage of capital, or that it was inherently uncompetitive. He suggested that the invention of the "wet" flax-spinning process, rather than the repeal of protective duties, led to the slow decline of cotton spinning in Belfast by making flax spinning a more attractive investment project, given the region's comparative advantage in the linen industry. More recently O'Hearn (1994, 2001) argued that the Irish cotton industry was able to compete for a short time only because low labor costs offset both its unfavorable access to the raw material and to markets, and its lack of linkages to other innovating sectors. Once innovation in the cotton industry was localized around Lancashire, free trade was introduced, enabling British manufacturers to penetrate Irish (and world) markets, first in cotton yarn, and then in cotton cloth. The Irish industry adapted, first by specializing in the intensive-intensive phase of handloom weaving, and then by switching investment to the "semiperipheral" linen industry. Thus, for O'Hearn, the dependent nature of Irish industrialization resulted from a combination of cheap labor and subjugation to British interests.

This chapter does not take a position on the debate over the Irish cotton industry. Instead, it explores the relationship between protoindustrialization and labor supply in each of the three linen-manufacturing regions under consideration. I argue that differences in how men's and women's labor was mobilized in the articulation of household and market may help to explain why the cost of labor appears to have played a different part in each case. I begin with an overview of the development of the linen industry in the three countries. I then compare the evidence in relation to demoeconomic trends, and continue by examining the evidence for low wages, and for the putative link between wages and productivity, in each of the regional linen industries.

FLEMISH, IRISH, AND SCOTTISH LINEN IN THE LONG EIGHTEENTH CENTURY

At the beginning of the eighteenth century, the Flemish industry was much more developed than that of either Ireland or Scotland. Flanders had a lengthy history of exporting linens, dating from the fourteenth century. Despite being a "European battlefield," urban production of linen cloth increased in Flanders during the seventeenth century. In the eighteenth century, the growth of industrial production took the form of "ruralization," as urban manufacturing stagnated. Spain and the Spanish colonies had constituted the most important market for Flemish linens since the sixteenth century. Flanders manufactured both fine and coarse linens for the Spanish market, but from the end of the seventeenth century onward there appears to have been a decline in the production of finer linens, and an increasing specialization in the coarser varieties destined for use as clothing for slaves (brabantes), and for packaging (presillas)(Mendels 1969, 64–65 and 167–219).

According to Mendels (1969, 187), "Flanders had a significant place in the world market but it could not affect the price on most markets." In the 1690s, England introduced protective measures which led to a decline in linen imports from mainland Europe, including Flanders, and which formed the beginning of a series of measures that fostered the growth of linen manufacturing in Ireland and Scotland (see table 6.1). During the first half of the eighteenth century, Irish and Scottish linens increasingly substituted for European imports on the English market. At mid-century a scheme of bounties was introduced to promote the export of Irish and Scottish linens to the American colonies. Between the 1760s and the 1790s, the colonial market accounted for a greater share of the linen exports of both countries (chapter 2;

Durie 1979, 148). During this period Scotland increasingly specialized in producing the coarse linens supported by the bounty scheme, and in exporting them to the West Indies, where they were used to clothe slaves. The growth in colonial demand contributed to an increase in the production of coarser, "plain linens" in Ireland for the North American market. However, Ireland never produced (on any scale) linens as coarse as the "Osnaburgs" manufactured in East Scotland. Irish and Flemish linens were more similar in degree of fineness. According to a pamphlet on the Spanish trade, published in Ireland in 1790, "brabante florete," or "gant white sheetings" sold in Spain from 11d to 18d Irish currency. The official value per yard of Irish linen exports was 15d in the 1790s (Merchant 1790, 8).

Table 6.2 gives an indication of the quantities of linens exported from Flanders, Ireland and Scotland during the eighteenth and early nineteenth centuries. It suggests that the Irish and Scottish linen industries began to outstrip that of Flanders in the second half of the eighteenth century. During the decisive "growing up" period between 1780 and 1815, when mechanized cotton spinning (but not flax spinning) was introduced in each case, Irish and Scottish linen output more than doubled, while that of Flanders appears to have grown by less than a third. However, given events at the time, it was remarkable that the Flemish industry continued to grow. Spain began to restrict access to her markets, which were completely closed off during the continental and maritime blockades of the 1790s. France occupied Flanders between 1795 and 1814. However, while these events had negative short-term effects, in the longer term access to French markets saved the Flemish linen industry. Exports of linen cloth accounted for a third of total industrial exports from the Southern Netherlands until 1840 (Mokyr 1976, 69).

Table 6.1. Linen Imports and Exports to and from England in the Eighteenth Century

	Linen Imports to England			*Linen Exports from England to North America*	
Years	*Total Value (£000)*	*From North West Europe (%)*	*From Ireland & Channel Islands (%)*	*Total Value (£000)*	*Reexports (%)*
1699–1701	903	88	6	157	100
1722–1724	1036	81	11	244	91
1752–1754	1185	58	28	490	61
1772–1774	1246	33	52	966	30

Source: Davis 1969, appendix.
Note: Re-exports do not include linens originating in Ireland.

LINEN, PROTOINDUSTRIALIZATION, AND POPULATION GROWTH

How did growing world demand affect demographic trends in the three linen manufacturing regions? Table 6.3 shows that, during the long eighteenth century, population grew by at least 75 percent in Flanders, and by more than 100 percent in Ireland. In Scotland population increased by just 30 percent.

Flanders represents the classic test case for the demoeconomic hypotheses of protoindustrialization theory, first proposed by Franklin Mendels (see chapter 1). However, a number of scholars have queried Mendels' analysis of the Flemish case. Mokyr argued that Mendels' theory of the relationship between rural industrialization and family formation was not necessary to explain population growth in Flanders. Whereas Mendels (1969, 241) insisted that peasants "did not take up rural industry as an alternative to marginally less rewarding work in agriculture," for Mokyr (1976), protoindustrialization represented a solution to the "Malthusian trap," in the context of relatively low agricultural productivity, albeit at the expense of a poor standard of living.

More recently Vandenbroeke (1997, 106) argued that in Flanders, while "protoindustry and population growth are unmistakably positively correlated . . . the explanation underlying this is not the one proposed in Mendels'

Table 6.2. Output of Flemish, Irish, and Scottish Linen Industries, 1700 to 1825*

Year	*Flanders*[1]	*Ireland*[2]	*Scotland*[3]
1700	7,700	13	n/a
1720	8,400	2,600	n/a
1750	9,300	11,200	7,600
1780	12,600	18,800	13,400
1800	12,600	35,700	24,200
1815	16,100	43,000	32,100
1825	17,700	55,100	n/a

*Measured in thousands of yards.

Sources: Vandenbroeke 1987, 165; Gill 1925, 341–43; Warden 1864, 480.

Notes: 1. To convert these figures to thousands of yards, I have assumed that a piece consisted of eighty ells, and that a Flemish ell was twenty-nine inches in length. Thus a piece was almost sixty-five yards long. These are the figures given by Mokyr (1976, 15). However, Mendels (1981) stated that an ell from Ghent was twenty-six inches (p. 72), and a piece of middling quality cloth seventy-five ells long (p. 200). This would make a piece less than fifty-five yards long. But according to a contemporary observer (Merchant 1790, 8), a half piece of Gant white sheeting was between thirty and thirty-three yards in length. Thus Mokyr's figures seem to provide the better estimate. 2. Yards of linen exported. 3. Yards of linen stamped for sale. These figures thus include linens retained for domestic consumption.

Table 6.3. Estimates of Population: Flanders, Ireland, and Scotland*

	Circa 1700	*Circa 1750*	*Circa 1800*
Flanders	0.65	0.83	1.06 (1806)
Ireland	1.75–2.06 (1706)	2.22–2.57(1753)	4.42 (1791)
Scotland	Not available	1.3	1.6

*Measured in millions.
Sources: Dowltrey, Dickson, and O'Grada 1981, 624; De Jongh 1999, 26; Tyson 1995, 67.

model." Between about 1700 and the middle of the nineteenth century, continuous declines in marriage and birth rates, and an increase in permanent celibacy, indicate that the growth of linen manufacturing in the countryside was in fact accompanied by the development of a more *restrictive* marriage pattern. The linen manufacturing districts experienced dramatic population increase in the first sixty years of the eighteenth century, but by the later decades there was a clear slow down. In 1796, participation in protoindustry by region appears to have been negatively correlated with nuptiality and fertility. Vandenbroeke (1997, 107–109) attributed population growth in the protoindustrial districts to thedeurbanization and "territorialization" of linen manufacturing, and to a decline in infant mortality.

Despite their critiques of the *mechanisms* hypothesized by Mendels, both Mokyr and Vandenbroeke accepted that there was a relationship between the linen industry and population growth in Flanders. As I showed in chapter 3, no such consensus exists on the Irish linen industry. However, it is clear that the linen-manufacturing districts in the north of the country had exceptionally high population densities by the middle of the nineteenth century. In addition, there is some tentative evidence of a relationship between the geographical extension of spinning and population growth in the early nineteenth century. Thus while it may not have been the single most important determinant, there is sufficient evidence to suggest that the linen industry played some part in facilitating Ireland's dramatic rate of population increase.

If protoindustrialization hypotheses concerning population growth have been problematized in the Flemish and Irish cases, they appear to have little application to the Scottish case. Ireland's annual rate of population growth was more than double that of Scotland in the second half of the century (Tyson 1995, 66–67). Whyte (1989, 240–44) observed that, while there is some evidence in the Old Statistical Account for population growth in protoindustrial parishes, this could be accounted for by inmigration. Moreover, the rate of population growth was also greater than the average for rural districts in those parishes where new agricultural technologies were being introduced (Gray 1997, 59–60). Clearly, as Tyson (1995, 69–73) observed, Scotland's demographic regime differed fundamentally from that of Ireland. A decline in infant mortality seems the most likely explanation for Scotland's relatively modest population increase during the eighteenth century.

By the beginning of the nineteenth century, then, high rates of population increase, and high population densities in rural industrial districts, had created pools of abundant labor in Ireland and Flanders. In Scotland, by contrast, a lower rate of population increase implied a smaller labor surplus than in either of the other two cases. According to Mokyr's argument (above), abundant and cheap labor was not *sufficient* to explain "successful" industrialization—that labor must also have been relatively productive. In the next section, I explore differences in wage rates, and evidence for variations in skill and productivity amongst the three cases.

LOW WAGES, SKILL, AND PRODUCTIVITY

Economic historians agree that, in comparison with their neighbors in England and the northern Netherlands, wages in Ireland, Scotland, and Flanders were low. However, there are some indications of variation amongst the three cases in terms of changes in wage levels during the eighteenth century, and in terms of the gap in wages between skilled and unskilled labor. It must be emphasized that, especially in the Irish case, data on prices and wages remain scanty.

Gibson and Smout (1995) have presented evidence that, in Scotland, wages were characterized by a long period of near stagnation from the middle of the seventeenth through the middle of the eighteenth centuries. After about 1760 wages increased faster than living costs. Evidence from the Old Statistical Account "places central Scotland among a rather small number of areas in Europe where the living standards of the common people were improving in the second half of the eighteenth century" (Gibson and Smout 1995, 341). Kennedy and Dowling (1997) published data for Ireland showing that wages remained "sticky" from 1700 to around 1760, and from 1820 through the Famine years of the mid-1840s. Both wages and prices were characterized by marked inflation during the wars with France.

Unfortunately, the quality of the Irish data do not permit any confident estimate of changes in the standard of living during this period. Ó'Gráda (1994, 16–17) concluded that "The most plausible inference to be drawn from Irish wage data between the 1780s and the early 1810s is a rise in nominal wages that just about kept pace with rising prices." In Flanders, according to Vandenbroeke (1997, 112–16), the middle of the eighteenth century was a "golden age" of rising real incomes for both linen weavers and agricultural laborers. Because of lower food prices and taxes, Flemish nominal wages remained low. At the end of the century, unskilled or semiskilled laborers in Flanders earned 60 to 70 percent of the wages of their English counterparts (Vandenbroeke 1987, 164–68). Nonetheless, Vandenbroeke's data show that both weavers and agricultural laborers experienced downward pressure on their incomes in the final quarter of the eighteenth century.

According to Cullen, Gibson and Smout (1988), the differential in earnings between skilled and unskilled workers may be taken as an indication of the level of development of a given region. As a region develops, skilled labor becomes more plentiful, unskilled labor becomes more productive, and the gap in pay between the two categories narrows. They determined that while Scottish craft workers (carpenters and masons), earned less than their Irish counterparts during the eighteenth century, agricultural laborers' wages were greater. Moreover, the wage gap between skilled and unskilled labor was markedly smaller in Scotland. Kennedy and Dowling's (1997) evidence suggests that in Ireland the gap increased even further at the end of the eighteenth and in the early nineteenth centuries. These data appear to support the view that Scotland was characterized by more abundant skilled labor, and more productive unskilled labor than Ireland.

In Flanders, the "skill premium" appears to have been high relative to Holland (although it was certainly lower than that of Ireland). Lis and Soly (1997, 226–27) cited evidence that the nominal wages of skilled workers in Flanders were not much lower than those of their counterparts in Holland. In Ghent, unskilled workers earned 60 percent of journeyman's wages, compared to 70 percent in Holland. They argued—contrary to Mokyr—that since skilled labor was what the textile manufacturing sector required, the southern Netherlands did not have any advantage over the north in this respect. They further contended that, apart from a brief period between the 1660s and 1725, urban textile manufacturing grew as rapidly as rural production in Flanders (and in Brabant, where the woolen industry predominated), and that the wage difference between urban and rural areas was very small in any case. Thus for these authors, labor costs have no bearing at all on the industrial transition.

Should these arguments be extended to the Irish and Scottish cases? Two points can be made. First, the evidence from all three cases suggests that linen weavers' wages were lower than those of other skilled craftsmen, although the difference was relatively small in Scotland. Thus cheap labor costs may have contributed to the industrial transformation in linen-weaving districts, despite high skill premiums. In Flanders, weavers' earnings (at least in the rural districts) appear to have been no greater than those of unskilled workers, if not actually lower (Mendels 1969, 206–207; Vandenbroeke 1997, 113–14). According to Young (1892, 50–52, 206), Irish linen weavers earned from 10d to 1s 6d per day, compared to an average of 1s 9d per day for carpenters and masons in the 1770s. Moreover, there is some evidence that linen weavers' wages did not grow as rapidly as those of other workers during the period of high inflation associated with the French wars. When Young visited Armagh in the 1770s, he was informed that weavers earned between 10d and 1s 4d a day. Thirty years later Coote (1804) reported that weavers in Armagh earned 1s a day, on average, though they could earn up to 2s 6d when trade was brisk.

While data on Scottish weavers' wages are sparse, Warden's (1864, 421–657) extracts from the Old Statistical Account suggest a range from 10d to 1s 4d per day in the 1790s, compared to an average of 1s 4d for carpenters, and 1s 6d for masons. Thus Irish weavers earned about 66 percent of the wages of other craftsmen, whereas Scottish weavers earned about 80 percent. In contrast to Scottish weavers, who enjoyed a period of unprecedented prosperity in the last quarter of the eighteenth century, Irish weavers' wages appear to have stagnated, despite competition for labor from the cotton industry, and a dramatic increase in the output of linen cloth. The most likely explanation for this is that the increase in demand for coarser linens made it possible to draw men into the weaving business with less training. The contention is supported by the evidence, presented in chapter 2, that outlying linen markets grew more rapidly than those of the core "linen triangle" during this period. In Flanders, weavers' real wages declined in the latter decades of the eighteenth century.

The second point is that, in all three cases, men represented a minority of workers in the linen industry. Women outnumbered them by a factor of at least four to one. In both Ireland and Scotland, women's daily earnings in spinning were as low, if not lower, than those in unskilled agricultural labor, although this must be set against the highly seasonal nature of day work for women. In Ireland, Arthur Young's (1892, 116–258) data indicate that, in the linen districts, women earned from 2 and a half pence, to 6 pence (on average about 4 pence) a day in spinning, and about 6 pence a day pulling flax in 1776. In Scotland, evidence from the Old Statistical Account suggests that the earnings of female day laborers ranged from 3 pence to 14 pence, while those of spinners averaged between 3 pence and 15 pence (rarely more than 8d) a day in the 1790s (Morgan 1971). Thus evidence relating to men's wages in weaving gives a distorted picture of the cost of labor in the linen-manufacturing sector during protoindustrialization.

What of rates of productivity within linen manufacturing? There is little evidence of technological change in either of the two main phases of the production process—weaving and spinning—in any of the three cases during the eighteenth century. The flying shuttle, which was invented early in the century (1733), and which halved the time required to weave a piece, was not introduced to Ireland and Scotland until the end of the eighteenth century, and was probably not widely diffused until the nineteenth century (Crawford 1994, 41; Durie 1979, p.99). It was not introduced to Belgium until the 1820s and 1830s (Mendels 1969, 199). Contemporary commentators have left estimates of the average number of yards woven per day in each case, but meaningful comparison is made difficult by variation in the quality and widths of the linen cloth. According to Young's (1892, 116–258) estimates, Irish weavers manufactured between 2 and 3 yards of linen a day, depending on the fineness of the cloth. Flemish weavers wove 5 ells, or about 4 yards per day (Mendels 1969, 200). Osnaburg weavers in Scotland wove between 6 and 8 yards of this coarse variety of linen per day (Warden 1864, 559).

In Scotland, a two-handed spinning wheel was introduced in the 1750s, although it is unclear how widely or how quickly it diffused. Use of the two-handed wheel was recorded in various parishes in the Old Statistical Account in the 1790s. While it appeared to double the output of yarn from an individual spinner, the two-handed wheel was efficient only in the production of coarse yarn, and required a considerable amount of dexterity to use (Endrei and Maines 1995, 31–41).

It is impossible to evaluate the productivity of spinners in the three cases, because the sources rarely give enough information about the quality of yarn being produced to ensure that the examples are comparable. Consideration of spinners' productivity is further complicated by the fact that contemporaries assumed it to be a task embedded in women's everyday household duties, not one pursued consistently throughout the day. Wakefield (1812, 684) described spinning as an activity filling up "small intervals of time . . . that would otherwise be lost." From County Fermanagh, Young (1892, 196–97) reported that "a women will earn 4d a day by spinning, and do something in the family besides," and that spinning servants were contracted to "do the business of the house and spin a hank a day" (Young 1892, 204).

For most women, household activities, including spinning, occurred in the context of a marriage bargain, rather than a wage contract. Observing that women's and children's small earnings probably accounted for much of the increase in standard of living in Scotland at the end of the eighteenth century, Gibson and Smout (1995, 354) stated that "If the women's [incomes] look like gender exploitation from one angle, they look from another like an increase in total family income of 30 to 45 per cent." The statement illustrates dramatically how women's labor has been constructed differently from men's. Because spinning was not separated from the daily round of household tasks, and because the earnings from spinning were not disaggregated from total family income, the "value" of women's work—and indeed of their leisure—could not be calculated.

The protoindustrialization theorists attributed growth to the interplay between market and subsistence sectors, mediated by household processes. Subsistence production depended on some access to the material means of survival—especially land—but it also depended on access to "underemployed" labor. The gendered construction of work in rural households meant that women's labor, in particular, was expandable. As I argued in chapter 5, it was precisely the unremunerated labor of women and children that made it cheaper (from the merchant's perspective) to have goods produced in rural small-farm households, rather than in urban manufactures, irrespective of nominal wages.

Mendels (1969, 200–201) illustrated this for Flanders by showing that an "ideal," self-contained linen-manufacturing household, where there were four adult women to spin, and one adult man to weave, and which purchased flax in the market place, could earn less than the wages of two unskilled workers, assuming they could produce about 5 ells, or about 3 and a half yards of linen cloth a day. A similar calculation can be made for Ireland, using data collected by Arthur Young (1892, 122) in County Armagh. He was informed that about one and half stones of flax were required to produce a piece of cloth twenty-five yards in length. This quantity sold for 10s 6d (126 pence) in the marketplace, while the finished piece of cloth sold for 11d a yard, or £1 2s 11d (275 pence). Deducting the price of the flax, this meant that a weaving household earned approximately 6d a yard, or 18d a day, assuming three yards could be woven in a day. By this calculation, then, an Irish weaving household of five adults could collectively earn as much as two unskilled male laborers.

These calculations remind us that some of the most important aspects of protoindustrial development are obscured by wage data. Rather than being determined by individual levels of skill and productivity, variations in wage rates under household production systems may reflect differences in the gendered interaction between market and subsistence sectors.

HOUSEHOLD AND MARKET: DIFFERENT RELATIONSHIPS

In a pamphlet published in 1705, the French Huguenot Louis Crommelin pleaded his case that Irish women should apply themselves to spinning and leave off the business of raising and dressing flax, on the grounds that they "are and forever will be" ignorant of the correct procedures. In other countries, he wrote, flax was raised and prepared by "Men of Good Stocks," who sold it to spinners in the marketplace (Crommelin 1705, 23). Twenty years later, Lionel Slator (1725), an English flax dresser employed by Thomas Coote, was equally vehement in denouncing the tendency for scutching and hackling to be carried out by women in Ireland:

> If there be such Differences in swingling and hackling, [as] between Artist and Artist, what must this Nation loose, by the barbarous Methods followed by the House Wives? who have neither Tools, nor Skill to use them if they had them.

In a response to Slator, Richard Hall (1725), an expert flax dresser employed by the Linen Board, pointed out that in the Netherlands, hackling (but not scutching) was carried out by women:

> I see no Reason why the Women here [Ireland] might not be instructed to hackle as well as the Men; the Labor is not so great but that the Women might undergo it. As to the breaking, swingling, or scutching, that I must acknowledge to be labourious.

These comments demonstrate the extent to which the gender division of labor was implicated in the social construction of skill in the eighteenth century. For Crommelin and Slator, improving the Irish linen industry required that women be excluded from activities involving the exercise of skill. Note that Hall claimed women could be trained to hackle flax on the grounds that the task was not laborious, not on the grounds that women could be as skilled as men.

The comments also highlight a distinctive feature of the Irish linen industry: namely, that the cultivation and preparation of flax, through to the manufacturing process of spinning, was carried out on small, subsistence-oriented holdings, by "housewives," together with their daughters and servants. By the time of Arthur Young's visit in the 1770s, scutching mills, and to a lesser extent, specialist male flax dressers, had begun to displace women from some stages of the process. Nonetheless, flax was still grown in very small quantities—a "peck's sowing," or about half a rood. Even where scutch mills were used, women were often still responsible for the preparatory stage of breaking, or beetling the flax. Outside the linen triangle scutch mills were less widespread, and women almost certainly continued to scutch flax by hand, as Young was informed in County Fermanagh. Near Randalstown, Young (1892, 204) reported that hackling was done "by flax dressers who go about."

However, a pamphlet published in Carlow in 1778, claimed that "housewives" had been "allured" by the specious promises of flax dressers, and that:

> The Spinners and Weavers of the North East Part of Ulster, viz. the Counties of Armagh, Antrim, and Down, are better skilled in the Linen Manufacture than

> those of any other Part of Ireland, and Women Dress their Flax; except some Poor Families, who dwell in Towns, have no Lands of their own to cultivate Flax, and are, therefore, obliged to buy it in Shops. (Privat, Sloan and Company 1778, 4)

The authors were not disinterested in their condemnation of flax dressers, since they were claiming compensation from the Linen Board for the invention of a machine for dressing flax! Nonetheless, it is unlikely that either scutch mills or itinerant male flax dressers had displaced women entirely from the processes of preparing flax for the wheel by the end of the eighteenth century.

Flax was an extremely labor-intensive crop. In Flanders, according to Mendels (1969, 134–35), cultivation of a French acre of flax required two and a half "man days" and eighty "woman days." Arthur Young's (1892, 116–258) estimates of the expense of an acre of flax give a minimum requirement of six man days and forty-two woman days, and a maximum requirement of thirty-four man days and 108 woman days in Ireland. The estimates exclude scutching and heckling, but those at the high end of the range include beetling—the preparatory stage to scutching. The estimates were largely hypothetical, as few households grew as much as an acre of flax.

In Ireland, then, women on small, subsistence-oriented farms carried out the most labor-intensive phases of the linen industry, from cultivating and processing the raw material, to spinning the yarn. As I showed in chapter 2, during the second half of the century, a division of labor began to emerge between spinning and weaving districts, as petty manufacturers in the linen triangle began to purchase yarn in the marketplace and put it out to cottier weavers. However, as exports of linen cloth surged toward the end of the century, the problem of meeting the proportionally huge increase in demand for labor in the early phases of the production process was met by the geographical expansion of the industry to incorporate ever more remote and marginal rural districts. Sustained high population growth in the context of continued access to land for subsistence production ensured an almost limitless supply of cheap labor to the industry. Thus Irish merchants were able to increase their exports of linen cloth without any major alteration to the household-based production system.

The problem was solved differently in Flanders and Scotland. The development of the Flemish industry in the eighteenth century was accompanied by regional specialization. The "ruralization" of the industry as urban manufacturing declined has already been noted. After the middle of the century, manufacturing activities declined in the southeastern rural districts, becoming increasingly concentrated in a central zone stretching to the south of Ghent. The northeastern districts cultivated flax on a commercial scale for export both to the central manufacturing zone and overseas. According to Mendels (1969, 192), "We are thus speaking of a specialization; northeast Flanders produced the flax, and the rest of the interior produced the linen."

Flemish spinning and weaving households cultivated some flax, but they were dependent on the marketplace for most of their raw material. Moreover, according to Mendels, fully half of the protoindustrial population was landless by the second half of the eighteenth century. Population increase and increasing landlessness ensured that increasing amounts of labor were applied to spinning and weaving within the manufacturing zone. From the merchant's perspective costs were kept low because weaving households purchased the raw materials in the marketplace, and because the cost of women's labor in spinning was not calculated separately when the web was sold.

In Scotland (Durie 1979) the problem of increasing productivity in the early phases of the production process was met by importing flax (at first from Holland and Flanders, and then increasingly from Russia and the Baltic), and putting it out to spinners. The yarn was then, in turn, put out to weavers. Serious efforts to promote commercial flax cultivation in Scotland were tacitly abandoned around the middle of the century, as promoters of the industry sought to capitalize on the opportunities presented by the newly introduced bounty system on exports. According to one commentator (Sinclair 1831), "real farmers" found the labor requirements of flax to be a distraction at the time of year when they were busiest. In order to meet the increasing demand for yarn in the second half of the eighteenth century, merchant manufacturers extended their operations to the north and northeast of the central belt where both commercial agriculture and linen weaving were concentrated. This strategy enabled them to take advantage of the opportunity to meet growing demand for linens in the American colonies, in the context of relatively slow population growth, and the disappearance of the subsistence-oriented small-holder class which elsewhere provided much of the labor for protoindustrialization (see Gray 1997).

Because Scottish merchants (in contrast to their Irish and Flemish counterparts) paid for spinning directly, keeping women's labor costs down was a matter of immediate concern. Osnaburg manufacturers organized a boycott in 1749 in an attempt to lower spinners' wages, and as we have seen, two-handed wheels were introduced in the 1750s. By the 1790s yarn was being imported from Bremen to meet the shortfall in supply, as women in the lowlands abandoned spinning in preference for new opportunities in agricultural day labor—and also, one assumes, as their husbands' and fathers' real incomes increased.

As I argued in chapter 5, the Irish linen industry was able to grow by means of an ongoing process of "underdevelopment." It depended on the continuation of extremely low labor costs, which discouraged the emergence of divisions of labor that might have improved efficiency. Thus Irish labor was characterized by low productivity because of a particular form of gendered interaction between household and market.

Divisions of labor between the supply of raw materials and spinning characterized both Scotland and Flanders. In the Scottish case merchants were obliged to lay out capital in importing flax and putting it out to spinners. They were thus confronted with an ongoing problem of keeping labor costs down in an economic environment where the trend was toward increasing real wages. Labor shortages may have spurred Scottish merchant manufacturers to invest in spinning machinery, but cheap and skilled immigrant labor from the Irish linen districts also helped to sustain Scotland's industrial transformation.

Finally, in Flanders, the emergence of specialist flax cultivating and commercial agricultural zones ensured that increasing quantities of labor were allocated to spinning and weaving within the manufacturing zone in the context of growing demand for linens. However, costs were kept to a minimum because weaving households purchased their own raw material, and effectively absorbed the cost of spinning by having it done within their own households (or by purchasing yarn if necessary).

CONCLUSION

Theories of protoindustrialization have emphasized the part played by rural industry in generating population growth and abundant labor, although they have differed in their understanding of the mechanisms leading to this outcome. The theories have also represented protoindustrialization as a stage in the industrialization process, providing capital and cheap labor for the first factories. Again, there have been important differences in how these relationships were understood.

This chapter has critically engaged with arguments about the role of cheap labor in the industrial revolution in order to reveal the significance of gender in the transition to the factory system. Mokyr suggested that differences in the *productivity* of labor might explain why some protoindustrial regions with abundant labor made an early and sustained industrial transition, whereas others—like Ireland—did not. By contrast, O'Hearn argued that the *substitution* of cheap labor for machines was a rational, adaptive response, given Ireland's exclusion from core innovations by dominant English elites. I have argued that we must also pay attention to how labor was *differentiated* by gender. In rural industrial regions, differences in the cost and productivity of labor did not inhere in individuals, but rather in the different ways that men's and women's labor was mobilized within the household economy.

NOTES

This chapter is a revised version of Gray 2003.

1. Under the 1801 Act of Union between Britain and Ireland the duties payable on cotton goods imported into either country from the other were progressively reduced from 1808. All duties ceased on cotton yarn in 1816 and on cotton cloth in 1824 (Geary 1989, 254).

Chapter Seven

Conclusion

In an intriguing article, Goldstone (1996) argued that differences in the extent to which women were available for work outside the household explain why, in contrast to Europe, China failed to develop a factory-based system of textile production until the twentieth century. Because in both cases women worked for very low returns in household manufacture, early factories could compete only if they were able to mobilize female labor at wages below those paid to men for comparable unskilled work. In Europe this was possible because a period of work outside the family household was a normal part of the female life course between puberty and marriage. In China, by contrast, women moved directly from their fathers' to their husbands' households shortly after puberty, and there were strong cultural sanctions against young women working outside the home. He concluded that "specific characteristics of the gender specification of labor" (Goldstone 1996, 18) might be a neglected factor in explaining uneven patterns of economic development.

This book has shown how the "gender specification of labor" in the Irish linen industry was a key factor in the overall development of the industry during the era of "protoindustrialization," and in the dependent form taken by the "industrial revolution" in Ireland. Gender mediated local and regional variations in the nature and timing of incorporation to the world economy, creating distinct historical patterns of socioeconomic development. The gender division of labor between spinning and weaving, together with the technological bottleneck between the two phases of the production process, ensured that spinning was dispersed across a greater number of households and territories than weaving. Because of the undervaluation of women's work, this created a situation of unequal regional exchange, whereby the *under*remunerated labor of women in the small-farm, semisubsistence households of the yarn districts was added to the *un*remunerated labor of the wives and children of individual weavers, keeping the cost of manufacturing linen cloth in Ireland extremely low. The Irish linen industry was able to achieve extraordinary levels of growth under this system, because the availability of marginal land for cultivation, together with high rates of population growth and the absence of institutional controls on the proliferation of small farms in the yarn districts, ensured an almost limitless supply of labor to the most labor-intensive phases of the production process, namely, flax cultivation and spinning. However, in the long run, this feature of the Irish linen industry contributed to its underdevelopment—even by comparison with other linen-manufacturing regions. Not only did it discourage investment in machinery, it also discouraged the emergence of a functional division of labor *between* flax cultivation and spinning, thus further depressing costs and overall productivity levels.

I have argued that the behavior of individual rural industrial households in Ireland depended on the significance of spinning—rather than weaving—in the family economy. Spinning was most important in small-farm households that relied on the system of "spade husbandry" to cultivate their land. By the first half of the nineteenth century, such households were found in two kinds of district within the protoindustrial zone: first, in mature weaving districts in the proximity of major linen markets that had been incorporated early to the linen industry, with a prolonged experience of land fragmentation and population increase; second, in marginal districts that were incorporated through spinning only. The evidence suggests that it was these households that displayed the "subsistence-oriented" strategies which Medick considered central to the protoindustrial family economy. By contrast, in agriculturally viable districts that were more remote from major linen markets, or that were incorporated later to the industry when demand for agricultural products was also growing, spinning was much less important in the household economies of both farmers and laborers, and did not, therefore, have the same effect on household dynamics.

If this argument is correct, it has the potential to clarify the debate between those who argue that rural industrialization was driven by a desire on the part of the peasantry to purchase new commodities and accumulate wealth, and those who argue that it was externally imposed on a peasantry that remained fundamentally oriented toward maintaining a customary standard of living. The members of small-farm households may well have been motivated to participate in rural industry by the possibility of substituting bought items for homemade ones, and of consuming exotic luxuries like tobacco and tea, but the small size of their holdings, together with the poor earnings to be gained from spinning, limited their potential to accumulate wealth. Where men did not weave—either because they lacked the resources to do so, or because it was no longer remunerative—they preferred to maximize their leisure consumption. Women were more likely to engage in "self-exploitation" under deindustrialization, because, I have argued, their labor in spinning was defined as an integral part of their "subsistence" household duties, even when it provided vital cash income to the household economy. In short, households that were motivated by the desire to purchase commodities in the marketplace and "save up riches," may nonetheless have displayed "subsistence-oriented" strategies when women's labor provided the main source of cash income.

Thus family strategies cannot be reduced to economic factors alone. The small-farm households I have described did have other options available to them. In the yarn districts, they could have increased their income by allocating some male leisure time to spinning. Under deindustrialization, farmer weavers could have allocated some of their leisure hours to weaving, as women did to spinning, even in the face of dwindling earnings. But, I have argued, the value of men's and women's labor—and of their leisure time—reflected status differences between them, and the division of labor between spinning and weaving served to perpetuate that hierarchy. I have insisted, however, that gender must not be treated as an exogenous, ahistorical factor in our explanations of social change. What Goldstone called the "specific characteristics of the gender specification of labor"—or what I have called the "gender contract" —was clearly subject to contestation and change, even though "perception bias" limited the pace and depth of that change.

Appendix A

The 1821 Cavan Sample

The data files analyzed in chapter 4 were collected from manuscript copies of the original enumerators' schedules from the 1821 census, held in the National Archives of Ireland (Cen 1821/1-15). Almost all of the original schedules from the nineteenth century were destroyed by fire in 1922. County Cavan has the greatest number of surviving returns from 1821. The first file, consisting of the population of households with at least one weaver resident, was collected in the summer of 1987. The second file, consisting of a one in five systematic sample with a random start of all households with no resident weavers, was collected in the summers of 1991 and 1994.

The enumerators' schedules were organized by parish and townland. Townlands are small, vernacular spatial divisions, whereas the larger, civil parishes were official administrative units at the time. They corresponded with the parishes of the established Church of Ireland, but not always with the parishes of the Roman Catholic Church to which the majority of the population adhered (see Duffy 1995). I recorded townland information in the first data file on weaving households, but not in the second on nonweaving households. For each household I recorded the number of acres and calculated the number of children less than twelve years of age. The enumerators also recorded the number of stories in each house, but since almost all houses were single-story dwellings, I did not record this information. For each individual aged twelve years or more I recorded their relationship to the head of household, sex, age, and occupation. The first person enumerated in each household was assumed to be the head. Sex was inferred from relationship to the household head or, in the case of unrelated persons, from the name, if possible. The combined working file contains information on 3,760 households and 15,257 individuals. All data were analyzed using SPSS for Windows. When making inferences about both weaving and nonweaving households, I weighted the weaving data by dividing Ns by five.

The bound manuscript copies for the fifteen surviving Cavan parishes appear to be complete, although it is possible that some pages are missing from the front of the volume on Annagelliff. Table A.1 compares the population of households and individuals implied by my combined sample, with the figures reported in the British Parliamentary record.

The first attempt to obtain a census of the Irish population was made between 1813 and 1815. However, the first true census was obtained in 1821, and thereafter a census was held every ten years during the nineteenth century. There has been some debate surrounding the accuracy of the 1821 and 1831 censuses (Lee 1981). However, even in the 1841 census, it is widely accepted that women's occupations were underenumerated (Clarkson 1996). This makes it difficult to use census data to evaluate the significance of rural industry in the political economy, especially given the central argument of this book.

In the 1821 Cavan sample, women were less likely than men to have an occupation recorded, but this trend did not occur evenly across parishes. Table A.2 shows the percentage of individuals for whom an occupation was recorded by parish, and by relationship to the head of household.

There are three distinct patterns within the study area. In the first (pattern A), comprising parishes in the southeast and northwest of the study area, 90 percent or more individuals on average had a recorded occupation. In the second (pattern B), comprising parishes in the central part of the study area, no more than 67 percent of all individuals had a recorded occupation. In Denn, and Drung and Larah, this was due to the omission of wives' occupations. In Kilmore, it was mainly due to an underrecording of sons' and daughters' occupations, whereas in Lavey wives and sons were primarily affected. In each of the parishes in pattern B, "other relatives" were less likely to have a recorded occupation than under pattern A. Finally, in pattern C, comprising parishes in the northeast and southwest of the study area, less than 45 percent of all individuals had an occupation recorded on average. In these parishes the enumerators tended only to record occupations for heads of households, and unrelated household members (such as servants, or journeymen). Table A.3 reveals the consequences of this spatial pattern for the distribution of occupations in the Cavan study area.

It is clear that the proportions of spinners and laborers are dramatically affected by the percentage of occupations recorded. As I discussed in chapter 4, it seems likely that spinner and laborer had the status of universal occupational categories for women and men who were not otherwise employed. All

Table A.1. Estimated Population of Households in the Cavan Study Area

Parish	*(A) Weaving Households in the Sample (Population)*	*(B) Nonweaving Households in the Sample(1 in 5 Sample)*	*(C) Estimated Population of Households C = A + (B*5)*	*Published Household Totals (H.C. 1824)*	*Difference*
Annagelliff	51	106	581	663	−82
Ballymachugh	56	92	516	517	−1
Castlerahan	67	177	952	955	−3
Castletarra	61	186	991	1002	−11
Crosserlough	246	236	1426	1438	−12
Denn	116	141	821	833	−12
Drumlumman	117	223	1232	1256	−24
Drung & Larah	204	370	2054	2074	−20
Kilbride	10	134	680	689	−9
Kilmore	105	216	1185	1223	−38
Kinawley	33	90	483	498	−15
Lavey	71	149	816	872	−56
Lurgan	38	201	1043	1058	−15
Mullagh	21	154	791	747	+44
Munter Connaught	6	83	421	429	−8
Total	1202	2558	13992	14254	−262

Sources: 1821 Cavan sample; Abstract of Answers and Returns, H. C. 1824, vol. 21.

Table A.2. Percent of All Individuals, Aged Twelve or More Years, with a Recorded Occupation, by Parish

Parish	*All Individuals*	*Heads of Household*	*Spouses*	*Sons*	*Daughters*	*Other Relatives*	*Others*
Pattern A							
Castlerahan	95.3	97.4	100.0	95.4	92.6	79.9	96.4
Crosserlough	97.7	98.6	98.6	96.8	98.5	91.1	99.4
Kinawley	88.4	97.98	97.3	82.8	75.0	85.0	85.0
Lurgan	94.5	99.5	97.3	85.7	89.5	90.9	99.0
Mullagh	90.2	99.4	99.1	81.3	77.5	86.2	94.5
Munter Conn.	95.5	100.0	94.5	91.6	91.5	94.0	96.1
Pattern B							
Denn	63.8	84.3	4.4	72.1	79.8	57.3	93.1
Drung & Larah	65.3	95.1	0.4	73.3	68.4	64.9	95.7
Kilmore	67.0	89.8	70.2	49.2	37.3	55.3	92.0
Lavey	65.3	92.5	24.4	25.7	92.9	49.6	95.9
Pattern C							
Annagelliff	37.2	87.6	11.9	12.7	7.1	17.9	86.8
Ballymachugh	41.7	86.2	1.3	15.1	0.0	0.9	86.6
Castletarra	44.3	95.5	7.0	17.3	7.1	21.4	90.2
Drumlumman	32.2	89.1	0.0	4.3	0.0	3.3	80.3
Kilbride	33.1	92.6	1.9	2.7	0.0	9.4	76.2

Source: 1821 Cavan sample.

Table A.3. Percent of Individuals Aged Twelve or More Years Reporting Certain Occupations, by Parish

Parish	*Weighted N*	*Spinners %*	*Laborers %*	*Weavers %*	*Other Artisans %*	*No Occupation %*
Pattern A						
Castlerahan	3843	38.5	25.4	2.2	3.9	4.7
Crosserlough	5191	40.8	20.1	6.5	3.9	2.0
Kinawley	1762	35.3	15.1	2.4	6.2	11.6
Lurgan	3743	38.8	22.6	1.2	4.1	5.5
Mullagh	2995	38.3	26.9	0.9	1.7	9.8
Munter Conn.	1581	35.7	27.5	0.5	2.2	4.5
Pattern B						
Denn	3094	20.1	13.6	5.0	2.3	36.2
Drung & Larah	8111	15.8	15.6	3.1	2.4	34.7
Kilmore	4768	25.2	14.9	2.7	3.4	33.0
Lavey	2831	23.6	6.8	3.3	2.9	34.7
Pattern C						
Annagelliff	2210	4.2	6.7	2.7	1.9	62.8
Ballymachugh	2161	0.8	6.9	3.1	1.7	58.3
Castletarra	3859	4.5	4.8	2.0	4.9	55.7
Drumlumman	1643	0.0	7.3	2.6	0.5	67.8
Kilbride	2732	0.2	9.0	0.4	1.2	66.9

Source: 1821 Cavan sample.

wives and daughters spun as part of their normal household duties, and all sons were expected to help their fathers by laboring on the land. Given this, there are two possible interpretations of the occupational patterns discussed above. On one hand, the patterns may simply reflect differences in the diligence of the enumerators. If this is true, then no inferences may be drawn about the distribution of spinning within the study area. On the other hand, it might be assumed that the likelihood of enumerators' recording women's occupations depended on the perceived importance of spinning in the local household economy. There are two arguments in favor of this more optimistic interpretation. First, the phenomenon of relatively remote and marginal districts reporting higher proportions of spinners is repeated at a more aggregate level in the 1841 census (cf. Almquist 1979). Second, the relationships identified by QCA among spinning, laboring, low land valuation, and population growth, suggest that the pattern of reporting women's occupations was not based simply on the enumerator's whim.

Appendix B

The Poems and the Poets

This appendix contains the full texts of the poems referred to in the book, with biographical information on the poets where possible. Most of these details were obtained from John Hewitt's (1974) *Rhyming Weavers*.

"AN TÚIRNÍN LÍN"

Anonymous Irish language folk song. Reproduced in Ní Ógáin (1921, 24.)

An Bhliadhain sul ar phósas stór mo chroidhe
Ba ghairid mar lón aici sé púint lín,
Acht annsoin nuair phósas as chuadhmar i dtigheas
Bhíodh bun ag an púnt i gcionn trí mhí.
    Och! mo bean as mo chlann as mo thuirnín lín
    Mo chúpla púnt no dhó gan sníomh,
    Dá lá 'n-a luighe 'n-aghaidh lae 'n-a suidhe-
    As go dtógaidh Dia dílís a cúram díom

Nuair a measas gur thoghas-sa togha mná tighe
Go tais as go modhamhail as 'na rogha thár díogha,
Ni hamhlaidh a bhí acht an fala 'n-a croidhe
Do leag me im' cheann gan meabharí gan bhríg.
    Och! mo bhean as mo chlann . . .

Ta bean agam féin as nar mhairidh mé í,
Nar mhairidhe sí agam as nar mhairidh me í;
Dá m'éigean dom Éire do shiubhal le n'a cloinn,

Go rabhad fé n-a crocas i gcionn trí mhí.
Och! mo bhean as mo chlann. . . .

Nuair airigheann sí me féin ag teacht chum an tighe
Teine mhaith mhóna cuireann sí síos,
Stiúruigheann na leinbh ar fuaid an tighe
Agus scaoileann ar siubhal an túirnín lín.
Och! mo bhean as mo chlann as mo thúirnín lín,
Mo chúpla púnt go deo gan sníomh;
Tobac or a bais as piopa len' ais,
'S is cuma san domhan ca ngabhann an cíos.

"THE AULD WIFE'S ADDRESS TO HER SPINNING WHEEL"

By Thomas Beggs, reproduced in Crawford (1994, 82–84).

Thomas Beggs (1789–1847) was born the son of a farm laborer in Glenwhirry, County Antrim. His mother was a first cousin of James Orr (see below). Beggs found employment at a number of bleachworks, first at Ballyclare, County Antrim, and then around Belfast. He was often unemployed, however, and seems to have tried to live by his writing, despite being married with five children (Hewitt 1974, 70–71).

Frae Tibbie Gordon I gat this wheel,
An' then I was young, an' my face was fair,
An' since the first day she cam' into my shiel,
We aye had something to keep an' to spare.
On the wintry night by the clear ingle side,
My wee bit lamp hung laigh in the lum;
An' I sung my sang, an' my wheel I plied,
An' Rorie was pleased wi' the hartsome hum
But now upon her I maun spin nae mair,
An' it mak's my heart baith sorry an' sair.

Now fare thee weel, my cantie wee wheel,
In age an' youth my staff an' my stay,
How gladly at gloamin, my kind auld chiel
Has reeled our pirn, sae bonnie an' blae
But men o' cunning, an' pelf, an' pride,
Hae made thee a useless thing to me'
For they carena what puir bodies betide,
Or whether they live on the yirth or die.
Now the feck o' my fae is a heart fu' o' wae
An' the fourth o' a groat is the wage o' a day.

The mountain lass, at her wee bit wheel,
        How blythe was her e'e, an' how rosy her cheek!
Her bosom was white, an' her heart was leal,
        Her mien it was modest, her manner was meek;
But now the pert maidens, wha ply in the mill,
        How wan is their visage,—how dim is their e'e
For the ban they maun bide is enough to chill
        The spring o' the heat an' to deaden their glee:
To toil for men that are hard to please,
In a hot-be rank wi' vice an' disease.

An' when they speak, it maun be wi a squeal;
        They maun rise an' rin at the toll o' the bell,
An' brook the insult o' a tyrant an' de'il,
        An' the jargon they hear is the language o' hell
To breed a bit lassie in sic a vile place,
        Instead o' her ain father's cot on the green,
It puts the puir thing in a pitifu' case—
        Ah! black was the day when they made the machine.
It has added mair pelf to the hoards o' the great
And left those that were low in a far lower state.

But weel I remember langsyne, that I,
        When Rorie had little outbye to dae,
Gat aye meat enough an' some claes forbye,
        By keepin' thee busy, an' birrin' away;
An' what though we never could boast o' our gear
        An' what tho' we never were blest wi a bairn;
For cault or hunger we hadna to fear,
        An' I sung my sang, an' I spun my yarn;
But nae mair for mysel' can I provide,
In these wearifu' days o' poortith an' pride.

An' when I was rade, an' hale, an' young,
        My thread cam' level, an' fine as a hair,
An' the kitten purred, an' the cricket sung,
        An' the care o' my heart, was a lightsome care.
Now men ha'e erected a new ingine,
        An' left but little for us to earn,
An' little for me but to pinch an' to pine';
        I wish I had died when I was a bairn,—
For my guid auld man he has breathed his last,
An' I on the cauldrife warld am cast.

An' now the poke an' the staff I maun tak'
        An' wander awa', an amous to beg,

For a plack in the day is the maist I can mak',
        When I ca' at my wheel till I'm blin' as a cleg,
An' work till the witching hour o' the night,
        A time rather late for a thing like me;
But the guid auld times are gane out o' sight,
        An' it mak's the saut tear aften start to mine e'e;
For lords o' the Mill and Machine ha'e decreed
That bodies like me maun beg their bread.

"THE AULD WIFE'S LAMENT FOR HER TEA-POT"

By David Herbison, from *Midnight Musings, Or Thoughts from the Loom*, Belfast, 1848.

David Herbison (1800–1880) was born in Ballymena, County Antrim. His father was an innkeeper and small farmer. Completely blind until he was eight years old, Herbison had just two years of schooling. He helped on his father's farm until he was apprenticed to weaving. "At the age of fourteen I was harnessed to the loom, and doomed for life to be an operative weaver—an occupation at which those engaged must either toil with incessant drudgery or starve" (Herbison 1848, viii). Herbison emigrated to Canada in 1827, returning after just a few months. He lived through the whole era of industrial transformation in the linen industry, and published five volumes of poetry (Hewitt 1974, 75–76).

Alas! alas! what shall I do,
My auld black pot is broke in two,
In which I did sae often brew
                The wee drap tea,
And thought it would ha'e cheer'd me through
                Life's weary way!

A better pot, sure, ne'er was made,
It wadna vent the sma'est blade;
Still, when the table-cloth was laid,
                And it appear'd,
A smile out o'er my visage play'd
                And a' things cheer'd.

Before I brought it frae the town
It cost me nearly half-a-crown,
Nor did I grudge't, it was sae roun',
                And very snug—

At every party it was down,
Throughout Dunclug.

Lang after it cam' to our house
I kept it for our Sunday's use;
But when my daughters a' got spruce,
And wanted men,
Ah! Then it got the sore abuse
Baith but and ben!

Whene'er their wooers cam' to see them,
A wee drap tea they be to gie them,
For fear, as I thought, they would lea' them,
Alone to rove,
They never fail'd wi' sweets to free them
Frae ithers' love.

'Twas then my tea-pot had to thole
The power of mony a blazing coal,
Which knaw'd me to the very soul,
To hear it crackin',
While they prepar'd the butter'd roll
For lads to smack on.

They burn'd it till it was as thin
As my auld wrinkled bluidless skin,
I still must say it was a sin
To use it sae,
For lads that didna care a pin
About their tea.

But now my daughters a' are wed,
And health and peace frae me are fled,
I find it hard to earn my bread,
And creamless tea,
And wish I wi' the pot was laid
Low in the clay.

For, ah! I'm sure I'll never see
Such joys as charm'd my youthfu' e'e—
The days are past when folks like me
Could earn their bread,
My auld wheel now sits silently
Aboon the bed.

And well may Erin weep and wail
The day the wheels began to fail,
Our tradesmen now can scarce get kail
Betimes to eat,
In shipfulls they are doom'd to sail
In quest o' meat!

For that machine that spins the yarn,
We're left unfit our bread to earn,
O Erin! Will you ne'er turn stern
Against your foe,
When every auld wife can discern
Your overthrow!

"ADDRESS TO BACHELORS"

By Sarah Leech, from *Poems on Various Subjects*, Dublin, 1828.

According to the biographical memoir accompanying her collection of poems, Sarah Leech was the daughter of "an industrious linen weaver," born in the village of Ballylennan, about three miles from Raphoe in County Donegal. Her father died when she was three years old leaving a widow with six children.

> When she attained her twelfth year, she was permitted, for a very short period, to receive instructions in writing, but as she had now become useful in assisting her mother . . . she was obliged to relinquish school when she began to appreciate its value, and submit to the drudgery of a spinning wheel, an employment at which she is able to vie with any of her compeers. (Leech 1828, 12)

She spent some time as a schoolmistress, but having been partially disabled by rheumatism, "she was under the necessity of giving up school, and returning to her spinning wheel, the only means she now has to depend on for her subsistence" (Leech 1828, 16). According to Hewitt (1974, 41), she "belongs to the host of humble versifiers so eagerly taken up by fashionable patrons, which happened to few of the [male] bards."

Ye bachelors baith ane and a'
Oppressed wi' grief on you I ca',
While down my cheeks the tear-drops fa'
Thro' pure compassion,
To see ilk flirt and country daw,
Ape at the fashion.

The gents may weel put on grimaces,
And in sad plight bewail their cases,
When flunkies dress in frills and laces,
Sae fine and braw
I fear soon in their ladies' places
Themselves they'll shaw.

Ilk lass maun ha'e a snaw-white gown,
Wi' span-lang flounces waving roun',
Some weel-plait straw upon her crown,
And ribbons gay,
While hose weel starched, and right-left shoon
Her feet display.

Next she maun ha'e a yard o' veiling,
Affected modesty concealing,
Tho' want o' this is a' the failing,
Laid to the lassie—
How can I help at times bewailing,
Poor fools sae saucy.

How to her mither Kate will bawl,
To purchase her a scarlet shawl,
In hopes she may some gull enthral,
Who gapes for riches,
But six months wed, she proves a brawl,
And wears the breeches.

Examples here I could bring in,
Which would create a mighty din,
But some at my poor muse might grin,
And sairly flyte her—
I wish them safe beyond Clyde's linn
That wad sae spite her.

Despite o' fear I ane shall state,
O Willie! How I mourn your fate—
Since you were tied to bucksome Kate,
Without compassion
She thrash'd you weel baith ear' and late,
When in a passion.

In truth she is a thrawart dame,
You're often witness o' the same;
For be it spoken to your shame,

She never spares you,
And should you try the shrew to tame,
She drubs or hairs you.

Her tongue at rest can never be,
And when she pries the barley bree,
Wi' nibours she will disagree,
But in the end,
Poor Willie gets a blackened e'e,
You may depend.

I therefore a' young fellows caution
To guard against sic dames o' fashion,
Or you may aiblins get a thrashin'
Frae tongue as glib,
When wed, you rouse the angry passion
Of captious rib.

Too late you may have cause to wail,
For should the tea or whiskey fail,
She, vixen like, will you assail,
Or chide and snap,
And swear, should you be dragged to jail,
She'll have her drap.

Keep these examples in your view,
For happiness is doom'd to few,
But hark! the clock is striking two,
And time goes rinning,
So I'm obliged to bid adieu,
And join my spinning.

"TEA"

By James Orr, from *Poems on Various Subjects by James Orr of Ballycarry, with a Sketch of His Life*, Belfast: Wm. Mullan and Son, 1935. This is a reprint of two volumes originally published in 1804 and 1817.

James Orr (1770–1816) is probably the best known of Ulster's "rhyming weavers." Born the only son of a farmer weaver, he lived in the village of Ballycarry, in the parish of Broadisland (or Templecorran) on the east coast of County Antrim. Like many of his coparishioners he supported the cause of the United Irishmen in 1798, when a small party of rebels from Broadisland, the neighboring parish of Islandmagee, and the nearby town of Larne, marched toward Donegore Hill on June 7. They intended to rendezvous for an attack on Antrim town, but after many desertions en route, they arrived to find the uprising already put down, and the rebels fleeing from government troops. The military authorities later pardoned all those who surrendered their arms, except their leaders, for whom rewards of fifty guineas were offered. Orr found his name on the list of "fifty pounders," and was obliged to flee to America. After a few months he returned to Ireland under a general amnesty, resumed his trade as a farmer weaver in Ballycarry, and became a respected and well-liked member of the community, although he had a weakness for alcohol to the end of his life. Orr never married, perhaps because of his love for a lady "too far removed by social position from the sphere of life he enjoyed" (Madden 1864, 64). According to John Hewitt (1974, 42), Orr's poems "The Penitent" (see below) and "The Irish Cottier's Death and Burial," "are far beyond the capacity of any other of our rural rhymers, in firmness of structure and consistency of language, undoubtedly the major successes in scale in our vernacular literature." Details of Orr's life, together with a discussion of the value of his poetry for social history, may be found in Akenson and Crawford (1977).

Welcome, my frien's,—ye're just in time,
The kettle's on, an' soon will chyme;
An' giv, tho' us'd to strains sublime,
Ye'll listen me,
I'll clear my throat, an' rudely rhyme
In praise o' Tea.

What mak's ye nice? I'm no yet stintet
To mashlin bread an' weel-won mint to't;
The far-fetch'd leaf is maistly grantet
Sev'n times a week'
An', tak' my word, the day I want it
The pipe does reek.

Leeze me on Tea!—the maskin pot
Keeps peace about the poor man's cot:
Nae waitin' wife misca's the sot,
Wha stauchers hame wi'
A grain o' pouther an' o' shot,
To charge the wame wi'!

The L-d leuk on her wretched bield,
Whase pence are out, and hank unreel'd!
Nae griddle's het, nae pratoe peel'd,

To mak' a bap o't;
Nor *weed* nor *head-ach* tak's the field
Without a drap o't.

But blast the smuggler, fause an' fell,
Wha brews't in tinfu's by hersel'
An' bribes the sma'-craft no to tell
Their drudgin' daddy;
Deel nor he'd ay bounce in, pell-mell,
Just when 'tis ready.

When Riggie's yell, an' kitchen dear,
'Tis the poor cotter's cheapest cheer:
The creamless blash, that sugar fair
Has little share in,
Sen's glibly owre, his bonnoch bare,
An saut, saut herrin.

The poorest bodies far or near,
Their pipes wi't ay on Sunday clear:
And a' the state-days o' the year;
But, chiefly, yule,
Wife, wean, an' cat, can hardly bear
To let it cool.

At breakin' clovin', kirn, an' quiltin',
'Tis ay the base that bliss is built on;
An' when the spae-wife to the Mill-town
In hiddlin's slips,
Without it, vain were her consultin'
Divinin' cups.

While roun' the hag the young things catch
The story o' their future match,
Tho' a' her skill's no worth a fitch,
Sud at her haunch
Bauld Moses rise to "slay the witch,"
They'd mak' him gaunch.

When claughin wives, wi' heads in flannin',
Forgether'd on a sabbath e'enin',
Pit spoonfu's twa a piece o' green in;
(While wi' the mother
The splain an' stuffin'—a' compleenin'
Sit whazzlin' throuther.)

Losh! how they rauner, rail, an' ripple
Their nybers names, an' mumph an sipple!
But, conscience! gif the auld delft nipple
Nae ooze wad bring,
The priest, an' parish, king, an' people,
Might tak their swing.

One wha oure-night has play'd the weary,
An' crept frae slumber, half deleery,
Wi' achin' banes, an blinkers bleerie,
An' tortur'd nerves:
While some slee jilt, wi' mirth sincere ay,
His plight observes.

When wash'd his face, and camb'd his hair,
An' in again frae takin' air,
Sax reekin' roun's, or may be mair,
Can mak' him able,
To think, an' speak, an' labour share,
In barn or stable.

Yet "*Tea* mak's man a nerveless wrig,"
The doctor says—p-x on the prig!
Its juice has gladden'd monie a big,
An' brave leel heart,
Wha'd firm as *Gabbin* keep the trig,
Or forward dart—

But, harkee! there's a blyther singer;
I tald ye 'twad be nae lang hinger:
Yestreen I daftly still'd the clangour
I' the auld twin'd blether;
Or pints a piece o' something stronger
We'd bouse thegither.

"THE PENITENT"

Inscribed to the Rev. J. Bankhead.
Written in the year 1800.

Earth feels the triple scourge wild warfare spreads,
Emaciate *famine* gnaws the husks and pines,

And ev'ry friend, forsaking, inly dreads
        The fated wretch, whom *pestilence* confines:
Say, will BANKHEAD, who piously declines
        Man's ev'ry vice, and mourns his woes severe;
Will he, the guide, who feels what he enjoins,
        The fervent love of ev'ry *faith* and *sphere*,
The Penitent's memoirs, tho' mean, be pleas'd to hear?

His name, if I min't right, was *Christy Blair*:
        Fu' aft I've pass'd the wa'-stead whare he leev'd;
An' auld ash tree stan's branchless now an' bare,
        Aboon the spring, unnotic'd an' unpreev'd:
The side wa' co'ers the causey that he pav'd,
        The beasts rub doon the cheeks o' ilka door;
Rank nettles hide the hearth on which he shav'd
        The nybers ance a week in years o' yore –
I learn'd his life frae *Brice*, the auld herd on the moor.

He weav'd himsel', an' keepet twathree gaun,
        Wha prais'd him ay for hale weel-handled yarn;
His thrifty wife an' wise wee lasses span,
        While warps and queels employ'd anither bairn;
Some stript ilk morn an' thresh'd, the time to earn
        To scamper wi' the houn's frae hill to hill;
Some learn'd the question-beuk in nyb'ring barn-
        Christy wrought unco close, whyles took a gill,
But when his wab was out had ay a hearty fill.

An' nae mean spunge was he; but was hae lent
        Sums to poor sots, wha basely brak their word;
Rich rakes admir'd his sprie, sae weel he kent
        The way to heel, an' hand', a guid game bird:
An' in the pit he wadna twice be dar'd,
        The odds were shamefu' when he cried "fair play";
His nieve, that nail'd the messons to the sward,
        Wad stapt to lift their weanies frae his way:
He harm'd himsel' at times was a' that folk cud say.

But och! if vice the least indulgence claim
        'Twill wax, an' strengthen, like a wean at nurse;
Belyve he staid hale days an' nights frae hame,
        Tho ae nights absence, ance he deem'd a curse;
An' aft brought hame nought but an empty purse,
        O' a' the hale wabs price he took to sell;
Then, sick niest day, poor Mary boost disburse

Her pence, to get a glass his qualms to quell:
She grudg'd—he storm'd—the weans grat—hame grew hell.

At length he turn'd a doonright ne'er-do-weel,
For ilka draught, he swore, but made him dryer;
The kye gaed baith for debt. A sorry chiel'
Was he to cleave their stakes to men' the fire:
Mary ne'er min't the house—mair like a byre,
But clash'd wi' nyber wives. Unkent to him
For tea, an' snuff, the troubled dames desire,
She'd smuggled meal an' seeds; tho' hunger grim
Devour'd the duddy weans, now in a wretched trim.

Gif ye had pass'd his door, ye'd either heard
Him we his comrades madly makin' noise,
Or squabblin' wi' the wife. He seldom car'd
To wake the looms mair profitable voice:
The weans were wicked mair thro' chance than choice,
How marvellous wad been their mense an' grace!
He learn'd the lasses smut, an' gart the boys
Drink dreadfu' toasts, an' box for pence or praise;
They'd ca' their mother le'er, an' curse her till her face.

Whyles wi' his auld colleagues he blam'd his wife;
He kent that she was slack, an' they were fause:
She sometimes took a drap, an' by the life
A drinkin' wife's ay deem'd for greater flaws:
Ance when they differ'd, like a thoughtless ass,
He listed wi' the sogers on the street,
Yet when he ru'd, wrang'd Mary pledg'd her braws
To raise the smart money. To see her greet
Wad thow'd the hardest heart in army or in fleet.

Yet shame owrecam' him whyles, an' when advice
Was properly applied it rous'd his pride,
He'd kiss the beuk, an' swear by a' the skies,
He'd in *nae change house* drink till hallon-tide;
Then, then he thrave; but och! he cudna bide
Frae worthless spen'thrifts, nor cud they frae him;
At first he'd drink his glass in some backside,
But at the table when his brains 'gan swim;
When told o' a' niest morn he'd tremble ev'ry limb.

At lang an' last, when to the frightfu' edge
O' dreary ruin, by his courses brought,

(For a' was gaen he had to sell or pledge
    The times were hard and nane would trust him aught)
To pass a painfu' hour, the barn he sought
    Whare Smyth, the methodie, harangu'd the folk:
They mourn'd, an' cried amen—he fleech'd an' fought,
    Christy grew grave, an' thought he'd join the flock,
An' imitate their lives wham ance he us'd to mock.

An' change his life he did; the bull-beat came,
    He wadna gang; but ca'd it savage vice:
A serious nyber 'cause he stay'd at hame
    Gi'ed him a wab to weave, an' lent the price:
Late, late did he sit up, an' early rise,
    An' eat the bread o' care to get it weav'd;
Syne took it hame, gat meal, an' monie nice
    Auld claes, to thack the weans, we thanks receiv'd;
Somebody ay will help the poor an' weel-behav'd.

Nature a while, tho' thought forbearance hard,
    An' Habit, like a bough by force held straight,
Sprang till its ain auld thraw. When aff his guard,
    Twathree rash gills wad set him till't a' night;
An' much he'd said an' done that was na right:
    Ilk short relapse the clashes met to track o';
But practice soon made irksome trials light;
    As ane, at first, wha trys the pipe for lack o'
His health, halts, coughs, an' greus, yet *learns* to like
        tobacco

While perseverin' in his heav'n-ward way,
    He lea's pale want behin', his cant' an' zeal,
Sae quite remarkable, mak' grave an' gay
    Laugh hearty at him, tho' they like him weel;
Has he a band to fill? he soon fin's bail,
    Nae pross ere plagues him now, sloth leas his hame;
He has baith kye an' corn, an' sells some meal,
    His frien's outbye add *mister* till his name;
An' alter'd Mary's now a douse an' dainty dame.

(Hail! good old WESLEY—this they owe to thee,
    The wise of all professions bless thy birth;
Believing what you taught, without a fee,
    "A poor way-faring man," you ventur'd forth,
Striving where'er you went to free the earth

From sin, enslaver of the human mind:
As godlike HOWARD, friend of woe an' worth,
In many a realm consol'd the cells where pin'd
Poor persecuted slaves, kept there by kings unkind).

Whase arm ance rash as Christy's? now tho' strong,
Nae bangster tholes his nieve or sla'thorn black;
Wha ance blasphem'd like Christy? now his tongue
Without minc'd oaths the lee-lang day can crack:
His nights ance spent with gamesters owre the pack,
Are pass't wi' deein' wights, or at his beuk;
The lyin' cash he ance wad sent to wrack,
Lent, int'rest-free, sets up new-married folk—
He's far owre wise to jibe; but no owre grave to joke.

The weans and Mary kept the cottage neat;
She was affectionate, an' fond were they;
They work't an' sang their hymns, and crack't, an' gree't,
Fine was their speech, an' affable their way.
They werena stupes, wha fient na word can say
For what they b'lieve; tho' first to rail an' rage
At a' wha differ. 'Mang some bolefu's mae,
Ane *Fletcher's* warks, a bra unbiass'd sage,
Gart 'em wi' might an' mense the Calvinists engage.

An' searchin' for the Truth improv'd their taste:
How nat'ral Joseph's Life was weel they kent;
How *Moses'* muse her notes sublimely rais'd,
An' *Jeremiah's* deeply did lament;
The *spen'thrift son's* fine scene they weel cud paint,
An *guid Smaritan's*—an' nearer han's,
How *Young* made night mair solemn wi' his plaint;
How *Milton's* Eve was fair, his Adam fand;
How *Gray* was sad an' grave, an' *Shakespeare* wildly grand.

They min't baith warls. In warps boil'd by their han'
Did thrice ten shuttles lose their entrails sma';
An' on a scoup o' cheap, but mountain lan',
They graz'd yell kye, an' drain'd, an' lim'd the shaw.
Beasts, yarn, an' claith, aft call'd the sons awa';
The daughters wash'd, an' sew'd, an' span wi' care:
Christy did little, but directed a';
An' cute was he when unco folk were there;
For at the very warst he had baith sense an' lear.

"The e'e that saw them bless'd them." Much they shar'd
        Wi' frien's, wi' strangers, an' wi' a' in need;
Folk thought the fam'ly *fey* if e'er they err'd,
        Bonnier an' better ne'er brak warls bread:
Christy ne'er strave to cross their loves; but gied
        Mailin's, an' gear, to ev'ry lad an' lass,
He leev'd to train their weans, an' when he died,
        Was what they ca' the leader o' a class.
Brice gied me this account, an' right weel pleas'd I was.

May my wild brethren turn to wisdom's path
        An' grace poor Erin, plagu'd with want and dearth!
And banish from her shores religious wrath,
        Desponding sloth, and dissipated mirth!
May sun-like Science from the poor man's hearth
        Chase Ignorance, the owl that haunts the stys!
So patriots brave, when we lie low in earth,
        "Harmless as doves, and yet as serpents wise,"
Shall follow Truth and Right, and guard the land they
    prize.

"THE AUTHOR'S PREFACE"

By Hugh Porter, from *Poetical Attempts by Hugh Porter, A County of Down Weaver*, Belfast, 1813.

Relatively little seems to be known about Hugh Porter, a weaver who lived in the parish of Moneyslan, in County Down. Like Sarah Leech, his work was published at the instigation of an upper-class patron, in this case a Church of Ireland clergyman, the Reverend Thomas Tighe.

        Reader,
Since ye hae gie'n your five an' fi'ppence,
For this bit Beuk, that's no worth tippence;
Anither page or twa o' paper,
Wad mak it aye leuk something cheaper;
At least mak mair o't for the money—
Say, shall I then impose't upon ye?
'Yes, if ye please, and after a'
'Five shillin' will be thrown awa.
'But stop—I think I have enough,
'I b'lieve owre muckle o' sic stuff;
'Yet, neither here nor there a leaf is,
'Come, gie's it in the way o' preface.'

First then, I naething write by rule,
For o' the knowledge taught at school
Mine was a very scanty share,
I only learn'd the letters there:
Yet, by degrees, wi' tentie head,
At leisure hours I came to read;
And thus, by bit an' bit I grew
That I could write a little too,
A willin' mind a deal can do.

And secondly, plain truth to tell,
I made my sangs to please my sel,'
My dearest worthy frien's, and ithers
No' just sae dear, but rhymin' brithers
To whom, just as they are, I sent them,
But never for the public meant them.

And thirdly, in the style appears
The accent o' my early years,
Which is nor Scotch nor English either,
But part o' baith mix'd up thegither:
Yet it's the sort my neighbours use,
Wha think shoon prettier far than shoes.

But fourthly, for I'm keen to close—
'Do-do-ye'll say—an do't in prose
'For flesh an' bluid can bear nae langer,
'This doggerel sang a saint would anger.'
Content am I, and for the Muse,
I'm sure she's glad to hear the news.

Then fourthly, as I said before,
(But whist—for I must rhyme no more)
If I be guilty of plagerism, it is only where I am unable to distinguish between the imagination and memory.

References

ARCHIVAL MATERIAL

Public Record Office of Northern Ireland

D562/5577. 1796. "An account of the number of wheels claimed in the year 1796 throughout the several counties in this kingdom, with the sums issued to the Inspectors General on account of payment thereof."

D562/1577. 1763. "Petition from London Merchants."

T2812/19/1. 1752–1773. "A Survey of the economic development of County Sligo in the eighteenth century, by Charles O'Hara of Nymphfield (the elder)."

National Archives of Ireland

CEN 1821/1–15. Shelf Numbers 2/436/4–7. Copies of 1821 census enumerators' schedules, County Cavan, various parishes.

National Library of Ireland

Mss. 353–76. Abstracts of Irish exports and imports in 24 vols. For the period 1764–1823.

BRITISH PARLIAMENTARY PAPERS

H.C. 1824. Vol. 21. Abstract of answers and returns, pursuant to act 55 Geo. 3, for taking an account of the population of Ireland in 1821.

H.C. 1825. Vol. 5. Report from the Select Committee on the Linen Trade of Ireland.

H.C. 1833. Vol. 39. Abstract of the Population Returns, 1831.

H.C. 1836. Vol. 31. Poor Inquiry, Ireland, Appendix D. Containing Baronial Examinations Relative to the Earnings of Labourers, Cottier Tenants, Employment of Women and Children, Expenditure.

H.C. 1840. Vol. 23. Handloom Weavers II. Part III. Reports from Assistant Hand-Loom Weavers Commissioners (West Riding and Ireland).

H.C. 1843. Vol. 24. Report of the Commissioners Appointed to Take the Census of Ireland, for the Year 1841. (Reprinted in 1968, Irish University Press Series of British Parliamentary Papers. Population 2. Shannon: Ireland).

PRINTED SOURCES

Besnard, Peter B. 1816. *Minutes of the Trustees, Containing the Report of a Tour of Inspection through the Provinces of Leinster, Munster, and Connaught, by Mr. B. P. Besnard*. Dublin: The Linen Board.

Coote, Sir Charles. 1804. *A Statistical Survey of the County of Armagh*. Dublin: Dublin Society.

———. 1802. *A Statistical Survey of the County of Cavan*. Dublin: Dublin Society.

Corry, James. 1816. *Minutes of the Trustees, Containing Reports of Their Secretary on a Tour of Inspection through the Province of Ulster*. Dublin: Linen Board.

County of Cavan. 1796. *A List of Persons to Whom Premiums for Wowing Flaxseed in the Year 1796 Have Been Adjudged by the Trustees of the Linen Manufacture*. Dublin: Linen Board.

Crommelin, Louis. 1705. *An Essay towards the Improving of the Hempen and Flaxen Manufactures in the Kingdom of Ireland*. Dublin: Andrew Crook.

Day, Angelique, and Patrick McWilliams, eds. 1990. *Ordnance Survey Memoirs of Ireland, Volume 4. Parishes of County Fermanagh 1, 1834–5. Enniskillen and Upper Lough Erne*. Belfast: Institute of Irish Studies.

———. 1990. *Ordnance Survey Memoirs of Ireland, Volume 5. Parishes of County Tyrone 1. 1821, 1823, 1831–36. North, West, and South Tyrone*. Belfast: Institute of Irish Studies.

———. 1991. *Ordnance Survey Memoirs of Ireland, Volume 11. Parishes of County Londonderry III, 1831–5. Roe Valley Lower*. Belfast: Institute of Irish Studies.

———. 1992. *Ordnance Survey Memoirs of Ireland, Volume 12. Parishes of County Down III, 1833–8. Mid–Down*. Belfast: Institute of Irish Studies.

———. 1998. *Ordnance Survey Memoirs of Ireland, Volume 40. Counties of South Ulster 1834–8. Cavan, Leitrim, Louth, Monaghan, and Sligo*. Belfast: Institute of Irish Studies.

Dubourdieu, John. 1812. *A Statistical Survey of the County of Antrim*. Dublin: Dublin Society.

———. 1802. *A Statistical Survey of the County of Down*. Dublin: Dublin Society, 1802.

Gamble, John. 1813. *A View of Society and Manners in the North of Ireland*. London: Cradock and Joy.

General Valuation of Ireland, County of Cavan. 1841. Newry: James Henderson, 1841.

Hall, Richard. 1724. *Observations Made by Richard Hall, of the City of Dublin, Hemp and Flax Dresser, on the Methods Used in Holland, in Cultivating or Raising of Hemp and Flax. And Likewise, his Remarks on Mr. Slator's Book.* Dublin: George Grierson.

Leech, Sarah. 1828. *Poems on Various Subjects*. Dublin: J. Charles.

Merchant, S. (C). 1790. *Informations to the People of Ireland Concerning the Linen Trade of Spain, Portugal, and the Spanish West Indies. Published with the Allowance and at the Expence of the Linen Board*. Dublin: Mat Williamson.

Ní Ógáin, Róis. 1921. *Duanaire Gaedhilge*. Baile Átha Cliath: Comhlucht Oideachais na h-Éireann.

Orr, James. [1804, 1819] 1935. *Poems on Various Subjects by James Orr of Ballycarry, With a Sketch of His Life*. Belfast: Wm. Mullan and Son.

Porter, Hugh. 1813. *Poetical Attempts by Hugh Porter, A County of Down Weaver*. Belfast: Archbold and Dugan.

Privat, [Monsieur], John Sloan, and Company. 1778. *A Short Treatise upon Improvements made in the Linen Manufacture of Ireland*. Carlow: William Kinnier.

Sinclair, Sir John. 1831. *Analysis of the Statistical Account of Scotland*. Edinburgh: William Tait.

Slator, Lionel. 1724. *Instructions for the Cultivating and Raising of Flax and Hemp in a Better Manner Than That Generally Practis'd in Ireland*. Dublin: George Grierson.

Stephenson, Robert. 1784. *Observations on the Present State of the Linen Trade of Ireland*. Dublin.

———. 1762. *The Reports and Observations of Robert Stephenson, Made to the Right Hon. and Hon. the Trustees of the Linen Manufacture, For the Years 1760 and 1761*. Dublin: Alex McCulloh.

———. 1754. *Considerations on the present state of the Linen Manufacture. Humbly addressed to the Trustees of the Linen Board, by Robert Stephenson, Linen Manufacturer*. Dublin.

Thompson, Robert. 1802. *A Statistical Survey of the County of Meath*. Dublin: The Dublin Society.

Wakefield, Edward. 1812. *An Account of Ireland, Statistical and Political*. 2 vols. London: Longnon, Rees, Orme and Browne.

Young, Arthur. 1892. *Arthur Young's Tour in Ireland (1776–1779)*, ed. Arthur W. Hutton. London: George Bell and Sons.

SECONDARY SOURCES

Abrams, Philip. 1980. "History, Sociology, Historical Sociology." *Past and Present* 37: 3–16.

Akenson, Donald H., and William H. Crawford. 1977. *Local Poets and Social History*. Belfast: Public Record Office of Northern Ireland.

Almquist, Eric L. 1979. "Pre-Famine Ireland and the Theory of European Proto-Industrialisation: Evidence from the 1841 Census." *Journal of Economic History* 39: 699–718.

——. 1977. "Mayo and Beyond: Land, Domestic Industry, and Rural Transformation in the Irish West." Ph.D. Dissertation, Boston University, Boston, MA.

Amenta, Edwin, and Jane D. Poulsen. 1994. "Where to Begin: A Survey of Five Approaches to Selecting Independent Variables for Qualitative Comparative Analysis." *Sociological Methods and Research* 23: 22–53.

Avdela, Efi. 1999. "Work, 'Gender & History' in the 1990s and Beyond." *Gender & History* 11: 528–41.

Barker, Walter S. 1917. "Flax: The Fiber and Seed: A Study in Agricultural Contrasts." *The Quarterly Journal of Economics* 31: 500–29.

Becker, Gary. 1981. *A Treatise on the Family*. Cambridge, Mass.: Harvard University Press.

Berg, Maxine. 1994. *The Age of Manufacturers, 1700–1820*. Revised ed. London: Routledge.

Bielenberg, Andy. 1991. *Cork's Industrial Revolution, 1780–1880: Development or Decline?* Cork: Cork University Press.

Biernacki, Richard. 1997. "Work and Culture in the Reception of Class Ideologies." Pp. 169–92 in *Reworking Class,* edited by John R. Hall. Ithaca, N.Y.: Cornell University Press.

Boyle, Emily. 1997. "Vertical Integration and Deintegration in the Irish Linen Industry, 1830–1913." Pp. 211–28 in *The Warp of Ulster's Past: Interdisciplinary Perspectives on the Irish Linen Industry, 1700–1920,* edited by Marilyn Cohen. New York: St. Martin's Press.

Brenner, Robert. 1977. "The Origins of Capitalist Development: A Critique of Neo-Smithian Marxism." *New Left Review* 104: 25–92.

Brown, Judith. 1970. "A Note on the Division of Labor." *American Ethnologist* 72: 1,073–78.

Chase-Dunn, Christopher. 1989. *Global Formation: Structures of the World Economy*. London: Basil Blackwell.

Clark, Anna. 1995. *The Struggle for the Breeches. Gender and the Making of the English Working Class*. London: Rivers Oram Press.

Clark, Samuel. 1979. *Social Origins of the Irish Land War*. Princeton, N.J.: Princeton University Press.

Clarkson, Leslie A. 1996. "Ireland 1841: Pre-Industrial or Proto-Industrial; Industrializing or De-Industrializing?" Pp. 67–84 in *European Proto-Industrialization*, edited by Sheilagh C. Ogilvie and Markus Cerman. Cambridge: Cambridge University Press.

——. 1989. "The Environment and Dynamic of Pre-Factory Industry in Northern Ireland." Pp. 252–70 in *Regions and Industries: A Perspective on the Industrial Revolution in Britain*, edited by Pat Hudson. Cambridge: Cambridge University Press.

Cohen, Marilyn. 2003. "The Dynamics of Capitalism in the Irish Linen Industry: A 'Space-Time Structuration' Analysis." *Journal of Historical Sociology*. 16: 432–59.

——. 1997a. *Linen, Family and Community in Tullylish, County Down 1690–1914*. Dublin: Four Courts Press.

——. 1997b. "Introduction." Pp. 1–36 in *The Warp of Ulster's Past: Interdisciplinary Perspectives on the Irish Linen Industry, 1700–1920*, edited by Marilyn Cohen. New York: St. Martin's Press.

——. 1990. "Peasant Differentiation and Proto-Industrialisation in the Ulster Countryside: Tullylish 1690–1825." *Journal of Peasant Studies* 17: 413–32.

Cohen, Marilyn and Nancy J. Curtin. 1999. "Introduction: Reclaiming Gender: An Agenda for Irish Studies." Pp. 1–12 in *Reclaiming Gender: Transgressive Identities in Modern Ireland*, edited by Marilyn Cohen and Nancy J. Curtin. New York: St. Martin's Press.

Coleman, D.C. 1983. "Proto-Industrialization: A Concept Too Many." *Economic History Review* 36: 435–48.

Collins, Brenda. 1997. "The Loom, the Land, and the Marketplace: Women Weavers and the Family Economy in Late Nineteenth- and Early Twentieth-Century Ireland." Pp. 229–52 in *The Warp of Ulster's Past: Interdisciplinary Perspectives on the Irish Linen Industry, 1700–1920*, edited by Marilyn Cohen. New York: St. Martin's Press.

——. 1988. "Sewing and Social Structure: The Flowerers of Scotland and Ireland." Pp. 242–54 in *Economy and Society in Scotland and Ireland 1500–1939*, edited by Rosalind Mitchison and Peter Roebuck. Edinburgh: John Donald Publishers.

——. 1982. "Proto-Industrialization and Pre-Famine Emigration." *Social History* 7: 127–46.

——. 1979. "Aspects of Irish Immigration Into Scottish Towns (Dundee and Paisley) During the Mid-Nineteenth Century." M.Phil Thesis, University of Edinburgh.

Connell, Kenneth H. 1950. *The Population of Ireland, 1750–1845*. Clarendon: Oxford University Press.

Connolly, Sean J., ed. 1998. *The Oxford Companion to Irish History*. Oxford: Oxford University Press.

——. 1992. *Religion, Law and Power: the Making of Protestant Ireland, 1660–1760*. Oxford: Clarendon Press.

——. 1985. "Marriage in Pre-Famine Ireland." Pp. 78–98 in Art Cosgrove, ed. *Marriage in Ireland*. Dublin: College Press.

——. 1983. "Religion, Work-Discipline and Economic Attitudes: The Case of Ireland." Pp. 235–45 in *Ireland and Scotland 1600–1850*, edited by T. M. Devine and David Dickson. Edinburgh: John Donald Publishers.

Coverdill, James E., William Finlay, and Jack K. Martin. 1994. "Labor Management in the Southern Textile Industry: Comparing Qualitative, Quantitative and Qualitative Comparative Analyses." *Sociological Methods and Research* 23: 54–85.

Crawford, William H. 1994. *The Handloom Weavers and the Ulster Linen Industry*. Belfast: Ulster Historical Foundation. (First published 1972 as *Domestic Industry in Ireland: The Experience of the Linen Industry*. Dublin: Gill and Macmillan).

——. 1991. "Women in the Domestic Linen Industry." Pp. 256–64 in *Women in Early Modern Ireland*, edited by Margaret McCurtin and Mary O'Dowd. Dublin: Wolfhound Press.

——. 1988. "The Evolution of the Linen Trade in Ulster before Industrialization." *Irish Economic and Social History* 15: 32–53.

——. 1983. "Ulster as a Mirror of the Two Societies." Pp. 60–69 in *Ireland and Scotland 1600–1850*, edited by T. M. Devine and David Dickson. Edinburgh: John Donald Publishers.

——. 1982. "Economy and Society in Eighteenth Century Ulster." Ph.D. Thesis, Queen's University, Belfast.

——. 1976. "The Influence of the Landlord in Eighteenth-Century Ulster." Pp. 193–203 in *Comparative Aspects of Scottish and Irish Economic and Social History 1600–1900*, edited by Louis M. Cullen and T. C. Smout. Edinburgh: John Donald Publishers.

——. 1975. "Economy and Society in South Ulster in the Eighteenth Century." *Clogher Record* 8: 241–58.

——. 1971. "Ulster Landowners and the Linen Industry." Pp. 117–44 in *Land and Industry: The Landed Estate and The Industrial Revolution*, edited by John T. Ward and Richard G. Wilson. Newton Abbot: David and Charles.

Cullen, Louis M. 1972. *An Economic History of Ireland Since 1660*. London: B.T. Batsford Ltd.

——. 1968. *Anglo-Irish Trade 1660–1800*. New York: Augustus M. Kelley.

Cullen, Louis M., T. C. Smout, and A. Gibson. 1988. "Wages and Comparative Development in Ireland and Scotland, 1565–1780." Pp. 105–16 in *Economy and Society in Scotland and Ireland, 1500–1939,* edited by Rosalind Mitchison and Peter Roebuck Edinburgh: John Donald.

Cunningham, Terence P. 1960. "Notes on the 1821 Census of Lavey Parish." *Breifne: Journal of Cumann Seanchais Bhreifne* (Breifne Historical Society) 1: 192–208.

Daly, Mary E. 1997. *Women and Work in Ireland*. Vol. 7. *Studies in Irish Economic and Social History*, edited by Peter Roebuck and David Dickson. Dublin: Economic and Social History Society of Ireland.

De Jongh, Guy. 1999. "New Estimates of Land Productivity in Belgium, 1750–1850." *Agricultural History Review* 47: 7–28.

Davis, Natalie Zemon. 1983. *The Return of Martin Guerre*. Cambridge, Mass.: Harvard University Press.

Davis, Ralph. 1969. "English Foreign Trade 1700–1774." Pp. 99–120 in *The Growth of English Overseas Trade in the Seventeenth and Eighteenth Centuries*, edited by Walter E. Minchinton. London: Methuen and Co.

Deere, Carmen Diana. 1979. "Rural Women's Subsistence Production in the Capitalist Periphery. Pp. 133–48 in *Peasants and Proletarians: The Struggles of Third World Workers*, edited by R. Cohen, P. Gutkind, and P. Brazier. New York: Monthly Review Press.

Daultrey, Stuart, David Dickson, and Cormac Ó'Gráda. 1981. "Eighteenth-Century Irish Population: New Perspectives from Old Sources." *Journal of Economic History* 41: 601–28.

Devine, T. M. 1983. "The English Connection and Irish and Scottish Development in the Eighteenth Century." Pp. 12–29 in *Ireland and Scotland, 1600–1850: Parallels and Contrasts in Economic and Social Development*, edited by T.M. Devine and David Dickson. Edinburgh: John Donald Publishers.

De Vries, Jan. 1993. "Between Purchasing Power and the World of Goods: Understanding the Household Economy in Early Modern Europe." Pp. 85–132 in *Consumption and the World of Goods*, edited by John Brewer and Roy Porter. London: Routledge.

Dickson, David, Cormac Ó'Gráda, and Stuart Daultrey. 1982. "Hearth Tax, Household Size and Irish Population Change, 1672–1821." *Proceedings of the Royal Irish Academy* 82: 125–81.

Donnelly, James S. 1975. *The Land and the People of Nineteenth Century Cork: The Rural Economy and the Land Question*. London: Routledge and Kegan Paul.

Donnelly, Michael. 1997. "Statistical Classifications and the Salience of Social Class." Pp. 107–32 in *Reworking Class*, edited by John R. Hall. Ithaca, N.Y.: Cornell University Press.

Duffy, Patrick J. 1995. "Perspectives on the Making of the Cavan Landscape." Pp. 14–36 in *Cavan: Essays on the History of an Irish County*, edited by Raymond Gillespie. Dublin: Irish Academic Press.

Dunaway, Wilma. 2001. "The Double Register of History: Situating the Forgotten Woman and Her Household in Capitalist Commodity Chains." *Journal of World-Systems Research* 7: 2–31. csf.colorado.edu/jwsr/ (accessed June 11, 2004).

Duncan, Simon. 1996. "The Diverse Worlds of European Patriarchy." Pp. 74–110 in *Women of the European Union: the Politics of Work and Family Life*, edited by M. D. Garcia Ramon and J. Mond. London: Routledge.

Durie, Alastair, and Peter Solar. 1988. "The Scottish and Irish Linen Industries Compared, 1780–1860." Pp. 211–21 in *Economy and Society in Scotland and Ireland 1500–1939*, edited by Rosalind Mitchison and Peter Roebuck. Edinburgh: John Donald Publishers Ltd.

Durie, Alastair. 1979. *The Scottish Linen Industry in the Eighteenth Century*. Edinburgh: John Donald Publishers.

Emigh, Rebecca Jean. 2001. "Theorizing Strategies. Households and Markets in 15th-century Tuscany." *History of the Family* 6: 495–517.

Endrei, Walter, and Rachel P. Maines. 1995. "On Two Handed Spinning." Pp. 31–41 in *European Women and Preindustrial Craft*, edited by Daryl M. Hafter. Bloomington: Indiana University Press.

Fertig, Georg. 2003. "The Invisible Chain: Niche Inheritance and Unequal Social Reproduction in Preindustrial Continental Europe." *History of the Family* 8: 7–19.

Fitzpatrick, David. 1985. "Marriage in Post-Famine Ireland." Pp. 116–31 in *Marriage in Ireland*, edited by Art Cosgrove. Dublin: College Press.

Fontaine, Laurence, and Jurgen Schlumbohm. 2000. "Household Strategies for Survival: An Introduction." Pp. 1–18 in *Household Strategies for Survival 1600–2000: Fission, Faction and Cooperation*. Supplement 8. *International Review of Social History*, edited by L. Fontaine and Jurgen Schlumbohm. Cambridge: Internationaal Instituut voor Sociale Geschiedenis, Amsterdam.

Frader, Laura L., and Sonya O. Rose. 1996. "Introduction: Gender and the Reconstruction of European Working-Class History." Pp. 1–36 in *Gender and Class in*

Modern Europe, edited by Laura L. Frader and Sonya O. Rose. Ithaca, N.Y.: Cornell University Press.

Frank, Andre Gunder. 1998. *ReOrient: Global Economy in the Asian Age*. Berkeley: University of California Press.

———. 1966. "The Development of Underdevelopment." *Monthly Review* 18: 17–31.

Geary, Frank. 1998. "De-Industrialization in Ireland to 1851: Some Evidence from the Census." *Economic History Review* 51: 412–541.

———. 1989. "The Belfast Cotton Industry Revisited." *Irish Historical Studies* 26: 250–67.

———. 1981. "The Rise and Fall of the Belfast Cotton Industry: Some Problems." *Irish Economic and Social History*, 8: 30–49.

Gibbons, Luke. 1996. "Coming out of Hibernation: The Myth of Modernization in Irish Culture." Pp. 82–94 in *Transformations in Irish Culture*. Cork: Cork University Press.

Gibson, A. J. S., and T. C. Smout. 1995. *Prices, Food and Wages in Scotland 1550–1780*. Cambridge: Cambridge University Press.

Gill, Conrad. 1925. *The Rise of the Irish Linen Industry*. Oxford: Oxford University Press.

Goldstone, Jack A. 1996. "Gender, Work, and Culture: Why the Industrial Revolution Came Early to England But Late to China." *Sociological Perspectives* 39: 1–21.

Gray, Jane. 2003. "The Irish, Scottish and Flemish Linen Industries During the Long Eighteenth Century." Pp. 159–86 in *The European Linen Industry in Historical Perspective*. Vol. 13. *Pasold Studies in Textile History*, edited by Brenda Collins and Philip Ollerenshaw. Oxford: Oxford University Press.

———. 1999. "Spinners and Spinning in the Political Economy of Pre-Famine Ireland: Evidence from County Cavan." Pp. 161–84 in *Reclaiming Gender: Transgressive Identities in Modern Ireland*, edited by Marilyn Cohen and Nancy J. Curtin. New York: St. Martin's Press.

———. 1997. "The Irish and Scottish Linen Industries in the Eighteenth Century: An Incorporated Comparison." Pp. 37–70 in *The Warp of Ulster's Past: Interdisciplinary Perspectives on the Irish Linen Industry, 1700–1920*, edited by Marilyn Cohen. New York: St. Martin's Press.

———. 1993a. "Rural Industry and Uneven Development: The Significance of Gender in the Irish Linen Industry." *Journal of Peasant Studies* 20: 590–611.

———. 1993b. "Gender and Plebian Culture in Ulster." *Journal of Interdisciplinary History* 24: 251–70.

———. 1993c. "Folk Poetry and Working Class Identity in Ulster: An Analysis of James Orr's 'The Penitent'." *Journal of Historical Sociology* 6: 249–75.

Green, E. R. R. 1949. *The Lagan Valley 1800–1850*. London: Faber and Faber Ltd.

Gribbon, Henry D. 1997. "The Irish Linen Board, 1711–1828." Pp. 71–92 in *The Warp of Ulster's Past: Interdisciplinary Perspectives on the Irish Linen Industry, 1700–1920*, edited by Marilyn Cohen. New York: St. Martin's Press.

———. "The Irish Linen Board, 1711–1828." Pp. 77–87 in *Comparative Aspects of Scottish and Irish Economic and Social History 1600–1900*, edited by Louis M. Cullen and T. C. Smout. Edinburgh: John Donald Publishers.

Guinnane, Timothy. 1997. *The Vanishing Irish: Households, Migration and the Rural Economy in Ireland, 1850–1914*. Princeton: Princeton University Press.

Gullickson, Gay L. 1986. *Spinners and Weavers of Auffay*. Cambridge: Cambridge University Press.

———. 1983. "Agriculture and Cottage Industry: Redefining the Causes of Proto-Industrialization." *Journal of Economic History* 43: 831–50.

Hall, John R. 1997. "The Reworking of Class Analysis." Pp. 1–40 in *Reworking Class*, edited by John R. Hall. Ithaca, N.Y.: Cornell University Press.

Hareven, Tamara. 1991. "The History of the Family and the Complexity of Social Change." *American Historical Review* 96: 95–124.

Harrison, Mark. 1982. "Chayanov's Theory of Peasant Economy." Pp. 246–57 in *Rural Development: Theories of Peasant Economy and Agrarian Change*, edited by John Harris. London: Hutchinson University Library.

Harte, Negley B. 1973. "The Rise of Protection and the English Linen Trade, 1690–1790." Pp. 74–112 in *Textile History and Economic History*, edited by Negley B. Harte and K. G. Ponting. Manchester: Manchester University Press.

Hempton, David, and Myrtle Hill. 1992. *Evangelical Protestantism in Ulster Society, 1780–1890*. London: Routledge.

Hendrickx, Francois M. M. 2003. "Family, Farm and Factory: Labor and the Family in the Transition from Protoindustry to Factory Industry in 19th-century Twente, the Netherlands." *History of the Family* 8: 45–69.

———. 1993. "From Weavers to Workers: Demographic Implications of an Economic Transformation in Twente (the Netherlands) in the Nineteenth Century." *Continuity and Change* 8: 321–55.

Hewitt, John. 1974. *Rhyming Weavers, and Other Country Poets of Antrim and Down*. Belfast: Blackstaff Press.

Hirdman, Yvonne. 1998. "State Policy and Gender Contracts: The Swedish Experience." Pp. 36–46 in *Women, Work and the Family in Europe*, edited by Eileen Drew, Ruth Emerek, and Evelyn Mahon. London: Routledge.

Honeyman, Katrina. 2000. *Women, Gender and Industrialisation in England, 1700–1870*. Houndmills, Basingstoke: Macmillan.

Hood, Adrienne D. 2003. "Flax Seed, Fibre and Cloth: Pennsylvania's Domestic Linen Manufacture and Its Irish Connections, 1700–1830." Pp. 139–58 in *The European Linen Industry in Historical Perspective*. Vol. 13. *Pasold Studies in Textile History*, edited by Brenda Collins and Philip Ollerenshaw. Oxford: Oxford University Press.

Hudson, Pat. 1996. "Proto-Industrialization in England." Pp. 23–37 in *European Proto-Industrialization*, edited by Sheilagh C. Ogilvie and Markus Cerman. Cambridge: Cambridge University Press.

———. 1989. "The Regional Perspective." Pp. 5–38 in *Regions and Industries: A Perspective on the Industrial Revolution in Britain*, edited by Pat Hudson. Cambridge: Cambridge University Press.

———. 1981. "Proto-Industrialization: The Case of the West-Riding Wool Textile Industry in the 18th and Early 19th Centuries." *History Workshop Journal* 12: 34–61.

Hudson, Pat, and Steve King. 2000. "Two Textile Townships, c. 1660–1820: A Comparative Demographic Analysis." *Economic History Review* 53, 4: 706–41.

Hufton, Olwen. 1975. "Women and the Family Economy in Eighteenth Century France." *French Historical Studies* 9: 1–23.

Johnson, Richard. 1979. "Culture and the Historians." Pp. 41–72 in *Working Class Culture: Studies in History and Theory*, edited by J. Clarke, C. Critcher, and R. Johnson. London: Hutchinson.

Jones, Eric L. 1968. "Agricultural Origins of Industry." *Past and Present* 40: 58–71.

Kalb, Don. 1997. *Expanding Class: Power and Everyday Politics in Industrial Communities, The Netherlands, 1850–1950*. Durham, N.C.: Duke University Press.

Kennedy, Liam. 1985. "The Rural Economy 1820–1914." Pp. 1–61 in *An Economic History of Ulster 1820–1939*, edited by Liam Kennedy and Philip Ollerenshaw. Manchester: Manchester University Press.

Kennedy, Liam, and Martin W. Dowling. 1997. "Prices and Wages in Ireland, 1700–1850." *Irish Economic and Social History* 24: 62–104.

King, Steven A. 2003. "The English Protoindustrial Family: Old and New Perspectives." *History of the Family* 8: 21–43.

Klasen, Stephan. 1998. "Marriage, Bargaining, and Intrahousehold Resource Allocation: Excess Female Mortality among Adults during Early German Development, 1740–1860." *Journal of Economic History* 58: 432–67.

Knotter, Ad. 1994. "Problems of the Family Economy: Peasant Economy, Domestic Production and Labour Markets in Pre-Industrial Europe." *Economic and Social History in the Netherlands* 7: 19–59.

Koditschek, Theodore. 1997. "The Gendering of the British Working Class." *Gender and History* 9: 333–63.

Kriedte, Peter. 1981a. "The Origins, the Agrarian Context, and the Conditions in the World Market." Pp. 12–37 in *Industrialization Before Industrialization: Rural Industry in the Genesis of Capitalism* by Peter Kriedte, Hans Medick, and Jurgen Schlumbohm. Translated by Beate Schempp. Cambridge: Cambridge University Press.

———. 1981b. "Proto-Industrialization between Industrialization and De-Industrialization." Pp. 135–60 in *Industrialization before Industrialization: Rural Industry in the Genesis of Capitalism* by Peter Kriedte, Hans Medick, and Jurgen Schlumbohm. Translated by Beate Schempp. Cambridge: Cambridge University Press.

Kriedte, Peter, Hans Medick, and Jurgen Schlumbohm. 1993. "Proto-Industrialization Revisited: Demography, Social Structure, and Modern Domestic Industry." *Continuity and Change* 8: 217–52.

———. 1981. *Industrialization before Industrialization: Rural Industry in the Genesis of Capitalism*. Translated by Beate Schempp. Cambridge: Cambridge University Press.

Kynaston, Chris. 1996. "The Everyday Exploitation of Women: Housework and the Patriarchal Mode of Production." *Women's Studies International Forum* 19: 221–37.

Lehners, Jean-Paul. 2003. "Introduction. Part 1: Proto-Industrialization, Industrialization, and Family Change." *History of the Family* 8, 1: 3–6.

Leister, Ingeborg. 1962. "Landwirtschaft und agrarraumliche Gliederung Irlands zur Zeit A. Young's." *Zeitschrift fur Agrargeschichte und Agrarsoziologie*, 10: 9–44.

Levine, David. 1977. *Family Formation in an Age of Nascent Capitalism*. New York: Academic Press.

——. 1976. "The Demographic Implications of Rural Industrialization: A Family Reconstitution Study of Shepshed, Leicestershire, 1851." *Social History* 1: 177–96.

Lis, Catharina, and Hugo Soly. 1997. "Different Paths of Development: Capitalism in the Northern and Southern Netherlands during the Late Middle Ages and the Early Modern Period." *Review: Journal of the Fernand Braudel Center* 20: 211–22.

Liu, Tessie. 1994. *The Weaver's Knot: The Contradictions of Class Struggle and Family Solidarity in Western France, 1750–1914*. Ithaca, N.Y.: Cornell University Press.

Lynch, Patrick, and John Vaizey. 1960. *Guinness's Brewery in the Irish Economy 1759–1876*. Cambridge: Cambridge University Press.

Lysaght, Patricia. 1987. "'When I makes Tea, I makes Tea…': Innovation in Food: The Case of Tea in Ireland." *Ulster Folklife* 33: 44–71.

McCourt, D. 1981. "The Decline of Rundale, 1750–1850." Pp. 119–39 in *Plantation to Partition: Essays in Ulster History in Honour of J. L. McCracken*, edited by Peter Roebuck. Belfast: Blackstaff Press.

McGregor, Pat. 1992. "The Labor Market and the Distribution of Landholdings in Pre-Famine Ireland." *Explorations in Economic History* 29: 477–93.

McKernan, Anne. 1997. "Contested Terrain: The Making of a Market Culture in Ulster Linens." Pp. 93–110 in *The Warp of Ulster's Past: Interdisciplinary Perspectives on the Irish Linen Industry, 1700–1920*, edited by Marilyn Cohen. New York: St. Martin's Press.

——. 1995. "War, Gender and Industrial Innovation: Recruiting Women Weavers in Early Nineteenth Century Ireland." *Journal of Social History* 28: 109–24.

——. 1990. "The Dynamics of the Linen Triangle: Factor, Family and Farm in Ulster, 1740–1825." Ph.D. Dissertation, University of Michigan.

McMichael, Philip. 1990. "Incorporating Comparison within a World-Historical Perspective: An Alternative Comparative Method." *American Sociological Review* 55: 385–97.

Mager, Wolfgang. 1993. "Proto-Industrialisation and Proto-Industry: The Uses and Drawbacks of Two Concepts." *Continuity and Change* 8: 181–216.

Mastboom, Joyce. 1996. "Protoindustrialization and Agriculture in the Eastern Netherlands." *Social Science History* 20: 235–58.

Maynes, Mary Jo. 2004. "Gender, Labor and Globalization in Historical Perspective. European Spinsters in the International Textile Industry, 1750–1900." *Journal of Women's History* 15:47–66.

Medick, Hans. 1984. "Village Spinning Bees: Sexual Culture and Free Time among Rural Youth in Early Modern Germany." Pp. 317–39 in *Interest and Emotion: Essays on the Study of Family and Kinship*, edited by Hans Medick and David Sabean. Cambridge: Cambridge University Press.

——. 1981a. "The Proto-Industrial Family Economy." Pp. 38–73 in *Industrialization before Industrialization: Rural Industry in the Genesis of Capitalism* by Peter

Kriedte, Hans Medick, and Jurgen Schlumbohm. Translated by Beate Schempp. Cambridge: Cambridge University Press.

——. 1981b. "The Structures and Function of Population-Development under the Proto-Industrial System." Pp. 74–93 in *Industrialization before Industrialization: Rural Industry in the Genesis of Capitalism* by Peter Kriedte, Hans Medick, and Jurgen Schlumbohm. Translated by Beate Schempp. Cambridge: Cambridge University Press.

——. 1981c. "The Transition from Feudalism to Capitalism: Renewal of the Debate." Pp. 120–29 in *People's History and Socialist Theory*, edited by Raphael Samuel. London: Routledge and Kegan Paul.

——. 1976. "The Proto-Industrial Family Economy: The Structural Functions of Household and Family during the Transition from Peasant Society to Industrial Capitalism." *Social History* 3: 291–315.

Mendels, Franklin. 1981. *Industrialization and Population Pressure in Eighteenth-Century Flanders. Dissertations in European Economic History*. Originally presented as the author's thesis, University of Wisconsin, Madison, Wisconsin, 1969. New York: Arno Press.

——. 1972. "Proto-Industrialization: The First Phase of the Industrialization Process." *Journal of Economic History* 32: 241–62.

Mies, Maria. 1982. *The Lacemakers of Narsapur: Indian Housewives Produce for the World Market*. London: Zed Press.

Miles, Ian, John Irvine, and Jeff Evans. 1979. *Demystifying Social Statistics*. London: Pluto.

Miller, David W. 1983. "The Armagh Troubles 1784–95." Pp. 155–91 in *Irish Peasants: Violence and Political Unrest 1780–1914*, edited by Samuel Clark and James S. Donnelly. Madison: University of Wisconsin Press.

Mintz, Sidney. 1985. *Sweetness and Power: The Place of Sugar in Modern History*. New York: Penguin.

——. 1978. "Was the Plantation Slave a Proletarian?" *Review-Journal of the Fernand Braudel Center* 2: 81–98.

Misra, Joya. 2000. "Gender and the World-System: Engaging the Feminist Literature on Development." Pp. 105–27 in *A World-Systems Reader: New Perspectives on Gender, Urbanism, Cultures, Indigenous Peoples, and Ecology*, edited by Thomas D. Hall. Lanham, MD: Rowman and Littlefield.

Moch, Leslie Page. 1987. "Historians and Family Strategies." *Historical Methods* 20: 113–15.

Moen, Phyllis, and Elaine Wethington. 1992. "The Concept of Family Adaptive Strategies." *Annual Review of Sociology* 18: 233–51.

Mokyr, Joel. 1993. "Editor's Introduction." Pp. 1–131 in *The British Industrial Revolution: An Economic Perspective*, edited by Joel Mokyr. Boulder, Colo.: Westview Press.

——. 1991. "Dear Labor, Cheap Labor, and the Industrial Revolution." Pp. 177–200 in *Favorites of Fortune: Technology, Growth and Economic Development since the Industrial Revolution*, edited by Patrice Higonnet, David S. Landes, and Henry Rosovsky. Cambridge, Mass.: Harvard University Press.

——. 1985. *Why Ireland Starved: A Quantitative and Analytical History of the Irish Economy, 1800–1850*. London: Allen and Unwin.

——. 1980. "Industrialization and Poverty in Ireland and the Netherlands." *Journal of Interdisciplinary History* 10: 429–58.

——. 1976. *Industrialization in the Low Countries, 1795–1850*. New Haven, Conn.: Yale University Press.

Monaghan, J. J. 1942. "The Rise and Fall of the Belfast Cotton Industry." *Irish Historical Studies* 3: 1–17.

Morgan, Valerie. 1971. "Agricultural Wage Rates in late Eighteenth-Century Scotland." *Economic History Review*, 24: 181–201.

Morgan, Valerie, and William Macafee. 1984. "Irish Population in the Pre-Famine Period: Evidence from County Antrim." *Economic History Review* 37: 182–96.

Murdock, George P., and Caterina Provost. 1973. "Factors in the Division of Labor by Sex." *Ethnology* 12: 203–25.

Murray, Alice. [1903] 1970. *A History of the Commercial and Financial Relations between England and Ireland from the Period of the Restoration*. Freeport, N.Y.: Books for Libraries Press.

Nash, R. C. 1985. "Irish Atlantic Trade in the Seventeenth and Eighteenth Centuries." *William and Mary Quarterly*, Third series, 42: 329–56.

Ní Ógáin, Róis. 1921. *Duanaire Gaedhilge*. Baile Átha Cliath: Comhlucht Oideachais na h-Éireann.

Ó'Cadhla, Stíofán. 1999. "Mapping a Discourse: Irish Gnosis and the Ordnance Survey 1824–1841." *Irish Journal of Anthropology* 4: 84–109.

Ó'Gráda, Cormac. 1994. *Ireland: A New Economic History, 1780–1939*. Oxford: Clarendon Press.

——. 1993. *Ireland Before and After the Famine: Explorations in Economic History*. Revised edition. Manchester: Manchester University Press.

——. 1989. "Poverty, Population and Agriculture." Pp. 108–36 in *A New History of Ireland, Volume 5. Ireland Under the Union, I, 1801–70*, edited by W. E. Vaughan. Oxford: Clarendon Press.

O'Hearn, Denis. 2001. *The Atlantic Economy: Britain, the U.S. and Ireland*. Manchester: Manchester University Press.

——. 1997. "Irish Linen: A Peripheral Industry." Pp. 161–90 in *The Warp of Ulster's Past: Interdisciplinary Perspectives on the Irish Linen Industry*, 1700–1920, edited by Marilyn Cohen. New York: St. Martin's Press.

——. 1994. "Innovation and the World-System Hierarchy: British Subjugation of the Irish Cotton Industry, 1780–1830." *American Journal of Sociology* 100: 587–621.

O'Malley, Eoin. 1989. *Industry and Economic Development: The Challenge for the Latecomer*. Dublin: Gill and Macmillan.

O'Neill, Kevin. 1984. *Family and Farm in Pre-Famine Ireland: The Parish of Killashandra*. Madison: University of Wisconsin Press.

Ogilvie, Sheilagh. 2004. "How Does Social Capital Affect Women?: Guilds and Communities in Early Modern Germany." *American Historical Review* 109: 325–59.

——. 2003. *A Bitter Living: Women, Markets, and Social Capital in Early Modern Germany*. Oxford: Oxford University Press.

——. 1997. *State Corporatism and Proto-Industry: The Wurttemberg Black Forest, 1580–1797*. Cambridge: Cambridge University Press.

——. 1996. "Social Institutions and Proto-Industrialization." Pp. 23–37 in *European Proto-Industrialization*, edited by Sheilagh C. Ogilvie and Markus Cerman. Cambridge: Cambridge University Press.

Ogilvie, Sheilagh C., and Markus Cerman, eds. 1996. *European Proto-Industrialization*. Cambridge: Cambridge University Press.

——. 1996a. "The Theories of Proto-Industrialization." Pp. 1–11 in *European Proto-Industrialization*, edited by Sheilagh C. Ogilvie and Markus Cerman. Cambridge: Cambridge University Press.

——. 1996b. "Proto-Industrialization, Economic Development and Social Change in Early Modern Europe." Pp. 227–39 in *European Proto-Industrialization*, edited by Sheilagh C. Ogilvie and Markus Cerman. Cambridge: Cambridge University Press.

Oxley, Deborah. 2004. "Living Standards of Women in Prefamine Ireland." *Social Science History* 28: 271–95.

Patriarca, Silvana. 1994. "Statistical Nation Building and the Consolidation of Regions in Italy." *Social Science History* 18: 359–76.

Peet, Richard. 1991. *Global Capitalism: Theories of Societal Development*. London: Routledge.

Perlin, Frank. 1983. "Proto-Industrialization and Pre-Colonial South Asia." *Past and Present* 98: 30–95.

Pfister, Ulrich. 1996. "A General Model of Proto-Industrial Growth." Pp. 73–92 in *Proto-Industrialization: Recent Research and New Perspectives in Memory of Franklin Mendels*, edited by Rene Leboutte. Geneve: Librairie Droz.

——. 1992. "The Protoindustrial Household Economy: Toward a Formal Analysis." Pp. 114–45 in *The European Peasant Family and Society: Historical Studies*, edited by Richard L. Rudolph. Liverpool: Liverpool University Press.

Ragin, Charles. 1994. *Constructing Social Research*. Thousand Oaks, Calif.: Pine Forge Press.

——. 1987. *The Comparative Method: Moving Beyond Qualitative and Comparative Strategies*. Berkeley: University of California Press.

Reddy, William. 1984. *The Rise of Market Culture: The Textile Trade and French Society, 1750–1900*. Cambridge: Cambridge University Press.

Rose, Sonya. 1992. *Limited Livelihoods: Gender and Class in Nineteenth-Century England*. Berkeley: University of California Press.

Roseberry, William. 1989. *Anthropologies and Histories: Essays in Culture, History and Political Economy*. New Brunswick, N.J.: Rutgers University Press.

Sabel, Charles, and Jonathan Zeitlin. 1985. "Historical Alternatives to Mass Production: Politics, Markets and Technology in Nineteenth-Century Industrialization." *Past and Present* 108: 133–76.

Sanderson, Stephen K. 1995. *Social Transformations: A General Theory of Historical Development*. Cambridge, Mass.: Blackwell Publishers Ltd.

Scally, Robert. 1995. *The End of Hidden Ireland: Rebellion, Famine and Emigration*. Oxford: Oxford University Press.

Schellekens, Jona. 1993. "The Role of Marital Fertility in Irish Population History, 1750–1840." *Economic History Review* 46: 369–78.

Schlumbohm, Jurgen. 1996a. "Proto-Industrialization as a Research Strategy and a Historical Period: A Balance Sheet." Pp. 12–22 in *European Proto-Industrialization* edited by Sheilagh C. Ogilivie and Markus Cerman. Cambridge: Cambridge University Press.

——. 1996b. "Micro-History and the Macro-Models of the European Demographic System in Pre-Industrial Times: Life-Course Patterns in the Parish of Belm (Northwest Germany), Seventeenth to the Nineteenth Centuries." *History of the Family* 1: 81–95.

——. 1981. "Relations of Production, Productive Force, Crises in Proto-Industrialization." Pp. 94–125 in *Industrialization before Industrialization: Rural Industry in the Genesis of Capitalism* by Peter Kriedte, Hans Medick, and Jurgen Schlumbohm. Translated by Beate Schempp. Cambridge: Cambridge University Press.

Schneider, Jane. 1989. "Rumpelstiltskin's Bargain: Folklore and the Merchant Capitalist Intensification of Linen Manufacture in Early Modern Europe." Pp. 177–213 in *Cloth and Human Experience*, edited by Annette B. Weiner and Jane Schneider. Washington, D.C.: Smithsonian Institution Press.

Scott, Joan W. 1992. "Experience." Pp. 22–40 in *Feminists Theorize the Political*, edited by Judith Butler and Joan W. Scott. New York: Routledge.

——. 1988a. "Women in 'The Making of the English Working Class'." Pp. 68–92 in *Gender and the Politics of History*. New York: Columbia University Press.

——. 1988b "Gender: A Useful Category of Historical Analysis." Pp. 28–52 in *Gender and the Politics of History*. New York: Columbia University Press.

Seccombe, Wally. 1992. *A Millennium of Family Change: Feudalism to Capitalism in Northwestern Europe*. London: Verso.

Sen, Amartya K. 1990. "Gender and Cooperative Conflicts." Pp. 123–49 in *Persistent Inequalities: Women and World Development*, edited by Irene Tinker. New York: Oxford University Press.

Slater, Eamonn, and Terence McDonough. 1994. "Bulwark of Landlordism and Capitalism: The Dynamics of Feudalism in Nineteenth Century Ireland." *Research in Political Economy* 14: 63–118.

Slater, Eamonn. 1988. "Coexistence of Pre-Capitalist Modes of Production with Capitalist Production in Nineteenth Century Ireland." Ph.D. Dissertation, Trinity College, Dublin.

Smith, Joan, and Immanuel Wallerstein. 1992. *Creating and Transforming Households: The Constraints of the World-Economy*. New York: Cambridge University Press.

——. 1991. "Households as an Institution of the World-Economy." Pp. 225–42 in *Gender, Family and Economy: The Triple Overlap*, edited by Rae Lesser Blumberg. Newbury Park, Calif.: Sage Publications.

So, Alvin Y. 1990. *Social Change and Development: Modernization, Dependency and World-System Theories*. Newbury Park, Calif.: Sage Publications.

Solar, Peter. 1980 "The Irish Linen Trade, 1820–1852." *Textile History* 21: 57–85.

———. 1988. "A Belgian View of the Ulster Linen Industry in the 1840s." *Ulster Folklife* 34: 16–25.

Steinberg, Marc. 1991. "The Re-Making of the English Working Class?" *Theory and Society* 20: 173–97.

Thirsk, Joan. 1961. "Industry in the Countryside." Pp. 70–88 in *Essays in the Economic and Social History of Tudor and Stuart England*, edited by F. J. Fischer. Cambridge: Cambridge University Press.

Thompson, Edward Palmer. 1974. "Patrician Society, Plebian Culture." *Journal of Social History* 7: 382–405.

———. 1967. "Time, Work-Discipline and Industrial Capitalism." *Past and Present* 38: 56–97.

———. 1966. *The Making of the English Working Class*. New York: Vintage Books.

Thorner, Daniel, Basil Kerblay, and R. E. F. Smith. 1966. *A.V. Chayanov on the Theory of Peasant Economy*. Manchester: Manchester University Press.

Tilly, Charles. 1984. *Big Structures, Large Processes, Huge Comparisons*. New York: Russell Sage Foundation.

———. 1983. "Flows of Capital and Forms of Industry in Europe, 1500–1900." *Theory and Society* 12: 123–42.

Tilly, Louise. 1987. "Beyond Family Strategies, What?" *Historical Methods* 20: 123–26.

Tilly, Louise, and Joan W. Scott. 1998. *Women, Work and Family*. New York: Holt, Rhinehart and Wilson.

Tomich, Dale. 1997. "World of Capital/Worlds of Labor: A Global Perspective." Pp. 287–312 in *Reworking Class*, edited by John R. Hall. Ithaca, N.Y.: Cornell University Press.

———. 1994. "Small Islands and Huge Comparisons: Caribbean Plantations, Historical Unevenness, and Capitalist Modernity." *Social Science History* 18: 339–58.

Trimberger, Ellen Kay. 1982. "E. P. Thompson: Understanding the Process of History." Pp. 211–43 in *Vision and Method in Historical Sociology*, edited by Theda Skocpol. New York: Cambridge University Press.

Truxes, Thomas M. 1988. *Irish American Trade, 1660–1783*. Cambridge: Cambridge University Press.

Tyson, R. E. 1995. "Contrasting Regimes: Population Growth in Ireland and Scotland during the Eighteenth Century." Pp. 64–76 in *Conflict, Identity and Economic Development: Ireland and Scotland, 1600–1939*, edited by S. J. Connolly, R. A. Houston, and R. J. Morris. Preston: Carnegie Publishing.

Ulrich, Laurel Thatcher. 1998. "Wheels, Looms, and the Gender Division of Labor in Eighteenth-Century New England." *William and Mary Quarterly* 55: 3–38.

Vandenbroeke, Christiaan. 1996. "Proto-Industry in Flanders: A Critical Review." Pp. 102–17 in *European Proto-Industrialization*, edited by Sheilagh C. Ogilvie and Markus Cerman. Cambridge: Cambridge University Press.

———. 1987. "The Regional Economy of Flanders and Industrial Modernization in the Eighteenth Century: A Discussion." *Journal of European Economic History* 16: 149–70.

Van Der Wee, Herman. 1996. "The Industrial Revolution in Belgium." Pp. 64–77 in *The Industrial Revolution in National Context: Europe and the USA*, edited by Mikulas Teich and Roy Porter. Cambridge: Cambridge University Press, 1996.

Vardi, Liana. 1993. *The Land and the Loom: Peasants and Profits in Northern France 1680–1800*. Durham, N.C.: Duke University Press.

Wallerstein, Immanuel. 1997. "Merchant, Dutch or Historical Capitalism?" *Review-Journal of the Fernand Braudel Center* 20: 243–54.

———. 1991. "The Industrial Revolution: *Cui Bono?*" Pp. 41–50 in *Unthinking Social Science: The Limits of Nineteenth-Century Paradigms*. Cambridge, UK: Polity Press.

———. 1983. *Historical Capitalism*. London: Verso.

———. 1974. *The Modern World-System.* Vol. 1. *Capitalist Agriculture and the Origins of the European World-Economy in the Sixteenth Century*. New York: Academic Press.

Ward, Kathryn B. 1993. "Reconceptualizing World-System Theory to Include Women." Pp. 43–68 in *Theory on Gender/Feminism on Theory*, edited by Paula England. New York: Aldine De Gruyter.

Warden, Alexander J. 1864. *The Linen Trade, Ancient and Modern*. London: Longman, Green, Longman, Roberts and Green.

Whelan, Kevin. 1997. "The Modern Landscape: From Plantation to Present." Pp. 67–105 in *Atlas of the Irish Rural Landscape*, edited by F. H. A. Aalen, Kevin Whelan, and Matthew Stout. Cork: Cork University Press.

———. 1994. "Settlement Patterns in the West of Ireland in the Pre-Famine Period." Pp. 60–78 in *Decoding the Landscape*, edited by Timothy Collins. Galway: Centre for Landscape Studies, Social Sciences Research Centre, University College Galway.

Whyte, Ian. 1989. "Proto-Industrialisation in Scotland." Pp. 228–51 in *Regions and Industries: A Perspective on the Industrial Revolution in Britain*, edited by Pat Hudson. Cambridge: Cambridge University Press.

Wickham-Crowley, Timothy. 1991. "A Qualitative Comparative Approach to Latin American Revolutions." Pp. 82–109 in *Issues and Alternatives in Comparative Social Research*, edited by Charles C. Ragin. Leiden: E. J. Brill.

Wolf, Diane. 1992. *Factory Daughters: Gender, Household Dynamics, and Rural Industrialization in Java*. Berkeley: University of California Press.

Wolf, Eric. 1982. *Europe and the People without History*. Berkeley: University of California Press.

Wolpe, Harold, ed. 1980. *The Articulation of Modes of Production*. London: Routledge.

Index

About the Author

Jane Gray is a Lecturer in Sociology at the National University of Ireland, Maynooth, where she continues to teach and carry out research on family formation, households, and social change.

www.ingramcontent.com/pod-product-compliance
Ingram Content Group UK Ltd.
Pitfield, Milton Keynes, MK11 3LW, UK
UKHW012040150926
475560UK00001B/97

9 780739 109472